Masculinities

Football, Polo and the Tango in Argentina

Eduardo P. Archetti

BERG

Oxford • New York

First published in 1999 by
Berg
Editorial offices:
150 Cowley Road, Oxford OX4 1JJ, UK
70 Washington Square South, New York NY 10012, USA

© Eduardo P. Archetti 1999

Berg is the imprint of Oxford International Publishers Ltd.

Library of Congress Cataloging-in-Publication Data

A catalogue record for this book is available from the Library of
Congress.

British Library Cataloguing-in-Publication Data

A catalogue record for this book is available from the British Library.

ISBN   1 85973 261 5 (Cloth)
       1 85973 266 6 (Paper)

Typeset by JS Typesetting, Wellingborough, Northants.
Printed in the United Kingdom by WBC Book Manufacturers,
Mid Glamorgan.

For Kristi Anne

Contents

Acknowledgements

This book is the product of many years of fieldwork, heterogeneous reading, exploration in archives, dialogues and discussions, conferences and seminars. Grants from the National Research Councils of Norway and Argentina made possible several months of fieldwork in the period 1988 to 1994. I want to thank colleagues at the Department of Social Anthropology in Oslo for suggestive reflections and critical comments: Marit Melhuus, Signe Howell and Thomas Hylland Eriksen; the late Ladislav Holy, who gave me inspiration through long winter talks during his stay in Oslo in 1995; Gary Armstrong, Richard Giulianotti, Pierre Lanfranchi, Christian Bromberger, Sergio Leite Lopes, Jeffrey Tobin, Roberto DaMatta, John MacAloon and Patrick Mignon, members of the global minority of social scientists concerned with the complicated relations between modernity, sport and bodily practices; Rosana Guber and Sergio Visacovski, anthropologists from Buenos Aires who, like myself, are striving to understand the puzzling cultural clues of *la patria*; Beatriz Sarlo, who, at an early stage and perhaps without knowing, convinced me of the relevance of my concerns, and the same must be said of other *porteño* intellectuals and social scientists: Adrián Gorelik, Juan Carlos Torre, Enrique Oteiza, Carlos Altamirano, Donna Guy, Hugo Vezzetti, Laura Golberg, Elisabeth Jelin, Héctor Palomino, Ariel Scher, Dora Barrancos, Miguel Murmis, Rosalia Cortes, Leopoldo Bartolomé, Néstor Lavergne, Pablo Alabarces, Julio Frydenberg, Marcelo Masssarino, Roberto Di Giono and Oscar Terán. I am grateful to many Masters and PhD students from the Department of Anthropology of the University of Oslo, some of whom are now my colleagues, for their good and open-minded ideas. I remember especially the comments of Kjersti Larsen, Sidsel Roaldkvam, Marianne Lien, Hans Christian Hognestad, Anne Leseth, Roger Magazine and Sverre Bjerkeset.

Many friends have been important during this long journey. For almost thirty years, the love, knowledge and wide understanding of football by Luis Boada, my old friend from Paris 1968, economist and ecologist, critical supporter of Barcelona and Flamengo, not only kept me informed about the global developments of the 'universal sport' but revealed to me the existence of a 'deep poetics' in sport and football. Jorge Jasminoy, my best *porteño* friend since the 1960s, has offered me his generosity, his intelligence, his many passions, and his home – *la guardilla* – during my research stays in Buenos Aires. Amilcar Romero, an outstanding representative of critical sport journalism in Argentina, always supported my work, offered me his archive, corrected my errors, introduced me to new informants and taught me many secrets of Argentinian football. Finally, my Norwegian friends – comrades of Kulturstiftelsen Blindern – with whom the sharing of passion and practice of football has helped me so much in surpassing the cold and dark winters of the North.

Friends and colleagues from all over the world, in St Andrews, Barcelona, Oslo, Paris, Florence, Vienna, London, Buenos Aires, Uppsala, Amsterdam, Misiones, Bergen, Lund, Rio de Janeiro and Guadalajara, have read and commented on parts of this book; my thanks to all of them. Taller Escuela Agencia (TEA) and Editorial Atlántida in Buenos Aires allowed me to work during several months in their archives. Two anonymous referees, engaged by Berg, made strong critiques and generous suggestions that helped me to improve the final version. John Gledhill and Kathryn Earle, from Berg, believed in this project and I hope that I have not disappointed them. My English was considerably improved and transformed by the critical readings of Nancy Frank and Gary Armstrong.

I would like to express my profound gratitude to all my informants: friends from my time as student at the University of Buenos Aires, from the Canadian Bar, from the café of Lavalle street and from Almagro. You must know that without you this book would have never been written. Moira McKinnan introduced me to her mother Nora and her aunt Veronica, and through them the saga of the Traills was disclosed.

Finally, the most precious and constant intellectual, emotional and moral support was the long-term relationship with Kristi Anne Stølen, University of Oslo, with whom I share the interest in Argentina and an exciting and rich daily family life, and to whom this book is dedicated. Our adventure and cooperation began in Reconquista and Santa Cecilia, province of Santa Fe, in Argentina, more than twenty years ago. In this first fieldwork, among cotton farmers, originally from Friuli in northern Italy, we worked together and Kristi Anne taught me – with her clever queries and doubts, her enthusiasm and sensibility – how to become an 'observer' in my country.

Prologue

This book is the result of many years of research on the meanings of football, polo and the tango in Argentinian society. Parts of chapters 2, 5, 6 and 7 have been published earlier (see Archetti 1994, 1996, 1997a,b). The choice of sport and dance was the result of a research strategy that attempted to combine images of men and masculinities with concrete historical contexts, nationalist ideology and modernization of the city of Buenos Aires, and with recent anthropological debates on hybridity and morality. A pioneer book on football in Brazil with the programmatic introduction written by DaMatta (1982), a prestigious Brazilian anthropologist trained in the study of 'primitive' Amazonian people, opened the door to the study of sport and its relation to the 'national' in Latin America and in anthropology in general. Inspired by structuralism as the search for decisive cognitive maps, and by ritual theory as the importance of public dramatic performances in complex societies, DaMatta in an earlier book (1978) problematized the 'national' through the analysis of carnival – and samba – and the construction of popular heroes. The connection between football and dance as an anthropological field of empirical research in Latin American studies thus became evident. I shall first present some of the methodological orientations – the mixing of the oral and the written, the use of limited historical construction and the limitations of auto-anthropology – and, briefly afterwards, the theoretical concerns that have guided my research and that, in many ways, depart from the original preoccupations of DaMatta. The theoretical stances will be developed successively throughout the book.

Methodological Points of Entry

A prologue is needed for placing my research and my findings in a proper anthropological context. To write on masculinities through football, the tango and polo in order to grasp Argentinian identity is not very usual. The book you will read is not a traditional monograph resting upon the long-term presence of the ethnographer in the field. The practice of anthropology in the contexts of 'little traditions' implied an emphasis on the study of oral practices: speaking, singing and orating. The anthropological written texts originate, in principle, from oral transmissions – and, of course, behavioural observation. Orality was thus transformed by the writing of the anthropologist. However, in contexts of 'great traditions', social discourses were and are also embedded in, or expressed through, writing. Anthropologists working in complex societies with ample literary traditions are confronted with a variety of texts. These different texts have been produced nationally, even locally, in the community studied, or elsewhere, by the informants themselves or by 'others' in general: writers, journalists, scientists, politicians, bureaucrats or teachers. Confronted with this dense jungle of texts, research strategies can vary: the emphasis on the consumption of texts concentrates on the impact of reading, while the emphasis on the production of texts permits a discussion on the implications of writing in the shaping of cultural forms. Any cultural theory thus needs to reflect on the multiplicity of writings because identities, or the interface between the self and the social, are also created and re-created through writing and reading. So how heterogeneous literary works may affect the anthropological understanding of a given sociocultural setting is a relevant question to ask.

My book combines traditional fieldwork and orality – stories and histories told by the informants – with textual analysis – historical essays, ideological writings of the nationalist authors, journals, magazines and tango lyrics. A central concern is the process by which meaning is produced in various texts – including the narratives produced by my informants – rather than the simple representation of a cultural reality. I try to combine what my informants said or commented on, read in magazines or journals, and watched on television or saw in films, with what I read or saw. The traditional anthropologist will perhaps find my analysis more textualist than ethnographic, and the cultural studies scholar will find my textual analysis unsophisticated. However, I hope to have reached a balance between the written and the spoken in the presentation of some of the 'myths' of football, constructed historically in written texts and reproduced today in the figures of some outstanding players like Maradona. This, due to lack of research, is less developed in the cases of the tango and polo. This imbalance does not invalidate my key methodological device: the exploration of meanings in written texts as a way of understanding that which is derived from or transformed into orality, which I consider central to anthropological analysis in complex literate societies. I have, in other words, emphasized 'emphatic listening' more than the traditional device of unidirectional observing (Fabian 1983: 151–2).

My fieldwork and archival exploration in Buenos Aires were carried out in different periods from 1984 to 1994, a total of twenty months and almost fifty football matches watched. More details will be presented in the introduction. The reader will easily discover that my work attempts to integrate a more distant past with a near present without seeking to give a detailed historical analysis. There is a 'here and now' and, at the same time, a 'there and then' fashioned by the process of modernization of Buenos Aires – and Argentina – that, initiated at the end of the past century, was consolidated in the first three decades of this century. Sarlo has defined this process as *modernidad periférica* (peripheral modernity), in which European modernity and local differences, acceleration and anguish, traditionalism and change, *criollismo* and literary avant-garde are coalesced (1988: 15). Buenos Aires was thus in this period 'the great Latin American setting of a culture of mixture (*cultura de mezcla*)' (1988: 15). Buenos Aires was also a cosmopolitan city – with almost 3 million inhabitants in 1930 – in which 75% of the growth from 1900 is a result of European immigration. The histories of football, the tango and polo are related to this concrete period. My main hypothesis is that key stereotypes of masculinities were created through this modernization as part of a general quest for identities, imageries and symbols, making the abstract more concrete. There is, therefore, a historical gap in the book, and the reader must accept this limitation. I am particularly interested in the use of history in the cultural construction of identities in Argentina, and during my enquiry I became interested in the inverse process, the cultural construction of the past from the perspective of my informants. As will become clear later, I extended my focus of research, which initially was on football, to include

the tango and polo as a way of achieving an intracultural comparative perspective following the recommendations of some of my
informants.

As an Argentinian and, at the same time, an 'outsider anthropologist' – trained and working in Europe – I was on a kind of
familiar terrain because, in principle, I had fewer linguistic, social
and cultural obstacles than a non-Argentinian anthropologist.
Moreover, I have 'always' been interested in football, and the
majority of my informants during the first period of my research
belonged to my own 'social group' in terms of class, age and
education. I was a kind of 'anthropologist at home', like many
anthropologists of Brazil, Malaysia, North America or India in the
past, and now many more in Europe (see Jackson 1987), and my
anthropological research a kind of 'auto-anthropology'. Strathern
has defined 'auto-anthropology' as 'anthropology carried out in
the social context which produced it' (1987: 17). At the same time,
my training as a professional anthropologist, a point also emphasized by Strathern, implies that I am part of an 'anthropological
culture' and academic community, from which my informants are
excluded. This constitutes a dilemma, which Hastrup commented
on in the following way: 'while fieldwork among your own people
may provide you with an initially different "context of situation",
this context itself will eventually become textualized within the
general context of anthropology' (1987: 105). This implies that the
'insider' perspective in auto-anthropology is not necessarily that
of the 'natives'. Strathern has strongly argued that the personal
credentials of the anthropologists – being a male Argentinian in
my case – are less important for what, at the end, the written
product does: 'whether there is cultural continuity between the
product of his/her labours and what people in the society being
studied produce by way of accounts of themselves' (1987: 17).

In other words, being at home implies that my way of organizing
my enquiry, what Strathern calls 'techniques of organizing knowledge', coincides with the way the people studied organize knowledge
about themselves. I shall argue that, in spite of my theoretical
concerns, not necessarily shared by my informants, and in this sense
accepting the difference presented by Hastrup, the high degree of
auto-anthropology lies not only on the fact that my informants
agreed on – and directed – my objects of study but also on the
existence of Argentinian key cultural and social dimensions that,
to a large extent, I share with them. The reader will find in some

parts of the book a way of writing that has been called 'auto-
biographical ethnography', in the sense that some of my personal
experiences, in the context of fieldwork or in the realm of the
lived, are transformed into ethnographic writing. Some of my
informants also advised me on key aspects of my enquiry and
scrutiny and became temporarily 'native anthropologists' (see
Reed-Danahay 1997). I try to reproduce this process in the general
introduction of the book, and the different chapters explore various
interconnections, mixtures of genres and voices, in order to better
shape the complexity between historical reconstruction, fieldwork
and autobiography.

Masculinities: the World of Hybrids and Gendered Morality

García Canclini, in his influential book on hybrid cultures in Latin
America, has postulated that the 'uncertainty about the meaning
and value of modernity derives not only from what separates
nations, ethnic groups, and classes, but also from the sociocultural
hybrids in which the traditional and the modern are mixed' (1995:
2). He asked:

> How can we understand the presence of indigenous crafts and vanguard
> art catalogs on the same coffee table? What are painters looking for
> when, in the same painting, they cite pre-Columbian and colonial images
> along with those of the culture industry, and then reelaborate them
> using computers and lasers? The electronic media, which seemed to
> be dedicated to replacing high art and folklore, now are broadcasting
> them on a massive scale. Rock and 'erudite' music are renewing them-
> selves, even in metropolitan cities, with popular Asian and African
> American melodies. (1995: 2)

Latin American countries are in historical terms the result of the
'sedimentation, juxtaposition, and interweaving of indigenous
traditions, of Catholic colonial hispanism, and of modern political,
educational and communicational action' (1995: 46). The mixing
of tradition and modernity designates processes of hybridization.
He prefers, like myself, this term to 'syncretism' or 'mestizaje'
because it 'includes diverse intercultural mixtures, not only the
racial ones to which mestizaje tends to be limited, and because it
permits the inclusion of modern forms of hybridization better than

does "syncretism", a term that almost always refers to religious fusions or traditional symbolic movements' (1995: 11). His empirical, historical and sociological analysis is focused on expressive cultural forms: art, handicrafts, literature, film, comic strips and graffiti. García Canclini, however, has not developed a theory of hybridity based on the existence of different models permitting a comparative analysis. It will be clear later in this book that working with the models proposed by Young (1995) and Strathern (1992) is more fruitful.

García Canclini also postulates that hybridization can be better understood through a transdisciplinary framework which blends art history and literature, folklore and anthropology, and sociology and mass communication (1995: 3). My transdisciplinarity is also limited, as I have pointed out above, and my empirical arenas are football, polo and the tango, typical modern bodily practices; in a world of increasing competition and transnational exchanges, these are powerful expressions of national capabilities and potentialities – as powerful as art and literature. Football and polo are originally British codifications exported to Argentina and the rest of the humanity, while the tango is a genuine Argentinian cultural product exported to the world. Hybridization is thus related not only to the expansion of genres but also to the deterritorialization of social and symbolic processes – key processes for explaining hybridization, according to García Canclini (1995: 207). I think that, in addition, the emphasis on sport and dance makes possible an analysis of hybridization in which the various ways of classifying men and women, and the relations between men and women, and placing these classifications in the 'national' and international cultural global landscape, provide an innovative way to look at hybrid circuits. I shall try to demonstrate that 'male hybrids' – football and polo players – have a transgressive power, subverting categorical oppositions and creating conditions for cultural reflexivity and change (see Werbner 1997). Hybrids have unique, special or exceptional qualities, and can be seen as ideological constructions of social order – and in this way also producers of tradition. The 'ideal' Argentinian football or polo player is a hybrid who becomes a symbol of tradition and continuity. The paradox of hybrids lies in the possibility of investigating change – and modernity – and tradition as being both transgressive and normal. To insist only on the subversive sides of hybridity, as the post-modern oracles Hall, Gilroy and Bhabha have done, is partial and in some ways misleading, because empirical research has been replaced by ideological visions of the future of modern societies. My research is not grounded on a political standpoint that claims to fight against conservative forces in Argentinian society (see Hall 1990). Neither is my book an intellectual product of the radical post-modern political imaginary.

In the introductory chapter I shall show that Argentinian modernization has been shaped by a massive process of European migration, and, because of this, hybridization and hybrids are less conditioned by colonial situations than has been the case in other Latin American countries with important indigenous and black populations. In this respect, the analyses of Mosse (1985, 1996) of the modern European construction of a masculine stereotype related to nationalism, as well as the recent anthropological contributions to the study of masculinities (Cornwall and Lindisfarne 1994), have been important in inspiring my work. Mosse has emphasized that 'masculinity was in fact dependent upon a certain moral imperative, upon certain normative standards of appearance, behaviour, and comportment' (1996: 8). He has also insisted on the fact that manly beauty and a physically fit body were important for the construction of modern masculinity because they reflected the 'linkage of body and soul, of morality and bodily structure' (1996: 26). Moral worth and moral health became central concerns of modernity. Because 'the male body assumed ever-more importance as symbolic of true masculinity, greater attention had to be paid to its development, as well as to setting a specific standard of masculine beauty' (1996: 28). He argues that 'the male body, beauty, and morals are linked' and that together 'they symbolize "manly courage" and a "manly spirit"' (1996: 41). In nineteenth-century Germany and other European countries, gymnastic exercises became the main means for achieving both beauty and moral strength. Mosse correctly points out that England was the exception; there team sport was regarded as education in manliness (1996: 46). Football and polo, British sports exported to Argentina, are, therefore, privileged contexts within which to reflect on Mosse's hypothesis on the interconnection between male beauty and morality in the image of modern man. My empirical analysis, in the second part of the book, will prove that in the Argentinian situation morality is more pertinent than beauty. I will also explore the field of morality as an anthropological theoretical domain.

Masculinity without femininity, men without women, is perhaps unthinkable. A man needs a woman to reaffirm his own masculinity, but the woman who fulfils this function does not always need to be the same. The lyrics of the tango, a dance made for a man and a woman, will permit me to discuss the tension existing between a conventional morality that defines woman as passive and chaste – the mother and the disciplined spouse – and a romantic drive in which man is fascinated by the seductive power of the *femme fatale*. Mosse has emphasized the fact that in the construction of modern masculinity woman was subordinated to man; at the same time, the demands she made upon him were thought to strengthen his masculinity (1996: 76). The coexistence in the tango of different moral codes provides, in many ways, alternative definitions of manhood.

Also masculinities in my book are seen in relation to nationalism, to the way national imageries function as models and mirrors for Argentinians. The model of hybrids, as well as reflections on morality, is central in the way football, polo and the tango are perceived as social and symbolic fields which place Argentina and Argentinians in a global scene. During this century a peripheral modern society has been exporting performing bodies to the world: male players in football and polo, and, in the tango, male and female dancers. This process has created native interpretations, both cultivated and popular, as well as external images: Argentinians are supposed to do well in all of these activities. In the last chapter on the meaning of Maradona, a football player defined as the best in the world in the 1980s and a national icon, I synthesize the way the local is mixed with the global and historical continuity is defined. I also try to understand how this is reflected in the consciousness of my informants.

Introduction: Frameworks and Perspectives

Buenos Aires and the Nation

The Argentina of today is a complex industrialized and highly urbanized society that is still, to some extent, dependent on the economic performance of its agrarian sector. It is not surprising, therefore, that the powerful imagery of rural Argentina, the *pampas* and the gauchos, still coexists with the overwhelming dominance of large cities, particularly Buenos Aires, the city capital, a metropolis with 13 million inhabitants. In the canonical historical interpretation of the past it is accepted that from the 1860s, after the end of the period of civil wars, and until the economic crisis of the 1930s Argentina was made a modern country through variously: massive European immigration; British investments in industry and infrastructure; and a successful integration in the international economy through massive exports of cereals, wool and beef. Between 1870 and 1914 around 6 million Europeans arrived in Argentina, almost 3.3 million settling permanently. In 1914 one-third of the Argentinian population was foreign-born, the majority being Italians (39.4%) and Spaniards (35. 2%) (Solberg 1970: 38). By 1900 hundreds of thousands of northern Italians had become rural workers and tenant farmers in the provinces of the *pampa* area (Buenos Aires, Córdoba and Santa Fe). Italians also settled in the city of Buenos Aires, built the wine industry in Mendoza and provided the bulk of manpower to develop the British–Argentinian railways. Most of the Spaniards came from Galicia and at least one-third of them settled in Buenos Aires, where they worked in the most unskilled occupations. Russian immigrants, primarily Jews escaping from political and ethnic persecution in the Russian Empire, formed

1

the third largest group (4.1%) and settled in agricultural *colonias* and in Buenos Aires. Syrians and Lebanese (2.7%) arrived after leaving another oppressive empire, the Ottoman. Few were Muslims and, avoiding agriculture, they became businessmen. Immigrants also arrived from France, Germany, Denmark and Austria-Hungary (mostly Serbo-Croatians and Friulans). An important and powerful minority were the British. They were in 1914 1.1% of the total foreign population (almost 30,000), working in British firms and living in the rich suburbs of Buenos Aires or on the estates they owned. They had their prestigious boarding-schools and their social clubs, maintaining segregated cultural boundaries. They brought in the Scottish and English bovine and ovine breeds that trans-formed livestock production, introduced modern finance systems, transformed transport and commerce, and, above all, introduced new sporting practices such as football, tennis, polo, rugby and cricket. Among the British the English, much more than the Irish living in the rural areas of the *pampas* or the Welsh farmers striving for survival in Patagonia, were able to establish social standards much admired by the Argentinian upper class. These standards were in many ways related to the powerful imagery of the British aristocratic way of life with its concomitant influence on equestrian sports competitions. However, the ascendancy of the British was much larger and more persuasive via the rapid expansion of the practice of football.

Argentina received, between 1869 and 1930, more immigrants in relation to its native population than any other modern country. A mirror of this historical pattern exists in the growth and develop-ment of the capital city of Buenos Aires. The city grew rapidly from 180,000 inhabitants in 1869 to 1,576,000 in 1914. By 1930 the city had almost 3 million inhabitants, one-third of whom were European immigrants (Ferrer 1972: 146). The proportion of foreigners was 13.8% in 1869, 24% in 1895 and 42.7% in 1914 (Vázquez Rial 1996: 24). A gender imbalance in the arrival of female immigrants primarily among the younger population meant that for long periods in Buenos Aires history there was an over-abundance of males. It is possible thus to imagine Buenos Aires as a kind of cultural Babel, wherein English was the language of commerce and industry, French was the language of culture, and the tongues of daily life were a mixture of Spanish (and Galician), Italian (various dialects) and a mixture of Western and Eastern European languages. Buenos Aires in the 1920s, like New

York, represented, before the recent discovery by anthropology of the impact of global culture, diasporas and multicultural encounters, in effect a 'truly global space of cultural connections and dissolutions' (Clifford 1988: 4). Urban life was rapidly transformed during the first decades of the twentieth century. Luxury hotels, restaurants, bistros, hundreds of cafés, a world-famous opera-house and theatres were built by European architects. This prompted changes in the use of leisure time and created a new environment beyond the walls of privacy and home. The Argentinian economic boom permitted this type of conspicuous consumption. During the first three decades of the twentieth century Argentina was among the ten richest countries in the world. This period is also characterized by the rapid expansion of sporting arenas and social clubs and the construction of the majestic hippodrome in the suburb of Palermo. With the building of stadiums and the creation of a national championship, football developed, so that by the end of the 1920s Argentina was a world leader in the game.

The appearance of public arenas created new conditions for public participation. Three institutions, in particular, provided the public with new excitements and opportunities for the deployment of sexual fantasies: the modern legal brothels with thousands of imported European prostitutes, the 'dancing academies' (*academias de baile*) or 'cafés with waitresses' (*café de camareras*), and the cabaret. These arenas were not only appropriated by men but also provided a space for women, albeit of a special kind. The potent image of a metropolis like Buenos Aires was dependent on a social and cultural complexity that transcended the limited and close world of provincial towns. In this representation the possibilities arising from the uses of leisure time and the consolidation of institutional frameworks for individual creativity and mobility were also important. In the Argentine of that time, success for a singer, a dancer, a musician or a football player was related to performances and recognition by the *porteño* (Buenos Aires) audiences and experts. Buenos Aires had, from the point of view of its inhabitants and the Argentinians visiting from the provincial and rural interior and even from larger cities like Rosario or Córdoba, everything: cafés, theatres, opera, cabaret, luxury brothels, football clubs, sophisticated restaurants, opulent hotels and equestrian sports including, from 1928, the Open Polo Championship on the fields of Palermo.

The Argentinian élite imagined that Paris was the only city

comparable to Buenos Aires. Paris had achieved, at the end of nineteenth century, the title of the world's capital of elegance, sophistication and pleasure. But Paris was more: it was a scientific centre, a place for technical innovations, an international milieu where ideological debates flourished and artistic fashions were shaped. Paris was perceived as the core of modernity. It was also the city where the hitherto most successful World Exhibition was held in 1900, attracting more than 50 million visitors. But above all Paris promised entertainment and enjoyment, with its cafés and restaurants, its theatres, vaudevilles and cabarets, its department stores and colourful local fairs and markets. Paris functioned, in what was the world of travellers at that time, as a fabric of fantasies and illusions. Buenos Aires operated in the same way in Argentina and later, once its prestige was consolidated, in South America. For the South Americans fun and elegance were not enough: the fact that Buenos Aires was seen as a typical European (and white) city was crucial in their positive image.

Buenos Aires was inhabited by Europeans but in its origins was not a typical European city. Buenos Aires was never a medieval labyrinth like many European cities, including Paris before the Haussmannian transformation provoked by the upheavals of the Commune of 1871. Buenos Aires had always had a square-grid design and by the end of the nineteenth century was a flat and extended city. From the 1900s the rapid expansion of electricity not only replaced gas as the main source of energy but made possible the construction of high buildings with lifts. In 1905 the city had 126 buildings with more than three floors and a lift. The number of such buildings had increased threefold by 1909 (Liernur 1993: 66). By 1930 Buenos Aires was 'finished' and looked like a large European city with great boulevards, big buildings, huge palaces in the northern quarter, parks and monuments; it had a modern system of transport, with the electric tramway inaugurated in 1897 and the subway and the railway connecting the centre with the suburbs in 1913, and a centre (*el centro*) where bureaucracy, business, department stores and entertainment venues coexisted. But Buenos Aires was more; it was a city with an extended and busy port, unlike Paris, and contained many residential suburbs (Silvestri 1993).

The continuous and accelerated expansion of the city created new residential areas. In the northern part, towards the central railway station of Retiro and the cemetery of Recoleta, the fashionable Santa Fe Avenue become the heart of a very bourgeois and even aristocratic *barrio* (neighbourhood). This *barrio* was adjoined through the parks of Palermo with Belgrano and other localities in the north that later become expensive neighbourhoods. Towards the west, along the Rivadavia Avenue, new middle-class *barrios* were consolidated: Congreso, Once, Almagro, Caballito and Flores. The *barrio* of Once, with the construction of the western railway station, generated an important commercial and residential area where Jewish, Armenian, Syrian and Lebanese immigrants settled. In this quarter the colossal food market of Abasto, a kind of Parisian Marché des Halles, was located. Towards the south the city become more industrial, and around the factories were found the immigrant working class dwelling in the *barrios* of Boca and Barracas. If the city could expand unhindered towards the west and the north, the natural frontier in the south was the River Riachuelo, although the city grew beyond its natural limits when new industries settled in Avellaneda, Quilmes and Lanús. To the east the obstacle presented by the River Plate was beyond the limits of technical possibilities. All these new quarters were rapidly integrated into the life of Buenos Aires through an expansion of the transport system, primarily the railways and late in the 1920s via expansion of the small buses (*colectivos*). The growth of the city in all these directions created the *arrabal*, areas that were at the edge of the *pampa* and marked the transition from the urban to the rural (Gorelik 1996). The city of Buenos Aires is thus historically produced through the juxtaposition of three landscapes: the centre (*el centro*), a general space open to all inhabitants, visitors and tourists; the *barrio*, a locality, a particular 'closed' space populated in some cases by different social classes and ethnic groups; and the *arrabal*, a dangerous and liminal area occupied by a marginal population. The importance of these divisions in the imagery of the city will be explored later.

Gorelik (1996), an original historian of the city of Buenos Aires, has shown that the *barrios* appeared in the 1910s, not only as a more or less automatic consequence of the urban expansion but mainly as political and cultural creations. He argues that the *barrio* was, above all, a well-defined public space that was preceded by more or less socially articulated neighbourhoods (1996: 218). In the *barrio* the local civil organizations, launching all kinds of initiatives for providing the *barrio* with different services and arenas of sociability – cooperatives, public libraries and clubs – and the common, park and plazas, would define the boundaries and the identity of the vicinity (see also Armus 1996). In this new space, Gorelik maintains, the *barrio* became a quiet, domesticated and pleasant space conquered and dominated by the urban walkers (*paseantes*). The family house would ideally be built not far from a green space (a park or a plaza). This residential pattern was central in the aspirations of middle and working classes of European origin (1996: 220–33). In the neighbourhood the street was the common public space, while in the *barrio* the parks and plazas created an encompassing communal membership. The culture of the *barrios* was, in the 1920s, strengthened by the consolidation of organized football, the clubs representing different *barrios*, and by the dancing of the tango in clubs, dancing halls and bars (*confiterías danzantes*). To these institutions it is important to add the local public primary schools, which also defined an area of local participation. Through public education the Argentinian state aimed to develop a sense of nationality among the sons and daughters of immigrants. Civic commitments in local institutions, school and work – when industries were located in the *barrio* – coexisted with leisure-time possibilities afforded by green spaces, clubs and bars. The role of the bars in daily life was to provide a privileged arena for friendship, gossip and socializing. Gorelik writes:

> For different reasons, then, these institutions are moulded by an import-
> ant urban component, in the sense that they constitute societies defined
> locally in relation to a concrete territory that is in and against a major
> city; producing a localized public space, a space ploughed by formalized
> social and cultural relations, and transforming the small universe of
> streets and buildings of the *barrio* into a historical space. This historical
> space will not be defined either by a *tradition*, like the quarter of the
> traditional European city, or by a *destiny*, like the vicinity of a process
> of urban modernization without sense, but by a *project*. (Author's
> emphasis; own translation Gorelik 1996: 236–7).

By the 1920s the social and economic transformation of Argentina had been achieved and an incipient democracy consolidated.
The country had 'resisted' the 'invasion' of millions of immigrants
and the 'cataclysms' provoked by new technologies, global connections, immersion in the world market and massive urbanization
(by 1914, 53% of the population of Argentina was urban). The
country and the city of Buenos Aires were not only heterogeneous
in the objective sense of being the product of ethnic and cultural

mixings, they were also *imagined* as such by intellectuals, writers, politicians and, of course, by the population in general (see Halperín Donghi 1987; Sarlo 1996; Bernand 1997). To imagine a homogeneous 'imagined national community' in this historical setting was not, and is still not, easy. Much more imagination is required than is necessary when imagining the national in more ethnically homogeneous societies with fewer dramatic demographic changes. The analysis of the Argentinian national male imagery is, thus, an important arena for dealing with and perhaps challenging the assumptions and working methods of the anthropological approaches which emphasize the fact that identities are constructed and nations are products of modernity (Eriksen 1993: 99–102). The Argentinian situation, like the American or the Canadian situation, obliges the researcher to think about the 'national', taking into account, as the primary and overwhelming social factor, immigration, and, consequently, asking questions about how this process conditioned and still conditions imageries, identities (both personal and collective), symbols, meanings, and models of social and cultural transformation, in particular that from foreigner into 'national'. Moreover, the pursuit of the 'national', if possible, requires a less dogmatic and standard anthropological methodology where data are necessarily generated through participant observation and discussions with selected informants.

Locating the Field and the Informants

I realized very early in the research process that it was important to reflect critically on my relative distance to the 'national' in Argentina. It was necessary to find a perspective, a specific point of view in the process of understanding and selecting things and events which should be shown in their connections to one another and should enact a field of study. In my case the process of thinking and pursuing the national was even more intricate because I am an Argentinian citizen, born in Santiago del Estero, a provincial and old city of the north west, who then spent seven years in Buenos Aires as a university student and left the country in 1968. I returned from Paris at the end of 1972 and did two years of fieldwork in the northern part of the province of Santa Fe, among rural cotton producers, descendants of immigrants from the region of Friuli in northern Italy. I left Argentina again at the end of 1974, worked as an anthropologist in Zambia, Norway and Ecuador, and settled permanently in Norway. I returned to Argentina in 1982 and I was surprised to discover while attending a football match in Buenos Aires that I experienced it more as an anthropologist than as a supporter. For the first time in my life as a football enthusiast I saw something that I could call 'culture' in the behaviour of the crowd and in the bodily performances of the players. During two hours in the stadium I experienced the collective flow of movements, ideas, concepts and emotions. I perceived differences and similarities, noises and smells, brutality and fair play, the past and the present, and I realized that I was comparing what I saw with other distant places and stadiums. My anthropological understanding at that very moment was the result of explicit and implicit cross-cultural comparison (Holy 1987: 19–21). In 1984 I decided to initiate a study on the cultural and social meaning of football in Buenos Aires.

I am also a typical mixed or hybrid ethnic Argentinian. My mother is a descendant of an 'old' *Santiagueño* family, which originated in the 1820s by the marriage of a French adventurer, military man, journalist and natural scientist with a woman of the local aristocracy. From my father's side I am a more 'standard' contemporary Argentinian. My grandfather, born in Lombardy, Italy, immigrated at the end of the nineteenth century, worked with the British on the construction of the northern and central railways and settled in an inhospitable town in the province of Santiago del Estero. This decision was and still is a mystery in the family. He married an Argentinian creole woman, born in the neighbouring province of Tucumán, and never returned to Italy. My father went to the university in Buenos Aires, studied medicine and, on his return to the province, became a relatively active and engaged local politician. His marriage was, from the point of view of local social history, an upward move, an allegory of the fate of many sons of immigrants who got an education or made money. The social and ethnic heterogeneity of Argentina had (and still has) the quality of transforming differences in something visible because social and cultural mobilities were possible. The history of my ancestors clearly illustrates how the concrete social trajectories and the symbolic capital accumulated by individuals in a time of global connections conditions the mixings – marriages and settlements – and the real possibilities of successful upward mobility or, as in many other cases, direct social catastrophe.

When I began my work on football I discovered that the historical
and personal narratives on the origins and style of Argentinian
football were placed in a centre – Buenos Aires. This explicitly
excluded the peripheries, and with it hundreds of provincial and
local histories. The history of Argentinian football was the history
of Buenos Aires football, presented through the glory of prestigious
clubs founded at the end of the nineteenth century and the first
decade of the twentieth century. I thus realized the meaning of
madly supporting River Plate, one of the celebrated clubs of Buenos
Aires, since I was four years old. I was socialized as a *provinciano*, a
santiagueño, learning that in the building of the modern Argentinian nation Buenos Aires dominated and exploited the provinces,
but I was, paradoxically enough, supporting, suffering and enjoying,
and psychologically dependent on the fate of a club from the city
of Buenos Aires. I also became aware of the importance of having
santiagueño players, not only in River Plate but also in the other
first-division clubs of Buenos Aires. The national was conflated
because Buenos Aires football was almost by definition national
football – with the exception of two clubs from the city of Rosario
and two clubs from the city of La Plata, capital of the province of
Buenos Aires, which were incorporated early into the creation of
the professional league in the 1930s. I was suddenly conscious of
something different, of a particular history not found in other
places. An Englishman, I thought, born in London is not supposed
to support a club from Manchester, and vice versa. Suddenly, my
personal identification with a particular club was part of a national
identification, and I felt that a part of myself was shared with
millions of others supporting one of the most popular clubs of
Argentina. My research on football was then open to more general
questions and enquiries.

I found an undeniable centre, Buenos Aires, and a physical
activity, football: bodies, rituals, male performances, masculinity,
international connections, world competition, an international
market for players, a popular and national passion including the
élite, a kind of contemporary social madness in the confluence of
capitalism, media and politics, and a long history initiated in 1867,
when the first football match was played by English immigrants in
the fields of the Buenos Aires Cricket Club. I also realized that a
British sport brought by the British immigrants and transformed
into a national obsession should be a privileged arena for studying
ideologies around ideas of a 'melting-pot'. I began my fieldwork

in 1984 by attending football matches. I collected a considerable amount of data on what I call the folklore of supporters and the ritual performances in the stadiums. In six months, I attended twenty first-division football matches and, based on supporter's chants, published on masculinity and the meaning of ritual violence in Argentinian football (Archetti 1985, 1992).

In 1988 I started a much more systematic work with selected informants. In a city like Buenos Aires working on football and male national identity, the door-to-door method seemed to me unsuitable. I felt obliged to fall back on intermediaries in the form of friends or old professional colleagues. Given my middle-class background, it was normal to begin with persons I had had a lot to do with in the past: old friends and companions of university football. They were middle-class professionals, journalists, business-men and public servants. They introduced me to other informants and helped me to broaden my original sample. During eight months I worked with fifteen informants, my original nine friends and the six introduced to me, supporting different clubs of the Argentinian professional league – first division. I had supporters of the most important teams, such as Boca Juniors, River Plate, San Lorenzo de Almagro, Racing and Independiente, but also of less important ones, such as Vélez Sarsfield, Estudiantes de la Plata, Rosario Central, Quilmes and Huracán. My informants knew that I was interested in the national dimension of football and not in the parochial – but important – aspect of club identity. Therefore, in the majority of the interviews they were arbitrarily placed in the position of reflecting more on Argentinian football than on the history and meaning of their own teams. This situation was for some of my informants rather unusual. They reacted in different ways: they attempted to enhance my knowledge of Argentinian football history by providing more information and suggesting sources, they looked for clues that would indicate my football preferences – players and teams – and biases, they asked me a lot of questions about anthropology and the objectives of my research, and they employed a lot of humour and familiarity to show that they were confident of the importance of my study. But, above all, they sought to limit the 'disorder' occasioned by an abnormal situation. I found that the interviews functioned much better after attending a football match together or sitting in a café, and I tried to gather information on such occasions.

Our conversations were on football and only on football. We

were together in a kind of adventure that excluded topics related to family, profession, work or politics. The passion of football excluded other narratives, and I imagine that what we talked about was uninteresting to others not sharing the language we used. The language of football, as any specific language, creates important barriers for those who are not interested (see Augé 1998: 58–9). Therefore, to talk about the family, or any other topic unrelated to football, was inappropriate. The reader will not find in this book a description of the total social and cultural life of my informants, or even their lives and destinies as football supporters of given teams. This is another story.

During the year of 1988 I lived in the *barrio* (neighbourhood) of Boedo while working as visiting researcher in a research centre located in the centre of Buenos Aires. The *barrio* of Boedo is, in many ways, mythological due to the fact that San Lorenzo de Almagro, one of the great clubs of Argentina, was located here, and the tango is associated with the social life of the neighbourhood. In order to expand my sample I decided to find a place where I could meet other kinds of supporters, and not only my middle-class informants. I selected a bar located in the *barrio*, the Canadian Bar, where from 1988 onwards I met new informants. This group of ten constituted what I called 'the third age' group of informants. All of them aged more than 60, they were retired lower-middle-class labourers: one butcher, one electrician, two account clerks, one foreman labourer, two taxi-drivers and three small shop owners. Five of them were supporters of San Lorenzo de Almagro, three of Boca Juniors, one of Huracán and one of River Plate. With very few exceptions, all the interviews were done in the café. I developed a routine, if possible arriving once a week in the afternoon and joining the table where members of the group were seated that day. Most of the interviews were organized through group discussions, supplemented by individual interviews. During this period my focus of research expanded to the world of the tango.

Later, in two stays in Buenos Aires, two months in 1993 and four months in 1994, I expanded my circle of informants, working with supporters of San Lorenzo de Almagro, the majority of them working-class or unemployed students. They belonged to my group of 'teenagers', aged from 19 to 25. My intention was to begin a systematic research focused on the culture of young male fans of San Lorenzo de Almagro. The supporters of this club are known for being more creative in inventing chants and among the less violent of first- division football in Argentina. For different reasons, my research on the creation of team identity was interrupted. However, we saw six matches of San Lorenzo de Almagro together and two of the Argentinian national team. Our discussions on 'national style' convinced me of the changes that had occurred in Argentina in the epic period from 1980 to 1994, when Maradona was the dominant player of the national team. During these two stays I decided to work on the social and symbolic meaning of Maradona, the most famous and controversial Argentinian football player of this century, and an icon in contemporary Argentina. I also carried out systematic work in the archives of Editorial Atlántida, reading the leading Argentinian weekly sports magazine *El Gráfico*, founded in 1919, and in the archives of the National Library.

The Role of Narratives

I shall focus my analysis on narratives – textual strategies, meta-phoric constructions and displacements, metonymic structures and figurative devices – and their own history. A narrative is a way of telling temporal events so that meaningful sequences are portrayed (Kerby 1991). I worked with three generations of Argentinians, and, in a way, I was able to trace a kind of genealogical memory based on lived experiences. The anthropologist gathers a discourse – narratives and opinions – he is responsible for stimulating and provoking. For a certain number of hours over different days – and in different years, as was my case – the informants will put together an account of Argentinian football or the tango, and the meaning of such practices in the construction of male national identities. The existence of an archaeology of memory, being differ-ent in terms of generations, as much as the actual variations in representing relations between individuals and society, past and present, convinced me of the importance of a historical analysis. In a single society, such as Argentina, people do not remember in the same way and, moreover, are not obliged to remember (see Augé 1998). The diversity in remembering is related, among other things, to two factors: the scope and precision of a genealogical viewpoint, and the narrative method use to recount (see Le Wita 1994: 118–21). I shall give two examples. Héctor, belonging to my original group of informants, was socialized in football, like many

Argentinians, through a very close relationship with his father, a committed supporter of Independiente. His father, dead at the time of my research, was a fantastic narrator of football stories, and Héctor also had this quality: his memory was prodigious and his ability to relate a natural gift. In his tales, the football of the 1920s and 1930s lived by his father was joined to his experience in the 1950s and 1960s. Héctor's stories are central in the second part of the book. They were always poetic and embedded in moral reasoning. Tomás, one of my key informants in the chapter on Maradona and a member of the 'third age' group of Boedo, remembered fewer historical facts and football stories, but was profoundly reflective on what he called 'the essence of Argentinian football' (*las esencias del fútbol argentino*). He gave me many clues to the understanding of conceptual continuity in Argentinian football. Every memory is thus a translation, a way of connecting individual experiences with social and cultural processes. I therefore confine my attention to small stories, to discussions in a group when I introduced a topic, a finding or a doubt, and to anecdotes.

I also found it important to confront my informants with historical events because these arrangements eventually create their owns paths in memory, those evocations that nothing, it seems, can stop. Thus, particular experiences and moments are put together in such a way that what arises from memory's stream is continuously filtered and reordered (Cohen and Rapport 1995: 8). Crites (1971) calls this process the narrative quality of experience. Narrating – and remembering, as Connerton (1989) reminds us – is by definition an embodied event. As I pointed out above, we can agree upon the fact that all memory proceeds via genealogy, and in this sense the past is always seen from the present. It is what Foucault called history as genealogy (see Borneman 1996). The present is therefore the decisive and multiple moment in the process of narrating, because it conflates the present lived by the informants and the present of an observer – myself – reading and interpreting words, behaviour and written texts. In this process there is a kind of double reciprocity because I – the observer – am an Argentinian (that which I have in common with my informants) and an anthropologist (that which constitutes me as an 'other') at the same time. This, in theory, makes possible awareness of the problem of cultural construction and construction of categories in the social order (Fernández 1995). Thus, and perhaps paradoxically, I needed to construct my informants as 'others'. In this sense anthropologists are never completely 'at home', in spite of what many believe, because we are obliged to ask unexpected questions, to question what is commonsensically expressed and accepted by the informants, to interrogate our own identities as members of a collective or to examine critically the meaning of given narratives. Narrations enter into discourses, constituting a corpus of multiple and heterogeneous 'texts'. I shall place special attention on spoken, written, iconic, musical – although only partially – and kinetic forms produced in different contexts. I consider that Holy has expressed with great clarity the main difference between discourse and culture when he defines discourse as:

> a socially constituted communication which leads to the production of a set of 'texts'. These need not be written or oral but may be constituted through other modes of expression, for example, through the representational or performative arts. Even in the written or spoken form they need not be restricted to a single genre. 'Culture' I take as a system of notions, ideas, and premises which is not exclusive to any particular discourse but underlines a multiplicity of them. (1996: 4)

My analysis is not only confined to particular narratives and discourses. In several parts of the book I use the words 'imagery' or 'imageries' purposefully because the narratives I collect or read have the quality of being very visual due to the fact that the empirical focus of my research is intrinsically made up of performances. The importance of performances for individuals in their production of images of themselves, other than the world's image of them, is undeniable. Actors imagine and reproduce verbally their own performances as well as performances of others in the production of narratives. In this process, when they observe or recall performances and objective constructions the experience is mediated through a complex mental imagery (see Palmer and Jankowiak 1996). Melhuus and Stølen have pointed out that the notion of imagery can be seen to balance precariously between the imaginary and the essentialization of the meanings of the imagined (1996: 1). They have strongly argued that it is the fixation of an image as natural which explains its power. They postulate that narratives and discourses – as well as discursive practices – are all significant loci for the production of imageries in general. I maintain that, in addition to this aspect, the term 'imagery' refers to particular scenes that are activated through cognitive models (analogical representa-

tions, metaphors or metonymies). I will attempt to de
different cognitive models at work.

Masculinities at Work: Football, Polo and the Tango

As I mentioned earlier football, without a doubt, is the 'national'
sport of Argentina. Football is an activity and a passion that cuts
across class, ethnic status or regional origin. Through football
Argentina became an important actor in the modern world history
of sports. Thus, football is a powerful masculine expression of
national capabilities and potentialities. Argentinian football has
constituted a symbolic and practical male arena for national pride
and disappointments, happiness and sorrow. The nationalist discourses on sport, in addition to the discovery of the foundation of
a 'national style of playing', can then be seen as an influential
mechanism through which male cultural power is established.)
Then, was it only football?

One of my informants, in a passionate exchange of views on
Argentinian male performances in the café of Boedo, pointed out
that the country had been exporting to the world not only football
players:

> we exported, as you know, beef and cereals, and we were known due to
> these merchandises, but we have been exporting men and women all
> the time during this century. We exported football players by their
> hundreds, to Europe, to South America and to Mexico, but also we
> have been exporting music, the tango, our national music, since 1900,
> and of course musicians, singers and dancers. We are seen, and we
> think of ourselves, as a country exporting beef, cereals and human
> performers of all kind.

I argued back that we were also exporting highly qualified researchers in fields as different as mathematics, physics and semiology,
and artists. I suggested famous Argentinian ballet dancers, like Julio
Bocca, Maximiliano Guerra or Paloma Herrera, and classical music
pianists, like Daniel Barenboim, Bruno Gelber or Martha Argerich.
He accepted that perhaps 'we' (Argentinians) were known because
'they' (the Argentinians artists) were known and appreciated by
a sophisticated audience, but he was not totally convinced. He
argued that 'there is something universal in these important people,

researchers or artists' and pointed out that, after all, there are
thousands and thousands of good mathematicians or pianists that
are not Argentinians. I refused to accept this argument and I told
him that Brazil, Uruguay and the former Yugoslavia have also
exported hundreds and hundreds of football players and that
football was a 'universal game' as much as mathematics or a
symphony of Beethoven. He then replied:

> Yes, I know this very well, but there is something special with football
> because in this game the individuals will represent the nation, a way
> of performing, competing and doing things differently from others.
> Martha Argerich playing the piano is just herself, a unique being, and
> nobody will deduce from her way of playing that there is an Argentinian
> way of playing, let me say, Beethoven. If you insisted on comparing
> football with music you must find a music that expresses us in a different
> way. This music is the tango. With the tango, and I hope you will accept
> that I am right, there is something special, because the tango is our
> music, our gift to the world. And, moreover, the tango has become
> almost universal, it is liked in the most remote corners of the world.

He convinced me that I should expand my research and include
the tango. And, following his advice, I did so but not in a conventional anthropological way. He insisted on the importance of the
poetics of the tango in forming an 'emotional map of Argentinian
identity'. I was easily persuaded that the complexity of the tango
was such – it is dance, music, lyrics and show – that in working
with the texts, with the meaning of the poetics of the tango, I had,
in the Andersonian sense, 'printed capitalism' in the lyrics of the
tango. The work with hundreds and hundreds of tango texts helped
me discover that tango was an important field of creativity that
included many 'cultivated' Argentinian writers – and not only the
'popular' ones. Authors with great international success were on
the list: Jorge Luis Borges, Julio Cortázar, Ernesto Sábato and
Manuel Puig. I discovered a strong area of cultural commonality
that, unlike the different expressions of Argentinian folklore music,
was also international. I had two embodied products that had
travelled well in the world: the tango and football. The difference
with regard to their historical origins was also relevant for comparison: football was an English creation while the tango was typically
Argentinian.

In the tango Argentinians created a 'modern' cultural commodity
that has been travelling for almost a century and, paradoxically,

changing while remaining the same. The tango travels and transforms in Paris and Birmingham, Barcelona and Berlin, Cracow and
Tokyo, Colombia and Mexico, Finland and Germany, Russia and
the USA, and Egypt and Turkey. The history of this nomadism is
waiting to be narrated. We can agree that the very existence of
human society is bound to human creative capacity. It is a rare
achievement of a different kind to generate 'exportable' and 'permanent' artefacts and cultural practices that can travel for a long
period of time beyond the cultural and political boundaries of
Buenos Aires, the city of the tango. Argentinians can proudly state
that they participated in this rarity through the expansion, transformation and permanence of the tango as music and as a dance.
A product of Buenos Aires became a symbol and an expression of
a nation. In a modest way, compared with the massive English
export of sport activities, Argentinians were exporting, at the
beginning of the twentieth century, a music and a bodily cultural
performance that became widely accepted.

In the nationalist narrative the construction of the 'relevant
other' appears once closure has been achieved, once what is 'national'
with its clear borders has been defined and ritualized. The nationalist Argentinian discourse cannot travel, and Brazil or Chile will
not import nationalists and Argentinian symbols. In a world of
nations, similarity (all are nations) is accompanied by exclusion
(there is just one Argentinian nation). The study of travelling
'national products' and bodies offers a different perspective
because, in a world of interconnections and global networks,
Argentinian identity is placed in the wide context. Identity is not
closed; it is open in the sense that 'reflectivity' is not reduced to
the way Argentinians 'see' and 'define' the world. Football and
the tango are mirrors and masks at the same time. Identity is
connected, globally connected, because it reflects a long historical
process. Strauss has written:

> Identity is connected with the fateful appraisals made of oneself – by
> oneself and by others. Everyone presents himself to the others and to
> himself, and sees himself in the mirror of their judgments. The masks
> he then and thereafter presents to the world and its citizens are
> fashioned upon his anticipations of their judgments. The others present
> themselves too: they wear their own brand of masks and they get
> appraised in turn. (1977: 9)

Argentinians can see themselves in football and the tango, and in these activities the 'others' can similarly see them. A complex interplay of mirrors and masks is thus created and re-created over time. The tango and football as arenas for 'national male' identities reveal the complexity of these kinds of 'free' zones in relation to 'otherness'. The ordering tendencies of society are related to public arenas like school, military service, work, public ceremonies and rituals of nationhood. 'Free' zones, like the anti-structural properties of liminality and hybrid sacra in the work of Turner (1967), permit the articulation of languages and practices that can challenge an official and puritanical public domain. 'Free' zones are also spaces for mixing, for the appearance of hybrids, for sexuality and for the exaltation of bodily performances. In modern societies sport, games and dance are privileged loci for the analysis of 'freedom' and cultural creativity. The tango and football can thus be conceptualized as a threat to official ideologies. Therefore, an accomplished analysis of national male imageries will attempt to integrate the various aspects of 'otherness' because it needs all the fragments, and all the dislocated and mismatched identities, and it relies on the changing character of Argentinian society and Argentinian men and women.

Lugones, Rojas and Gálvez, the Argentinian nationalist writers of the 1910s, attempted to recreate the 'national', the essence of the 'nation' and of *argentinidad*, in the figure of the gaucho, a romantic male free rider and heroic figure of the Argentina of the wars of independence, at a time when he was in actuality losing his freedom and becoming a rural proletarian (see Slatta 1985; Delaney 1996; Miller 1997). The authors were reacting and pioneering in resisting immigration and the cultural effects of Argentinian modernization. They were responding like many other intellectuals in situations when a rural traditional society confronts rapid industrialization and urbanization (see Gellner 1983: 57–61; Hutchinson 1992). I shall, in the next chapter, return to some of their ideas. However, a study of Argentinian national male images needs to problematize the continuity of the rural and the contemporary exaltation of the *pampas* and the gauchos. I decided on an indirect strategy: to find the powerful rural imagery in other activities and not in the *pampas*. While I was searching for men, horses and riding in contemporary Argentina, one of my informants put me on the right track. Amilcar, a clever and perceptive journalist, commented to me that in only one sport is Argentina insuperable: polo – an equestrian game associated with British aristocrats and Texas millionaires. As I mentioned before, the British introduced polo, with great success, in Argentina. I thought that this expansion should permit me to make some fruitful comparisons between football and polo, the popular and the aristocratic, the urban and the rural. I decided, as late as 1994, to introduce polo as one of the 'free' zones of my study, and I interviewed retired polo players and personnel of the Argentinian Polo Association. I also worked on the history of this sport in Argentina. In 1997 I was fortunate enough to get acquainted with the descendants of the Traill's, the English family who founded modern polo in Argentina. They opened up a new perspective for me and gave me some important information.

I now had three fragmented, dislocated and mismatched ventures where I could search for, and perhaps find, Argentinian male masks and mirrors: football, the tango and polo. At the same time these activities more or less represented the stratification of Argentinian society in terms of its practioners: polo was the aristocratic landed-class sport, football was popular, and tango poetics were a product of the middle classes. Moreover, I had three sets of relevant relations: men–men in football, men–women in the tango and men–horses in polo.

My data are heterogeneous and generated from participant observations, discussions, various archives, as well as from newspapers, magazines and films. This writing combines oral and written traditions, draws on the past and the present, on ideas and visions, on concepts and moralities, and, above all, on topics that are central to many Argentinians. This book illustrates some of the problems associated with ideas of the nationhood and masculinities by focusing the research strategy on marginal or liminal topics. Significantly such a strategy of 'capture' does not exclude other alternatives.

My research is not on the official ideology of national male identities and nation state but on the margins of the national, the fields where the national can be perceived and related to specific individual features, cultural creativity and public performances. In the nationalist discourse and the ideology of the state individuals are defined as passive selves, as objects of socialization and indoctrination. Cohen has argued the importance of studying the 'thinking self' in relation to nationalism, the individuals as creative and producers of meanings. He writes: 'religious, nationalist or political doctrine may give people ways to think about themselves, forms within which to locate themselves. But there is a vital distinction to be made between these *forms* of thought and expression, and their content' (1994: 146). I would like to add that 'indoctrination' regulates arenas defined as vital by the nation state, like the school system or the military barracks, leaving 'free' zones of creativity. To define a project around these 'free' zones implies a change of perspectives in the research on nationalism and masculinities.

My empirical findings will be presented along the two axes presented in the prologue, which, I think, are central for the production of national male imageries in general: hybridization – or its contrary purity – and male hybrids, and gendered masculinities – comprising same-sex and cross-sex relations. I shall, in the following chapters, elaborate on these dimensions. However, other relevant issues are also revealed in the analysis of discourses of hybridization and masculinities. One of the central themes has to do with the importance of moralities in the production of hybridity and gendered identity. We shall see that in many cases narratives and discourses are pervaded by moral reflections. Therefore, it is highly plausible that hybridity and gender may be the vehicles through which morality is socially articulated.

PART ONE

Hybridization

CHAPTER ONE

Situating Hybridity and Hybrids

It has been stated that the existence of two or three different racial groups inhabiting the same geographical space as early as the sixteenth or seventeenth century is a unique characteristic of the American experience. Consequently, 'more than living side by side, members of different races came to know each other in the most intimate sense. The result was interracial progeny' (Socolow 1996: 3). Schwartz (1996) has called this process of interracial sexual relations 'ethnogenesis'. Latin American societies were, then and now, populated by 'hybrids', by people of mixed blood – mestizos, mulattos, mamelucos and pardos – and Argentina was no exception as we have seen in the previous chapter. The category of mestizo – Spanish and Indian mixed – indicated both a biological and cultural hybrid (Bouysse-Cassagne and Saignes 1996). The fact that this term is twofold, biological and cultural, suggests that the awareness of miscegenation and biology tends to predominate. Moreover, the existence of the concepts of mestizo and mestizaje as emic conceptualization implied that, in the long run, these terms could include any kind of racial or ethnic mixture. The same can be postulated in relation to folk categories like creole and creolization. In this chapter I shall show the power and limitations of these conceptual models in Argentina.

As we saw in the prologue, García Canclini prefers to use hybridization instead of syncretism and mestizaje because it includes 'diverse intercultural mixtures' and 'permits the inclusion of the modern forms of hybridization' (1995: 11). His approach is based on the idea that, in contemporary Latin America, modern culture is heterogeneous as a 'consequence of a history in which modernization rarely operated through the substitution of the traditional and the ancient' (1995: 47). García Canclini put special emphasis on cultural processes in general without, in a systematic way, relating hybridization to hybrids – concrete actors – and without problem-atizing the existence of different models of hybridization. A more complete analysis calls for a conceptualization of the 'hybrids', and in my case male hybrids, and 'hybrid moments', spaces or objects through which rituals are elaborated and 'free zones' separated from other domains of society.

Models of Hybridization and the Creation of Hybrids

General

Papastergiadis has convincingly argued that the history of the hybrid must be as old as the narratives of origin and encounter (1995: 9, 1997: 257). It is obvious that the existence of a clear boundary between 'us' and 'them' calls for the hybrid, the mixed, the less pure, which is created by the transgression or the possibility of transgression of this boundary. In a negative sense, the hybrid can be seen or defined as a representation of danger, chaos, loss and degeneration. However, if the mixing is perceived positively the hybrid can represent creativity, complexity, amalgamation, vitality and strength. Given these situations the hybrid is always thought of in relation to purity and along the axes of inclusion and exclusion. Therefore, the model of hybridity – and the codifica-tion of the hybrids – can only emerge from circumstances in which discontinuities have been produced and policies of purification enacted. Hybridization, as Latour (1993) has reminded us so many times, was a response to practices of purification. There are no hybrids without natural and pure categories.

Young (1995: 25) has summarized the debate on hybridization in the nineteenth century in three dominant models:

1. Hybrid as a category is conceptualized as mixed but as creating a 'pure' form that reproduces itself, repeating its own cultural origins.
2. Hybridization as creolization involves fusion: the creation of a new form, which is set against the old form of which it is partly made up.
3. Hybridization as a chaotic process in which no stable new form, but rather something closer to a radical heterogeneity, discon-tinuity, a kind of permanent revolution of forms, is produced.

It is clear that hybridity makes difference into sameness, and sameness into difference, but 'in a way that makes the same no longer the same, the different no longer simply different' (Young 1995: 26). The concepts of hybridity and hybrids were developed in the natural sciences and in the practice of biology in the nineteenth century. A hybrid was an animal or a plant produced from the mixture of two species. Hybridity implies the creation of a pseudo-species as a result of the combination of two discrete species. However, in Darwin's perspective, the emphasis was put on degrees of hybridity because the species could no longer be seen as absolutely distinct. Central to Darwin's hypothesis is the idea that there is no essential distinction between species and varieties.

By 1861 hybridity was used to denote the crossing of people of different races (Young 1995: 6). This use implied the acceptance that the different races mixing were of different species. For reasons closely associated with the question of racism, and especially because the 'human hybrids' produced were successful in terms of fertility, this was taken to prove that humans were all one species. Therefore, from the end of the nineteenth century until today 'hybridity' and 'hybrid' have moved from the field of biology into key concepts for cultural criticism and political debate. In this respect, Young has stressed the significance of Bakhtin's theory of hybridity (Young 1995: 20–2). Bakhtin's emphasis on the mixture of languages within a text, which defies authority, evidences a new way of relating the concept of hybridity to politics. The language of hybridity transforms and disrupts the singular order of a dominant code. Bakhtin writes:

> Unintentional, unconscious hybridization is one of the most important modes in the historical life and evolution of all languages. We may even say that language changes historically primarily by hybridization, by means of mixing of various 'languages' co-existing within the boundaries of a single dialect, a single national language, a single branch, a single group of different branches, in the historical as well as palaeontological past of languages. (1981: 358–9)

Bakhtin distinguishes 'organic hybrid' from 'intentional hybridity' as historical, unconscious products. Organic hybridity will tend over time towards fusion while intentional hybridity will almost by definition be a contestatory activity, a clear affirmation of cultural and linguistic differences (1981: 361). Hybridity is thus associated with resistance and cultural creativity; it is made contestatory in, for example, the case of carnival (Papastergiadis 1995: 13; Young 1995: 21). Moreover, hybridity can be defined as a kind of permanent condition of all human cultures, one which contains no zones of purity. Instead of hybridity versus purity, as in the biological use, Bakhtin's view suggests that hybridity is one of the conditions of human creativity.

Bhabha (1985, 1994) has politicized the concept of hybridity, using it as a critique of the colonial situation and the hegemony of the national discourse based on cultural homogeneity. Hybridity appears as a discourse exposing the conflicts in colonial discourse and the various ways of living with difference. Hybridity includes explicit forms of counter-authority, moments of political change as well the importance of transgressing fixed borders. Against the concept of a homogeneous nation Bhabha stresses the importance of the migrants and the diasporic communities. Hybridity itself becomes a form of cultural difference, challenging dominant cultural values and creating liminal spaces (a 'third space'). In this way, it is a mode for dealing with the juxtapositions of space and the combination of 'time lag', out of which a sense of identity that is always liminal is constructed. Friedman has correctly observed that: 'the language of in-betweenness, even of liminality, dominates and would even seem to organize Bahbha's call to hybridity. Words such as displacement, dis-juncture, tran-sition, tran-scendence are rife in the texts, where the enemy is that which is generally bounded and thus, for him, essentialised, (1997: 78).

The main limitations of Bakhtin's semiotic approach and Bhabha's literary analysis from an anthropological point of view is the distance from the commonsensical uses (the way actors themselves perceive mixing and create local categories) and, above all, the fact that they are definitions from the outside and, in this sense, powerful normative frameworks. However, I believe that we still need a view from outside that helps us to get a better understanding of the processes of self-definition and self-identification. I find Strathern's use of the concepts, partially following Latour, most fruitful. According to Strathern hybrids as entities are products of relations. The English conceptualize themselves as hybrids in terms of their origins; 'an astonishing mixed blend', this 'glorious amalgam', which is seen as the natural generator of manifold talent (1992: 30). Strathern emphasizes the fact that in the representation of English history there are always additions to an already infinite social and cultural complexity, sustaining the imagery of 'constant infusions of new blood'. The country's institutions were invigorated by cross-fertilization. However, in this mixing each individual – a hybrid him/herself in the sense that he/she is the product of different beings – 'contributed his/her unique portion without losing the transcendent characteristic of individuality that was preserved in the singularity of "the English" themselves' (1992: 36, 83). It is central, therefore, to ask for the native conceptualization of the relationships between the particular and the general, the unique and the representative. The English have two models. On the one hand, they aggregate in the sense that individuals carry out the resonance of a tradition or a community, and in this sense their attributes contribute to its aggregate character. The individual attributes contribute to the collective. On the other hand, they imagine a transcendent and organic order (the national or the collective) that allows for degrees of relatedness or solidarity or liberty; it is like an organism that functions as a whole entity to determine the character of its parts. 'The English' can similarly appear as both aggregate and organism (1992: 29). Strathern writes: 'the aggregating concept stressed the "melting pot" symbolism of heterogeneity, the organic concept that of a redoubtable character that was only to be exemplified idiosyncratically in each individual English(man). The English were thus self-defined in an overlapping way as at once a people and a set of cultural characteristics' (1992: 30).

In a more recent article Strathern (1996) has related hybridity to the concept of network as used by Latour. Hybrid, she proposes, is a concept used in social sciences to refer to something that is of mixed origin. It is a critique of separations and of categorical divisions. Therefore, in analysis of ethnicity, identity and popular culture, for example, it is positively related to creativity, cultural strength and political vigour. Hybridity is invoked in many analyses as a positive force in the world. If hybridity invokes openness the concept of network is needed because it: 'summons the tracery of heterogenous elements that constitute such an object or event, or string of circumstances, held together by social interactions: it is, in short, a hybrid imagined in a socially extended state' (1996: 521). This analysis must be properly contextualized. Strathern's methodology is based on the powerful idea of 'cutting networks'. In this direction, Strathern proposes that if we take given networks as socially expanded hybrids then we must take hybrids as condensed networks. 'The Euro-American hybrid, as an image of dissolved boundaries, indeed displaces the image of boundary when it takes boundary's place' (1996: 523).

The most important lesson that we can draw from Strathern's framework is the insistence on the analysis of native models of hybridity, based on the way the complex relations between diversity and generalization are defined. A model of hybridity calls for diversity and pluralism, while the existence of society – and the national state – and culture calls for generalization. My main aim is to study how in Argentina diversity and generalization are conceived by the intellectual élite as well as my informants in concrete processes of hybridization. This is even more indisputable because, as in the case of England, Argentinians have explicit and implicit models of hybridization based on powerful concepts like creolization (*criollización*) and mixing (*mestizaje*). In this context according to Strathern: 'we are dealing with people who themselves make generalisations, who imagine that they are part of larger collectivities, who act with reference to what they assume to be widespread norms and such like, and who are consequently preoccupied with what they take to be a relationship between the particular and the general' (1992: 28).

I shall try to demonstrate that the intellectual debates of the nineteenth century and the beginning of the twentieth century in Argentina defined a *problématique*, a semantic field and a dominant discursive arena. I shall not attempt to bring about a historical synthesis of the controversies and I shall not present them in a lineal way. In this chapter I shall move from Ibarguren, a nationalist of the 1920s, to Alberdi and Sarmiento, the founders of the modern nation state in the second part of the nineteenth century, and to Lugones, Rojas and Gálvez, the modern nationalists of the beginning of the twentieth century. This perspective implies that the historical complexities of these debates will not fully be discussed.[1] My main attempt is to delineate a field of ideas in the area of political ideologies and to explore its manifestation in other arenas. Sports can be seen as constituting 'patriotic games' in the era of national states and internationalism, as social practices that can eventually re-create dominant ideas related to nationalism (see Jarvie and Walker 1994; Mangan 1996; Pope 1997). Once these practices are established, they will provide a kind of historical framework within which the new generations will interpret the practice in their own way. The semantic field constituted at the beginning of the twentieth century will partly condition new ideological developments defining topics and *problématiques*.

Local

As I pointed out before the colonial period in Latin America and in Argentina is marked by the mixing of populations, particularly the mixing of native Indians and Europeans, known by the Spanish term *mestizaje*. Creole cultures constituted national identities and imageries long before anthropologists discovered that the modern world we live in today is hybrid. Carlos Fuentes, the prolific Mexican writer, celebrated the quincentennial discovery of America in 1992 as the consecration of the racial mix of Spanish America, writing: 'We are Indian, black, European, but above all mixed, *mestizo*. We are Iberian and Greek, Roman and Jewish, Arab, Gothic, and Gypsy. Spain and the New World are centres where multiple cultures meet – centres of incorporation, not of exclusion' (1992: 348). The ideology of *mestizaje* is still today the dominant ideology of national identity in Latin America. Therefore, the groups that did not mix or are perceived as lacking the will to mix with others are considered a potential threat to this ideology. In the colonial as well as in the post-colonial periods the category *mestizo* was identified with the mixture of Spanish and natives and, in this sense, presupposed the existence and the reproduction of the pure Indian or other pure racialized classifications (Mörner 1971; Basave Benítez 1992; Harris 1995; Ochoa 1995; Schwartz 1996; Bouysse-Cassagne and Saignes 1996; Radcliffe 1997). This process is extreme in the case of the Dominican Republican, in which the category Indian (*indios*) as pure Dominican is used in order to exclude the black population, or in many countries, Brazil being a typical case, in which some mixtures are defined as better than others (Freire 1946; Krohn-Hansen 1997).

In the immigrant Argentina of the end of nineteenth century and early twentieth century, the native Indian population had been almost eliminated through the expansion of the frontier of the national state and the consequent War of the Desert in 1879. The remaining native population was portrayed as an immobile, doomed race, unable to accept mixing (*mestizaje*), education and modernization, stuck in the compulsion to repeat the same ineffective campaigns of resistance until, at last, they perished along with their names and their stories. For different reasons, among them wars, diseases and the massive immigration of the last quarter of the nineteenth century, the black population, which constituted 25% of Argentinians in 1838, numbered less than 2% by 1900 (Reid 1980). Therefore, when the massive flux of immigrants disembarked in Buenos Aires, immigration was perceived by the nationalist writers of the beginning of the twentieth century as the real threat to the original *mestizaje*, to the original creole population, to the old inhabitants of the country.

Rojas, one of the most important nationalist writers, conceived the massive immigration and the lack of a clear educational policy orientated towards the integration of foreigners as a menace to cultural reproduction (1909: 89–90). Images of 'invasion', language 'corruption', moral and sexual 'chaos' are present in Rojas and other writers like Lugones, Gálvez, Bunge and Ibarguren. Even in 1926, a modernist writer like Borges, who imagined the city of Buenos Aires as a cosmopolitan fusion, contrasted the margins of Buenos Aires, populated by a creole population, to the centre of the city where 'the babelic, the picturesque, the tearing off from the four points of the world, the Moor and the Jewish' dominated, (1993: 24).

By 1914, when the first waves of the vast immigration stopped as a consequence of the First World War, the positive image that European immigration had enjoyed among the Argentinian intellectual élite was tarnished. Foreign-born businessmen and foreign enterprises controlled a large share of the national economy. Urban foreign workers, especially in Buenos Aires, organized trade unions, were continually striking and became very militant. Moreover, from 1904, the Socialist Party became one of the dominant political forces in Buenos Aires, where anarchists were also very active. Liberal values and cosmopolitanism had guided the generous immigration policies since the 1850s. The modern Argentina was imagined as the result of massive European immigration: a rapid integration in the world market through foreign capital investment, technological change, increasing local production and the expansion of consumption of foreign industrial goods; a prompt urbanization as a way of changing rural traditional attitudes, *caudillismo* and political clientelism; and, as a main consequence of the changes, an increasing economic and social mobility of larger groups of the society. Ibarguren, criticizing Alberdi, one of the fathers of the nineteenth-century modernist Argentinian project, wrote:

> The doctrine of Alberdi, opposed to the national idea founded in the heroic meaning of life and patriotism which created our first pages of history, is based on the materialist and bourgeois concept of the economic well-being as the supreme objective of a nation formed by

cosmopolitans. Our fertile territory was, and still is, a great world producer of cereals and beef. Such a policy, carried out with the best intentions of creating progress and producing indeed great wealth, joined by the massive avalanche of immigrants that has transformed Buenos Aires and the great Litoral into a polyglot and heterogeneous region, a real chaotic ethnic Babel, has not promoted the formation of a spiritual unity, a proper Argentinian soul. This soul will emerge and will be powerful only when nationalism creates the moral and organic unity of all the social forces amalgamated in one only spirit. (Own translation; Ibarguren 1934: 154)[2]

Ibarguren did not conceptualize the nation as a necessary mixture, as a hybrid based on miscegenation. The idea of amalgamation so explicitly presented, and so crucial in any model of hybridization, is a kind of Renanian conception of the spirit of the nation as an expression of a collective psychology. In this sense the nation (and the nationality) is reduced to a psychological phenomenon, to a collective consciousness that must be created. The question of racial mixing is thus avoided.

The liberals primarily conceived of Argentina as constituted by the citizens of a modern state. The accent was put on the freedom and the autonomy of the individual as representing the limits of the sovereignty of the nation state. According to Alberdi (1915) the individual and his liberty were above the authority of the fatherland. His vision concerning the impact of immigration was cosmopolitan: the new Argentina should be the product of the socio-economic and cultural impact of the immigrants. In this sense he rejected the idea that Argentinian culture was something fixed, a stock of irreplaceable meanings, symbols and practices. Argentinian society and culture were conceived of as something to be produced and changed through immigration and modernization.

Regarding the status of the immigrants, Alberdi thought that Argentina should only guarantee citizenship and political rights. This image was consistent with the way of life of Argentinian cosmopolitans like himself. They were not bound by local habits (which many of them considered to be traditionalist and backward), they spoke foreign languages and lived long periods of their lives in exile or as travellers in Europe and/or the United States. Their life experiences, sensibilities and ideology made it possible for them to perceive, in many ways, the immigrants as similar to themselves. The European immigrants to Argentina had left their villages and cities, customs, food habits and local rituals, manifesting a great flexibility of mind and an open spirit. In this modernist imagery immigration permitted the definitive conquest, domestication and transformation of the fertile territory of the country, and the transformation of a traditional culture. The wild life of gauchos on the pampas was to be replaced by settled farmers, as was livestock by agriculture, extensive use of natural resources by private property, a closed economy by one integrated into the world market, and folk artistry by European theatre, music and opera. Ibarguren reacted against this creed:

> The struggle against the desert and the political barbarism of the gaucho led Alberdi to the contrary exaggeration, rejecting what was the authentic creole culture and trying to transform our country into a cosmopolitan conglomerate without national spirit and character . . . Without any doubt, immigration has brought about great material benefits. But I must emphasize a trait typical of the immigrant which hinders his spiritual integration and solidarity in the building of a nation: his individualism . . . He is free from tradition, which is always a constraint, sees freedom and social exchanges with the egoism and openness of mind of one who has broken all ties with his original community in order to find easily obtained economic wealth abroad. Therefore the immigrant is an intense individualist with great difficulty in being integrated within a national coherent social group. (Own translation; 1934: 152–5)

Argentinian nationalist writers constructed an image of the male immigrant as extreme individualist, materialist, only preoccupied with earning money, refusing to accept the spiritual and cultural heritage of the host country and without feelings of belonging to a new nation (see Rojas 1909; Gálvez 1910, 1930).

Nationalism appeared to protect the creole heritage against cosmopolitanism. Ibarguren remembered his nationalist struggle during the 1920s in the following way:

> more than forty years ago, we were very worried about the heterogeneous make-up of the Argentinian people. On the one hand, we had the historical people, traditional, with a continuity of destiny, and on the other, the sons of immigrants who in spite of being the legal fellow-countrymen of the old creoles, rejected or ignored the glorious national past. (Own translation; 1971: 8)

How should ideas and sentiments of belonging to the Argentinian nation be transmitted to the immigrants and to their sons and daughters? One strategy was the adoption of obligatory conscription for the sons of immigrants; those who were born in the country automatically became Argentinian citizens because the state used the *jus solis*. Even a war against Brazil was thought of as an important step in creating national sentiments. Gálvez, one of the most active nationalist writers of the first two decades of the twentieth century, wrote that a war against the neighbouring country would be desirable because it would accelerate the assimilation of the first-generation immigrants: 'war would convert the foreigners to Argentinians and the cosmopolitan spirit would be destroyed beneath the vast patriotic fervour' (1910: 78). The other strategy, led by Rojas, and for most intellectuals the most attractive, was the transformation of the elementary and secondary curricula into a nationalistic education emphasizing Argentinian history and geography, national civic duties, moral teaching based on the cult of Argentinian heroes, Spanish language and Argentinian literature, which for this explicit purpose was, in many ways, 'invented' by Rojas himself (Rojas 1909; Solberg 1970: 144–54; Halperín Donghi 1987: 227; Escudé 1990: 25–86).

One clear illustration of the educational ideology that dominated the Argentinian primary school from 1880 onwards is found in Sarlo's analysis (1997) of two incidents that occurred in a primary school of the city of Buenos Aires in 1921. During the first week of school, the female headteacher of a school of Villa Crespo, a neighbourhood inhabited by Jewish immigrants and herself the daughter of European illiterate immigrants, decides, in order to eliminate lice, to shave the heads of all the boys (not the girls) attending school. Weeks later, before the celebration of the national day, on her own initiative and with her money, she buys metres and metres of cotton ribbon with the colours of the Argentinian flag – white and blue – and sews chignons for the girls and ties for the boys. During the parade on 25 May all the children of her school proudly marched in the streets of Buenos Aires, decorated with the national colours of Argentina. A rite of separation for the boys – shaving their heads – was compensated by a rite of incorporation – the national parade and the ties with the Argentinian flag. Sarlo concludes that both bodily interventions were profoundly patriotic because hygiene and fatherland were united (1997: 188). Sarlo defines the schoolmistress as a 'kind of state robot' and her story shows the efficiency of the Argentinian state in the formation of public servants (1997: 189).

Between 1880 and 1910, the expansion of the educational system
in Argentina was impressive. By 1910, the rate of illiteracy of the
adult population was as low as 4% (Prieto 1988: 13). During this
period, and in accordance with the liberal creed, education was
supposed to be objective, positivist, scientific, universalist and
secular. Thousands of teachers were imported from Europe and
North America. As late as in 1914, 14% of the elementary school-
teachers were foreigners (Solberg 1970: 152). The 'nationalist
restoration' of the education produced a shift of emphasis in
pedagogic theory which implied a change in the teaching of history,
geography, national civic duties and morals, and in Argentinian
literature from 'positivism' into 'nationalist fiction'. The main
function of the teaching of history, according to Rojas, was 'to form
the national consciousness' and to produce authentic 'feelings
of patriotism' (1909: 35). By 1910, this nationalist project was
hegemonic. This nationalist revival coincided with the centennial
festivities of the independence from Spain in 1810, in which a
potently patriotic rhetoric and imagery was organized around the
negative sides of immigration. Bunge (1911), one of the most active
nationalist intellectuals in the field of education, defended the idea
that the teaching of history should not be limited to the transmission
of proved and real facts, its main function being to introduce
'tradition', a mixture of real events and fiction, and 'legends', stories
telling impossible and marvellous events. In this perspective, traditions and legends should have an important nationalizing value
(*alto valor nacionalizante*). Thus what was defined as 'poetic and
social fiction' was conceived of as a key pedagogical instrument
for creating a nation and integrating the immigrants (see Halperín
Donghi 1987: 226–35; Escudé 1990: 38–41). Halperin Dongui
writes:

> the new nationalism, far from displaying itself as an anti-immigration
> ideology, is presented as the most appropriate to a country that should
> reconcile itself with the rapid transformations undergone. Even so, it
> reflects the definitive exhaustion of the liberal progressive ideology
> that attempted – utilizing among other instruments the policy of massive
> immigration – to build up a nation against her past without taking it as
> a point of departure. The nation will not be moulded as a realization
> of given universal values: the imperative of the national cohesion is a
> priority and an ideological agreement on values expressing this cohesion
> should be necessarily reached. (Own translation 1987: 228–9)

Let us go back to Rojas for a moment. Rojas acknowledged that the process of immigration and the increase of wealth had radically transformed the city of Buenos Aires and the Argentinian society as a whole. Buenos Aires, he recognized, had become a modern and cosmopolitan city, no longer a homogeneous village (1909: 89).[3] He imagined, almost as an echo of the models of hybridity discussed by Young, two possible developments: consolidation of an organic heterogeneity (*heterogéneo orgánico*), a human blend that works; or simply 'chaos', the lack of mixing, the coexistence of separate ethnic groups (1909: 89). Rojas, a *mestizo* himself from a traditional province in north-eastern Argentina, did not reject inter-ethnic marriages. He even assumed that the mixing (*mezcla*) was the best solution, but it should be done from a local, creole perspective. The ideal mixture should be achieved 'with a content of local civilization, produced from a traditional substance'. If this was not done the alternative was that the local 'race (*raza*) succumbs in pacific slavery to the foreigner' (1909: 91). Rojas, in spite of having been strongly marked by Herder's concepts of *Volk* and *Volksgeist*, was not very far from some key ideas advanced by Gobineau (Miller 1997: 8). Gobineau, who later influenced the thinking of many Argentinian Catholic nationalists like Ibarguren, maintained that any mixing should be done by a 'dominant civilization' or 'race' which is able to condition or subordinate the other, the less 'dominant' race (Gobineau 1983: 1159–70; Todorov 1989: 153–64).

By the First World War, the nationalists had found, in the male gaucho – the free cowboy riding in the pampas, hunting, gathering and working for a wage when he needed - a symbol to represent the cultural heritage of the nation under threat by immigration (Solberg 1970; Slatta 1985; Prieto 1988; Delaney 1996).[4] For the liberals, in contrast, the gaucho was the antithesis of civilization and culture and represented the rural social disorder, clientelism and political violence characteristic of post-colonial Argentina. The policy of '*gobernar es poblar*' (to govern is to populate) promoted by Alberdi and Sarmiento had a strong 'racial' component. Sarmiento, who served as Argentina's president from 1868 to 1874, wrote that the 'principal ingredient towards order and moralization in the Argentine Republic is immigration from Europe' (1981: 240). The liberal Argentinian intelligentsia imagined that the arrival of immigrants from North and Central Europe would lead to the purification of the race and a radical improvement of the work ethic of the creole population. The result was not exactly as they expected. Italians, Spaniards, Jew, and Middle and Far Eastern immigrants prevailed (Schneider 1996), and the nationalists continued to claim the figure and the cultural meaning of the gaucho as the primary symbolic type of Argentinian nationality. Paradoxically enough, the nationalist discourse revived the 'barbaric' subjects which had been condemned to disappear through immigration, hybridization and modernization. Let me briefly present some of the ideas of the archetypical exaltation of the gaucho made by Lugones, who, together with Rojas and Gálvez, was one of the paladins of the nationalist intellectual resurgence.[5]

Lugones's lectures on the gaucho – always a male – given in a huge theatre of Buenos Aires in 1913 and attended by the President Roque Saénz Peña, had a great impact on public opinion. They were published as book in 1916. The gaucho of Lugones is the product of colonial hybridization, the mixing of Spaniards and the Indian population. According to him, the gaucho inherited the pride of the Spanish blood (*sangre fidalga*) and the sense of independence of the local Indian population (*la independencia del indio antecesor*). These qualities distinguished the *criollos* from the servile blacks and the false mulattos (a hybrid defined negatively). In Lugones's theory of hybridity the best mixture is between Spaniards and Indians because both are virile races (*razas viriles*) (1961: 61). Obviously, a mixture between non-virile races will not produce the same result. Lugones postulates with great clarity that a hybrid like the gaucho is better than the original pure races. The process of hybridization makes it possible for gauchos to possess:

> the psychological tints which the Indian (*salvaje*) lacks; the compassion, which I called sometimes tenderness of the force; the courtesy, this hospitality of the soul; the elegance, this aesthetics of the sociability; the melancholy, this mildness of the passion. And after all, the social virtues: the honour, the frankness, the loyalty, blended in the gift of gentlemanliness; the prodigality without stint of his possessions and his blood. (1961: 61–2)

However, negative features are also inherited in the mixture: from the Indian the savage atavism (*atavismo salvaje*) that transforms the gaucho in situations of violence and war into a person with great cruelty, and the love for idleness, and from the Spaniard a profound pessimism (1961: 62).

Lugones accepted that the gaucho as a sociological reality had disappeared with the transformation of Argentina, and he stressed that he was an archetype, a kind of ideal type. Even this is seen as positive because: 'his disappearance is good for the country, because he had an inferior element in his part – Indian blood; but his definition as a national type made possible, both ethnically and socially, our separation from Spain, constructing our own personality. Therefore, the Argentinian, with the same physical shape and language, is, however, so distinct from the Spaniard' (1961: 83). The gaucho is not only an ideal type but also a 'substance' that is still alive.[4] This 'substance' exists in the confusion of 1913, in the city of Buenos Aires and in the chaotic *pampa* invaded by foreigners, and will reappear in the new hybrids. Lugones writes:

> Our best family qualities, like the extreme love for the son; the contra-
> dictory and romantic depth of our personality; the musical sensibility,
> so curious in a country in which aesthetics is sometimes not appreciated;
> the fidelity of our women; the importance given to personal courage;
> the boastfulness, the inconsistency, the lack of scruples for acquiring,
> the extravagance, constitute peculiar traits of the gaucho. We are not
> gauchos, without any doubt, but this product of the environment
> contained in potence the Argentinian of today, so different from the
> confused appearance produced by the actual cross-breeding. When this
> confusion disappears, these traits will still stand out. (Own translation
> 1961: 79)

In Lugones's conception, like that of Rojas, there is a substance, a kind of essence that will never vanish and that, paradoxically enough, reappears in each mixture. This condition is associated with the existence of superior qualities in the mixed races that will condition the new male hybrid. In this logic an essence which is strong will never disappear. This force is not only biological, because in their imagined gauchos biology is also social and includes moral values and psychological features. The preocuppation of Lugones is to avoid mixtures that generate chaos or degeneration or, in other words, the crisis of the qualities of the original ideal hybrid, the gaucho. In the theory of Gobineau, biological degenera-tion is possible when the original blood stock tends to dissolve. Gobineau, however, accepted that this risk will always be present because racial mixing cannot be prevented (1983: 334).

   In this context of nationalistic revival, the epic poem *Martin Fierro* was written by José Hernández in 1872 in a style reproducing gauchesque rural language. Its narrative of a gaucho struggling against state injustice in order to keep his freedom was transformed into a model for a 'national literature'. Bunge, full of enthusiasm, wrote in 1909: 'The gaucho Martín Fierro is more than a given man, he represents the generic type of the gaucho in the middle of the nineteenth century, and his figure, real or fantastic, will be perpetuated in the memory of the Argentinian people as a great and barbarian god of the heroic times' (quoted in Escudé 1990: 41). This reinvention of tradition was made possible by the privileged place that creole literature (*literatura criolla*) occupied in popular urban and rural literary consumption from the 1880s. *Martín Fierro* was not the only epic male hero. He was accompanied by other mythical figures such as *Santos Vega* and *Juan Moreira*, both noble gauchos like himself, fighting for what they considered just and representing freedom and tradition (see Ludmer 1988; Rama 1996: 50–63). Prieto has shown that creole literature was also read in the cities, especially among European immigrants, to whom the colourful rural iconography was the only expression of something national, local Argentinian, in the middle of the 'generalized disorder produced by the cosmopolitan swallows' (1988: 98–9). The creole literature created moral human types in situations of conflict and tension introduced by modernization and cosmopolitan values. These figures were heroic, but also elegant and polite when treated decently. They were men of honour and courage, symbolizing idealized aristocratic images.

It is important to keep in mind that, by 1910, Argentina did not have a consolidated and strong literary tradition with an accepted master narrative. Argentina was a 'new country' with a history in the making. Thus, tradition had to be imagined and, in many ways, recovered from the past. In a turbulent present much affected by the influx of foreigners and a rapid and chaotic growth of cities, the nationalist writers believed that the cosmopolitan Buenos Aires was not the place to look for the new symbols of nationality. These symbols were in the past, in the landscape, in the soil of the pampas, and in the reading and the imaginary reconstruction of a rural culture with its epic masculine figures. Borges observed in 1926: 'Buenos Aires, in spite of being packed with two million individual destinies, will remain deserted and without a voice, until a symbol will inhabit her. The province is people: there are Santos Vega and the gaucho, Cruz and Martín Fierro, possibilities of gods. The city is still awaiting poeticization' (1993: 126).

With the publication of *Don Segundo Sombra*, 1926 was a significant year for gauchesque literature. The novel, written by Ricardo Güiraldes, depicts the encounter between Fabio, a young urbanite, and Don Segundo Sombra, a strong, courageous and honest gaucho living a traditional life in the *pampa*. Fabio, a kind of metaphor of the new and modern Argentina, enters the countryside to learn the fundamental Argentinian virtues represented by the gaucho way of life. Values like generosity, lack of interest in material things, skill in the complicated art of horsemanship, the endurance of physical hardship and the acceptance of a hierarchical society are central in Don Segundo Sombra's cosmology. The gaucho depicted by Güiraldes (an aristocratic landlord himself) represented many of the best and most heroic qualities of the nation which the nationalists imagined were in danger of being lost due to immigration and modernization.

Models of Transformation: the Creation of Hybridity and Male Hybrids

The sociological fact of immigration was undeniable to the nationalist writers I have been dealing with in this chapter. They accepted it as part of the Argentinian history. Millions and millions of immigrants arrived, and the majority decided to stay in Argentina. A definition of a historical male essence, national and *criolla*, made sense only if combined with the dynamics of the present. In other words, the main problem was how to combine some imagined creole identity with its own archetypes and the new hybrids being produced. In addition, the demographic imbalance, with a majority of men among the immigrants, was a powerful morphological reality.[6]

It is clear that once *mestizaje* is accepted as a crucial element of national identity in Argentina the idea of a persistent national essence is difficult to sustain. Even Rojas approached the idea of a multi-ethnic Argentina.[7] He recognized that the Argentinian colonial society was a product of a variety of ethnic groups: peninsular Spaniards, American Spaniards (born in Argentina), other Europeans, blacks, Indians, and then different mixtures: *mestizos*, *mulatos*, *zambos* and others (1912: 173). His perspective implied a recognition that the 'national' was multifaceted and impossible to reduce to pure types or to the different mixtures that were continuously produced in post-colonial Argentina. However, in the model of transformations discussed by Lugones and Rojas there is a latent creole (native) substance that, given certain conditions, will emerge in the continuous hybridization process. These models imply a reversal of the dominant myth of the immigrant as a civilizing influence. This is even clearer in the case of the physician and well-known intellectual Ramos Mejía, who wrote in 1899 what many considered the first 'scientific study of Argentinian society' (1974). He described the immigrant as susceptible to changes once he was put into contact with the positive influences of Argentinian culture and society. Ramos Mejía went even further, suggesting that in this contact and in the consequent racial mixture it was possible to see in the second generation of immigrants 'the imprint of a relatively more civilized and cultured life' (1974: 214).

If we go back to the three models of hybridization presented by Young it is evident that the third alternative, a kind of racial chaos, where the new forms created are close to radical heterogeneity, total discontinuity and permanent transformation, is rejected by the Argentinian nationalists; they perceive this alternative as possible and much more dangerous than the other two, for it implies either a mixture – the creole, gaucho or *mestizo* – that has the particularity of reappearing in other mixtures, or a fusion – the creation of a new hybrid that can be compared with the forms from which it has been developed. My hypothesis is that all these models are possible to find in activities and public arenas where male immigrants were active and were not controlled by the formal institutions of the state.

Conclusion: Male hybrids in Sport

The model of the gaucho advanced by the nationalists can be seen as a reaction of urban intellectuals in Latin American societies entering into modernity, as García Canclini has pointed out, and, at the same time, as a re-creation of traditional male virtues in a context of change. The gaucho culture of the pampas, eminently regional, was thus transformed as national. Oliven (1996) has shown that in the state of Rio Grande do Sul in Brazil the gaucho culture and traditions, re-created in the 1940s in urban centres, has been used as a basis in the construction of a regional identity (see also Fachel Leal 1989). His findings elucidate the problems created in Latin America when cultural and regional differences were eliminated from what was defined as common, as national.[8]

Bioy Casares has provokingly stated that the gauchos in Argentina
never existed. He asserted that urban intellectuals imagined them
as something typical in a given historical period, and perhaps as a
result of this invention the gauchos had 'a protracted life' re-created
through film, literature, rural rituals and local feasts and festivals
(Bioy Casares 1970: 35). He described the revival of gaucho culture
in the Argentina of the 1940s and 1950s in the following way:

> In the 1940s and 1950s to the old popular zenith of sports in Argentina
> was added the even more popular interest in folklore. The rural youth
> was confronted with the novelty that the gaucho condition was inter-
> esting and prestigious. With great courage they took part as sportsmen
> in the revival of the horse traditional competitions, but before doing
> that they went to the local stores in order to buy gaucho clothes.
> (Own translation 1970: 39)

Bioy Casares ironically pointed out that the 'gaucho clothes' were
invented by the owners of local stores, using as a model the way
Rudolph Valentino wore them in some of his classical films of the
1930s when he portrayed traditional Argentinian gauchos dancing
the tango. He contrasted this 'sportsman' figure with the 'real'
male gauchos he met in his youth on his family estancia in the
province of Buenos Aires. According to Bioy Casares, they never
wore the 'gaucho clothes' in Valentino style, and they were Italians
or French or mestizos, with names like Panizzo, Pardo, Jara or
Mendivil, having in common the fact that they were extraordinary
riders and horse tamers, artists in the art of knifing, experts in
curing horses by talking, very reserved, masters in the art of irony,
distinguished, almost noble, and lonely (1970: 44–58). In spite of
his denial of the existence of a 'gaucho essence' we can recognize
in the gauchos of Bioy Casares some of the key male virtues emphasized by Lugones.[9]

In a country of massive immigration we can see national discourses and images as examples of dislocating identities and we
can expect from these that the meaning of 'otherness' shifts. In
more homogeneous societies I expect dislocation to be less apparent
and the lack of an explicit model of transformation more evident:
nationality is defined and experienced as more obvious. In a society
like the Argentinian one an accomplished national imagery will
attempt to integrate the different 'othernesses' because it needs
all the fragments, all the dislocated and mismatched identities, and
it relies on the changing character of the groups that inhabit a

given territory. Argentina entered into modernity by producing
a series of identities and cultural contradictory tendencies that
impeded integration and containment in a single national imagery
as envisaged by the nationalists. My examples in this part of the
book show that 'high' and 'low' culture, 'popular' and 'élite', 'local'
and 'transnational' visions were at work when Argentinian society
was caught by the forces of globalization. Argentinian cultural
identity was thus highly dependent upon multiplicity (see Masiello
1992: 165-200).

The next two chapters will be devoted to a historical analysis of
the images of man conveyed by football, an urban practice, and by
polo, a rural game. The choice of football and polo makes it
possible to explore in a comparative perspective the connections
between masculinities and the process of hybridization. Mosse
(1996) has pointed out that the ideals of male beauty and fitness
created modern masculinity through gymnastics and sport. Latin
American countries were also integrated into modernity through
sport. The construction of manhood and nationhood through
sports was in principle a modernist project because it was fabricated
by the introduction of foreign cultural practices and not by the
revival or invention of traditions. I shall try to show that this process
is more intricate than what Mosse has done for Europe, and that,
in this direction, a systematic comparison of different sports is
crucial.

Notes

1. The most notorious figures associated with liberal ideas and modern-
    ization in Argentina are Sarmiento and Alberdi. Sarmiento (1811-88)
    was an educator, a military man, writer and statesman who become
    president of Argentina (1864-74). He went into exile to Chile in 1840.
    In 1842 in Chile he was appointed director of the first school for
    primary school teachers in South America and began to put into effect
    a lifelong conviction that national development was intimately related
    to the consolidation of a system of public education. He spent several
    years travelling in Europe and the United States. During his exile he
    wrote *Facundo* (1845), a biography of a tyrannical gaucho political
    leader. In this book, primitive life (*barbarie*) is associated with the
    gaucho way of life and civilization (*civilización*) with European values
    of modernity, industry and agriculture. *Facundo* has been called
    the single most important book published in Spanish America. The

readings of *Facundo* are numerous, varied and conflicting. Goodrich (1996) has shown how the readings have had a potent impact on the making of the Argentinian nation and its culture. Most of the fifty-two published volumes of Sarmiento are, however, devoted to educational topics. The most important political thinker of Argentina in the nineteenth century was perhaps Alberdi (1819–84). His writings influenced the assembly that drew up the modern constitution of Argentina in 1853. His book *Bases y puntos de partida para la organización política de la República Argentina* (1852) emphasized the need for a federal government and argued in favour of attracting foreign capital and immigrants. In the 1850s Alberdi was an Argentinian plenipotentiary in Paris, Madrid, Washington and London. He lost power and influence in the 1860s and spent his last years in semi-exile in Europe until his death in Paris in 1884.

2. Ibarguren (1877–1956) can be defined as a 'late' nationalist, when compared with Rojas, Lugones and Gálvez, and as a kind of 'muscular Catholic nationalist', who was very active in the late 1920s and 1930s, when he wrote *La inquietud de esta hora* (1934). I have always found his writings against liberalism and cosmopolitanism clear and formulated with the typical rhetorical prose of the early nationalist writers. For a history of nationalism and an exhaustive presentation of the ideas of the different writers and political wings see Navarro Gerassi (1969), Solberg (1970), Rama (1981), Rock (1987) and (1993).

3. Rojas (1882–1957), a writer, historian and educator, cultivated all literary genres and from 1917 to 1921 published a monumental history of Argentinian literature. The spirit of *argentinidad*, the roots of national identity, was developed in his thinking within the wider context of the Americas as a civilization in which there was a privileged place for the Indian cultural heritage. Rojas described Buenos Aires in 1909 as an alienating city, rootless, without community feelings, with cosmopolitan values, with a decadent sensualist atmosphere, with a spoken Spanish polluted by the 'dialectal barbarism of the immigrants', very rich and opulent, and with an extreme influence over the Argentinian provinces and the rest of the country. Rojas believed that, due to the dominant role of the city, the nationalist battle had to be fought there (1909: 88–90).

4. The idea of the Argentinian nation is not a consequence of the post-colonial period initiated with the declaration of independence from Spain in 1810. Chiaramonte (1989) has demonstrated that the anti-colonial movement that culminated in 1810 was not guided by a clear idea of the meaning of a nation. At least three identities were at work simultaneously: Spanish-American (*hispanoamericana*); *Rioplatense*; and provincial. He concludes by pointing out that the ideology of the Argentinian nation appears relevant when the political élite tries to

organize a national state. State-building and national identity go together (see Riekenberg 1993). This is complicated by the period of civil wars in Argentina, which ended in 1853, and by massive immigration.

5. Lugones (1874–1938) was a poet and literary and social critic, considered by many to be the outstanding cultural figure of his time. His influence in public life set the pace of national development in the arts and education. In his youth a radical socialist, he lived in Paris from 1911 to 1914 and returned to Argentina just before the outbreak of the First World War. During his stay in Paris he changed his political ideology and became a militant conservative nationalist. He then became a fascist in 1919. Gramuglio (1977) has shown that Lugones's nationalist project was based on the production of a literature where the epic courage of the gauchos in the struggle for independence was the central element. She has traced his rejection of modernism in favour of a treatment of national themes in the analysis of *La guerra gaucha* (1905) and the poems of *El libro de los paisajes* (1917).

6. The sociological and historical literature on the impact of immigration on Argentinian society is vast. Devoto illustrates an important shift from simple models of marriage, dominated by a high degree of endogamy, to pluralism and exogamy in the production of the 'melting-pot'. From the perspective of the second generation of immigrants, he argues, the choice of marriage strategy must be seen in relation to other important cultural and political dimensions (1992: 29). In other words, even a high degree of endogamy among given groups of immigrants does not necessarily imply the persistence of the original ethnic identity of their parents. Freundlich de Seefeld (1986) has shown that, in the period 1860–1923 in Buenos Aires, among the first generation of immigrants, with the exception of the French, there was a high degree of endogamy. Surprisingly enough, the most endogamic were the Spanish, more so than the English. However, in the second generation the degree of exogamy increased. She calls this process 'crisol de razas a la criolla' (creole melting-pot) because the rate of intermarriage between different European groups was higher than between them and the Argentinian native population. Another important variable is the impact of social and economic mobility on marriage strategies, ethnic images and the reproduction of ethnic boundaries over time. More comparative studies are needed on the spatial and time variations of these dimensions (see Schneider 1997).

7. Argentina is at a certain level a hyper-modern country. Massive immigration was accompanied by an unprecedented introduction of new plants and new breeds of animals. The cross-breeding of livestock and the import of pure British breeds are behind the modernization of the beef and wool production in Argentina. Many of the debates on the importance of keeping a bloodstock of creole cows or creole horses

in the new hybrids were important ideological trenches (*The Standard* 17/1/1904: 3 and 10/4/1904: 7). The creole breeds had resistance and strength, which improved the qualities of the imported breeds. These debates run parallel to the discussions on the impact of massive immigration and the mixing of different ethnic groups. During the first decade of the twentieth century *The Standard* published letter after letter containing the opinions of British landlords in Argentina on the different strategies for improving the creole breeds. These debates were also important among Argentinian landlords. The history of these parallelisms, with its continuities and discontinuities, is still waiting to be researched.

8. Cohen (1974) demonstrated the influence of the impact of immigration and the growing hostility towards immigrants, in the period 1890 to 1924, as a consequence of the rise of nativist ideas on the American self-image. She correctly observes that something similar happened in Argentina: 'the image of the "gaucho" underwent a similar transformation to that of the America cowboy, and the cult of the "gaucho" seems to have been used to contrast traditional creole values with those of the immigrants and to depict the immigrant as inept and unsuited for an idealized, vanishing epoch of Argentinian history' (1974: 39).

9. An interesting study on gaucho cultural persistence is the unpublished thesis of Strickon (1960), based on research on an estancia of the Province of Buenos Aires. As the reader could imagine, the bibliography on the gauchos in Argentina is vast (see especially Nichols 1942; Assuncao 1959; Coni 1969; Becco and Dellepiane Calcena 1978). Lack of space prevents me from even briefly discussing it.

CHAPTER TWO

Male Hybrids in the World of Football

Horacio, with whom I have attended so many football matches since 1984 and who, with great generosity, enlightened me about the history of Argentinian football, said in one of the endless conversations we had during October 1994:

> Argentina is a very odd country, full of contradictions. You remember, after the Falklands war, we changed all the names of the streets and places which reminded us of the British influence in our own history. Since then, periodically, the monument of Canning, I think a British Prime Minister in the past century, has been attacked and the British Tower of Plaza San Martin horribly vandalized. These acts are an expression of our nationalism, of our anti-British feelings. As you know, almost by definition, to be anti-British is to be a kind of anti-imperialist. However, there is an important monument in Buenos Aires which has never been vandalized or destroyed. In the park of Palermo, very close to the Planetarium, you will find a modest monument commemorating the first game of football played in Argentina on 20 June 1867. These fields belonged to the Buenos Aires Cricket Club, an old British club, and all the players who played this match were British citizens. You can read all their names. They introduced the game, our national passion and, as an act of justice, they deserve to be remembered for ever. I hope that this monument will enter the next century intact.

I told Horacio that I did not know that we had such a monument in Buenos Aires, and I confessed my surprise, telling him that this story was one of his inventions. He understood my scepticism and, as the man of action he is, invited me to visit the place. After finishing our drink, we took a taxi and, in the park of Palermo, I discovered that he was right. Just because Horacio knew of it, we were – I imagined like two idiots – in front of a modest and almost unknown monument of Argentina, impossible to find in any tourist guide of Buenos Aires where all kinds – both important and unnecessary – of historical monuments, museums and buildings are listed. I proposed to Horacio that we initiate a campaign to declare this monument a place of pilgrimage for all the Argentinian football lovers and supporters. He dismissed my idea as unrealistic and improper. He commented:

> Imagine, imagine for a second, the day we beat England in the 1986 World Cup of Mexico, with the famous goal of Maradona with his hand, 'the hand of God'; if the supporters knew of its existence . . . well, a disaster was possible because they, perhaps, might have decided to organize after the joyful street celebration a demonstration against British imperialism, resulting in its destruction. It is much better to keep this secret between us. I told you because I hope that you are not going to bomb it. I cannot imagine Argentinian history without this monument. We have so many unnecessary monuments in our country, so many false heroes and stupid battles to celebrate.

If this monument was a secret in 1994, it was revealed to the nation on 21 June 1997. *Clarin*, a serious and much-read newspaper of Buenos Aires, published two articles about this event with the titles: 'Together with the railways arrived the English pioneers. The country of immigrants' and 'Memory: The first football match ever played in Argentina. 130 years since the first kick'. A picture of the monument illustrated both articles. The journalist concluded the second article with a clear message: football contributed to the integration of the immigrants and to the growth of a national football style and identity.

Today, we cannot imagine the Argentinian nation without this unknown monument. The spread of football and other sports was a product of Britain's world power status and its active presence in commerce, industrial production, territorial control and international finance. The English Football Association was formed in 1863. Their founders, ex-public school and university players working in London, hoped to produce a set of clear rules from the different varieties of football played in Great Britain. The aim was to produce one unified game. They did not fully succeed, because the supporters of Rugby football decided to maintain its distinguishing features of hacking and handling (Mason 1989: 146). Since then Great Britain has exported football and Rugby as different games.

The editor of *The Standard*, a leading British newspaper issued in Buenos Aires, received the rules of football in 1867 and sent them to Thomas Hogg, a well-known and enthusiastic sportsman.

The Buenos Aires Football Club, a division of the Buenos Aires
Cricket Club, was founded in 1867 by Thomas Hogg himself,
together with his brother James and William Heald. They decided
to play the first game on 20 June the same year. On this day two
teams, identified with 'red' and 'white' hats, played the first match
in the territory of Argentina. After two halves of fifty minutes each,
the 'white' team won four goals to nil. With the exception of a
player named Boschetti, probably an Italian, all the other names
were British: Hogg, Forester, Ramsbottom, Smith, Bond, Heald,
Best, Wilmont, Ramsay and Simpson. It was the beginning of an
unstoppable bodily habit (Escobar Bavio 1923).

Football expanded, and many clubs were founded in Argentina.
The majority of them sprang out of British schools located in
Buenos Aires and surrounding neighbourhoods. It is no surprise,
then, that the first association in Argentina was founded in Buenos
Aires in 1893 with an English name: the Argentine Association
Football League; the twenty original teams were British, and its
first president was A. Watson Hutton, from 1892 the headmaster
of the prestigious St Andrews Scottish School. After 1900 it was
decided that the clubs change their English names for Spanish ones.
However, the association kept English as its official language until
1906 and changed its name to the Argentine Football Association
in 1903 (Scher and Palomino 1988: 24–5).[1]

In the period 1893–1900 the Lomas Athletic Club in the suburb
of Buenos Aires won five titles. All the players had been students in
the Lomas de Zamora School, an important British boarding-school.
From 1895 onwards, football spread throughout the country. The
pioneering period of Argentinian football is inseparably linked to
the building of the railways, beginning in the 1860s in Buenos
Aires and reaching, in the course of forty years, the rest of Argentina. By 1910 there were clubs and provincial leagues as far away
as Santiago del Estero in the northern part of Argentina. However,
British and non-British clubs, located in Buenos Aires, or La Plata,
the city capital of the province of Buenos Aires, and the small
industrial cities close to the capital dominated Argentinian football
until the end of the 1930s; then, once professionalism was declared,
clubs from Rosario, the second largest city of the country, joined
the 'national league'. Nevertheless, the popularity of football was
rapidly increasing, with the incorporation of the immigrants in its
practice, and by 1907 twelve independent leagues of the Argentine
Football Association existed in Buenos Aires. These leagues consisted

of 350 teams (Frydenberg 1997: 7). At the same time, contacts with the nearby Montevideo, the city capital of Uruguay, created a core of football in the Rio de la Plata basin; since 1902 games between Argentina and Uruguay have been played for the possession of the Lipton trophy. The trophy was donated by the world-famous 'tea baron' and sportsman Sir Thomas Lipton, who visited Argentina in search of suitable land for tea plantations and discovered that the young British population of Buenos Aires and Montevideo loved to play football. Horacio stressed the importance of this trophy and Lipton himself tried to persuade the president of Southampton FC, an English first-division professional team, to visit Argentina. In 1913 *The Standard* wrote:

> In the same manner that British capital, British brains, pluck and energy have developed the commercial stability of Argentina, so have British sport and games tended to physically develop the youth of the country and to impulse an admiration for that fair play which sport breeds . . . An idea of the growth of sport in the Argentine is reflected in the fact that eight years ago there was not a single business in Buenos Aires to supply sporting materials and clothing and now we have three: George McHardy, Lacey and Sons and Watson Hutton & Co. (1/1/1913: 22)

The British pioneer families in Argentina organized clubs and introduced and played sports but also made money. Via sport the British saw themselves as both gentlemen and players, and considered such activities as vital in achieving a very important cultural task: transferring the ethic of fair play to the native population (see Coleman 1973; Mangan 1989).

From 1901 until 1913 Association football was dominated by another British team, the Alumni Football Club, created by former students of the Buenos Aires High School. Alumni represented the best of the football played in Argentina from the time the Association began to organize the championships, and the majority of its players played for the national team. The visit of Southampton in 1904 was perceived in Buenos Aires as the test. The match of Alumni against Southampton was thus anticipated with great anxiety. *The Standard* defined the match as a crucial game in order to evaluate local standards, particularly as Southampton was captained by G. Molyneaux, an international player, with a 'strength and comprehension of the game excelled by no other player' (8/5/1904: 5). The match, played on 26 June, saw a 3–0 victory for Southampton. According to *The Standard* the English team manifested 'values' worthy of emulation: 'exact combination', 'a real display of how to head' and 'fair play, the players always went for the leather' without violent charges. In turn Molyneaux was impressed by the Argentinian footballers, who 'were a long way ahead' of many players from different European countries, like France and Denmark. The chronicler concluded:

> Yesterday's match was a landmark in Argentine football. We have left the infant stage behind us and it is now probable that a first-class team will visit us every year. I look forward to the day not many years hence, when the first Argentine team leaves our shores to give battle to the giants of the game in the Motherland. May I be there to see. (29/6/1904: 1)

The editorial of *The Standard* of 29 June under the title 'Football' recognized that football was the British sport that Argentinians and Anglo-Argentinians liked the most because it appealed to many of their natural talents: 'courage, quickness of perception and promptness in decision and action' and, in addition, could be played 'by the youth of all classes' because the needed expenditure in equipment was insignificant compared with polo, golf and cricket. The visit of Southampton was stressed because it permitted Argentinian players to be in contact with 'the masters of the game' and to learn from them. 'The young Anglo-Argentines who played against the Southampton team were defeated but they made a good fight.' To learn from Southampton was possible because they displayed a 'scientific style', a 'systematic understanding of the game' (29/6/1904: 3).

Southampton played four more matches. The second was against a mixed team of 'Anglo-Argentinians' from various clubs. The English team won 10 to 0! *The Standard* writes: 'The exhibition of the forwards in red and white was as near perfect as possible, their cool, deft, touches of the ball seeming almost supernatural as is the marvellous instinct which every man had of the position of his companions' (4/7/1904: 5). The third match, played against Belgrano, produced an easy 4–1 victory for the English side. The fourth test, against a mixed team of 'Anglo-Argentinians born in Argentina' produced an 8 to 0 victory. The last match of the tour, against the Argentinian national team, was more difficult but a 5–3 victory none the less. *The Standard* recognized that the 'Argentinians' played well but insisted on the need 'to copy' Southampton players, especially in the 'understanding of the midfielders', and the 'modern force of the forwards', 'the value of heading' and 'the importance of keeping one's place', this being of the 'very utmost importance' (13/7/1904: 3). The visit of Southampton thus revealed both the importance of playing against a professional team representing the qualities of the football played in the motherland and, at the same time, the importance of distinguishing Anglo-Argentinians born in Great Britain from Anglo-Argentinians born in Argentina. No match was played against a typical 'Argentinian' team: all the Argentinian national team players had British names. These matches were seen as a version of the traditional 'Gentlemen vs. Players' cricket match played annually in London from 1806 to 1962 in which the gentlemen hoped to win against the players (the professionals). The idea of the effortless superiority of the English gentlemen was transformed into a dominant value in the English society. The gentlemanly ideal was supposed to be transferred to the professional ideal. In other words, behind any professional player there is expected to be found the spirit of the gentleman (see Coleman 1973; McKendrick 1986).

Many of my old and younger informants knew a lot about the early period of Argentinian football. Such accounts are periodically reproduced in the sport pages of newspapers or presented in weekly sport magazines. Recently, television programmes have been showing, in a systematic way, the history of Argentinian football. A film documentary *Fútbol argentino* was watched by millions in the 1990s. The script, written by a well-known historian, was also published as a book with a great commercial success (Bayer 1990). Now it is possible to find in kiosks and bookshops a series of beautiful postcards introducing 'the history of Argentinian football'. Given this historical context, names of the famous early players have been conveyed, and are now part of a common memory shared by informed football supporters. The five brothers Brown, for instance, from the 'mythical' Alumni team, are still well known because they also played for the Argentinian national team and were the architects of the early victories against Brazil and Uruguay. Bayer writes in his book that:

> The first myth and the first heroes were Alumni and the brothers Brown. A team with eleven English names and ten championships won everything in twelve years. The prologue of the history of creole football was written by the English. But even in the first chapter names of

different origin appeared. Sarmiento and Alberdi (the liberal architects
of the modernizing project of Argentina) wanted Nordic and Saxon
immigrants but instead arrived Italians and Spaniards, who, together
with the creoles, would found the real Argentina. However, the years
of Alumni were examples of morality, gentlemanship and sport nobility.
(Own translation 1990: 20–1)

In writing these sentences, Bayer is reproducing a kind of synthesis
of the myth of the origins of football in Argentina: first football
was British, or English – because for Argentinians Englishness is
the essence of Britishness, and both terms are used interchangeably
– and only after a process of historical transformation become
criollo (creole). The real Argentinian football, the creole way, was
made by Italians, Spaniards and the male native population. However, this pioneering time is regarded as positive because the
English values of gentlemanly behaviour dominated and impregnated
the spirit of the game. In discussions, my informants emphasized
ideas of strength, virility and physical stamina as important aspects
of the pioneers' epoch. The football they played, while imagined
as 'primitive' and lacking in sophistication, was at least honest.
When I asked about visiting English teams, my informants imagined
them with the qualities stressed by *The Standard*. Amilcar, like
Horacio a well-read informant, stated, with great intuition, that all
good Argentinian players of the early period were English or British,
like the visitors, and, therefore, played in the same way. *The Standard*
would not agree with this characterization: Anglo-Argentinians
never reached the standards of the visiting professional players.

Another English first-division club, Nottingham Forest, visited
Argentina in 1905. They played six matches and won each of them
with scores like 13–0, 9–0, 7–0 and 6–0 twice. Against the Argentinian national team, which included for the first time two players
of non-British origin, the score was 5–0. The journalistic description of their style read like that attributed to Southampton but
was even more panegyric: they showed 'discipline'; they were sophisticated, 'scientific', 'technical', 'intelligent' but also 'artistic'. The
forward line was composed of five 'artists' who were admired by
all the crowds (*The Standard* , 23/6/1905: 7).

Two other important teams, Tottenham and Everton, arrived in
1909 to play two exhibition games against each other and to confront the best club teams of Buenos Aires and Rosario. Expectations
were great. The first exhibition match, which ended 2 to 2, was
seen by the journalist of *The Standard* in the following way:

> There is no doubt that the game was a good one and some of the short passing was delightful to watch . . . There was much good work and a feature of the display was the fine head work of both teams and rapidity . . . The passing was accurate and clever and the ball was almost invariably parted with at the right moment, players rarely attempted individual effort or gallery tactics, when he had a comrade well placed to receive the leather from him. Attention to this rudimentary law of football is the great fault amongst local players and in this respect the example of our visitors can be followed to advantage. (7/6/1909: 2)

Again, the collective capacities of teamwork are promoted against the tendencies to individualism that existed in local football. To emulate an English way of playing football meant abandoning 'gallery tactics', i.e. the attempt to play in a manner intended to please the public but done to the detriment of team efficiency. As in the other visits, Tottenham and Everton would return to England undefeated. However, the matches against the Argentinian national team were defined by *The Standard* as 'real struggles', evidenced by the scores: Tottenham won 1–0 and Everton 4–2.

The next visit in 1912 confirmed the evolution registered since 1909. Swindon Town played six matches and drew in two of them. The first was against a team with players from first-division teams located in the northern area of Buenos Aires. The second was against the national team. Many English residents sent indignant letters to *The Standard* following the first draw, seeing the result not only as a defeat but as an expression of the decadence of the quality of the football played in the 'Old Country' (19/6/1912: 4). There were, however, other letters defending Swindon, pointing out that it is difficult to play against teams 'having an entirely different style and entirely different tactics', and that 'its players have probably practised to defeat the style and tactics to which they have been used and have had no training suitable to play with the teams playing in the Argentine way' (*The Standard*, 21/6/1912: 4). After the draw against the national team, *The Standard* concluded that football in Argentina had reached a 'high degree of excellence' and that the national squad 'played really well and there was hardly a weak spot in it' (1/7/1912: 2).

The time of learning was over and so local English dominance. In 1912, Alumni decided to leave the league; this event made it possible for other teams with players of non-British origin to dominate the local championship. *The Standard* commented that the road was now open to teams composed of creole and non-British immigrants. It was observed that, among first-division teams, Porteños and San Isidro had only three '*anglos*', Gimnasia y Esgrima one, River Plate three, Estudiantes de La Plata one and Racing Club none (*The Standard*, 10/6/1912: 2). In 1912 the championship was won by Quilmes, another traditional British team. The following year, however, is a historical one in the mythical construction of football's past because Racing Club, a team without a single player of British origin, won the championship for the first time. In the more recent history of Argentinian football Alumni and Racing are presented as the 'founders' of a national tradition, but the virtues of Racing are of greater significance because their victories arrived when football was more popular, the quality of the game was higher and more teams competed for the victory (*La Nación*, 1994, Vol. I, 1: 10).

In pioneering historical research Frydenberg (1997, 1998) has illustrated the changes in amateur football in Buenos Aires in the 1900s.[2] He discovered that, by 1907, 300 football clubs existed outside the official championship of the Association, playing organized football in various competitions. The points of reference for the creation of these teams were the workplace, the street, the neighbourhood and the parish. The youth of the time were seduced by the practice of the new sport, but emphasis is placed on the importance of the search for local identity through the practice of football. One of the main problems for a recently created club was to find open ground upon which to play. In almost all cases a primitive ground was enough in order to establish a club. Many of the clubs formed in the city centre were obliged to find open spaces in the city surroundings. Even Alumni had never had its own stadium and, from 1904, played on the pitch of the Ferro Carril Oeste club. According to Frydenberg the continual foundations of new clubs and the permanent crisis of many older clubs reflected an unparalleled enthusiasm as well as lack of organizational realism (1997: 12–4). Many clubs disappeared, and the ones which survived were able to combine football with other leisure-related activities. The social space created by the clubs transformed the life of the city. The majority of the first-division clubs in today's Argentinian football were founded in the period 1887 to 1915, and all of them offer to their members more than football (Scher and Palomino 1988: 236–9).

Frydenberg describes not only the expansion of football but also some of the problems: the increasingly violent participation of supporters in order to influence the development of a game; the lack of discipline among the players; and the inconsistency in the definition of rules governing results (1997: 16–7). It was a common practice to protest against the result of the match, using arguments such as the partiality of the referee or the threat of the local public against the physical safety of the visiting team. Many of the conflicts were exacerbated when the clubs were located in the same neighbourhood (1997: 18). However, Frydenberg concludes, 'the combination of competition and desire for winning with the will to defend the identity of the club provoked a rivalry different from the one related to sport values' (1997: 18). As I have stressed above, the value of 'fair play' was central to the diffusion of English sports in both Argentina and the rest of the world. Frydenberg reveals an increasing contradiction between those values and the popular practice of football:

> there was a model: the values of English sports . . . The youth admired Alumni, and the *gentlemen*. However, in reality football was fashioned out of the practice of daily competition, there was a constant tension between the idea of a clean game and the explosion of rivalry with certain doses of violence . . . While the new *footballers* dyed their lives with the values of rivalry and enmity, the creators of *fair play* promoted the custom of 'third time', a moment of confraternity among the players once the game was over. In the practice of competition the popular groups had a difficulty in imagining a friendly relation with the opponents when the match was over. (Own translation 1997: 24) [3]

It is normal to imagine that the invasion of the masses in the practice of football created many anxieties among the original practioners. Competition with clubs composed of new immigrants and creole players, who were guided by new values, produced ambivalent feelings among the British. *The Standard* critically observed that, during the visit of Tottenham and Everton in 1909, the behaviour of the Argentinian crowd was not an example of an educated public: they were booing and whistling constantly, and 'a number of the crowd descended to even lower depths of insults' (27/7/1909: 3). The newspaper advised the Argentinian crowd to change their behaviour if they were to remain interested in receiving visits from such famous teams in the future. This description is in sharp contrast with the one published in 1905 during the visit of Nottingham Forest. The crowd of nine thousand spectators was extremely civilized while watching the match between the professional visitors and a typical English club, the Belgrano Athletic; the grandstand was 'overflowing with the élite of both English and Argentine society', and the elegance of the clothes and automobiles parked outside reminded the journalist of attending 'a fashionable equestrian race meeting' (19/6/1905: 1). It seems that this highly civilized age was definitively over by 1912 when Alumni abandoned the practice of football. One by one the English upper-class clubs abandoned the practice of competitive football and concentrated on Rugby, tennis and cricket.

In 1914, Exeter City, a professional second-division team playing in the English Southern League, toured Argentina. They lost one match but beat the champions Racing, 2–0, and the national team, 3–1. English football was still superior. The Argentinians meanwhile complained about the extreme brutality and primitiveness of the football displayed by the visitors (*The Standard*, 18/7/1914: 4). During the farewell banquet the coach of Exeter said that the Argentinian amateur players should master amateur teams in England without difficulties, but they were not yet ready to defeat professional teams. He emphasized that the local players 'are clever in dribbling and fast, but their weak point is that they are individualists and try to shine each above their fellows. They will never achieve real success until they recognise that it takes eleven men to score a goal' (*The Standard* , 14/7/1914: 4). By 1914, if this statement holds true, two styles were constituted: the English, grounded on collective discipline and common effort, and the other, the local creole, based on individualism and lack of tactical sense. This opposition is central in the construction of the imagery of Argentinian football style.

Hybridity in Football: the Creation of a *Criollo* Style

The majority of my informants agreed upon the importance of mapping the ideological construction of football in the weekly magazine *El Gráfico*. Most of them were regular readers, and even the youngest knew the history of the magazine very well. One of the characteristics of *El Gráfico* is to celebrate itself with periodic publications about its own history. This not only reminds the reader of the importance of the publication but also makes it possible to have easy access to a 'written memory'. I accepted the path they opened to me without imagining how difficult it would be to get access to the archives of the magazine. To get permission took many years, and in the meantime a series of letters were unanswered. Later, I understood these difficulties very well: the only two complete sets of *El Gráfico* in the country are kept in the library of the publishing house. The need for a tight control is, therefore, important, and, at the beginning of my work, each volume was given to me by a journalist who was responsible for its remaining intact. This complicated my work until I got the confidence and trust of two young journalists. To complete the reading of *El Gráfico* was indeed painful for an anthropologist not trained in cultural or media analysis.

Founded in May 1919 in Buenos Aires, *El Gráfico* was in the beginning literally a magazine 'for men'. Produced by the Atlántida publishing house, which also brought out very successful magazines for children and for women, *El Gráfico* included, in different measures, political articles, news photos, sports, photos of artists, and reports on leisure and open-air activities. After 1921 *El Gráfico* gradually became a sports magazine, although photos of unknown and supposedly foreign female dancers would be published until the end of the 1920s. The circulation of *El Gráfico* increased in this decade and levelled out at 100,000 in the 1930s. The magazine's circulation reached its peak between the mid-1940s and the mid-1950s, with 200,000 copies published weekly. At that time the magazine had a continental circulation, and was read in Santiago de Chile, La Paz, Quito, Bogotá, San José, Guatemala City and Mexico City. *El Gráfico* has been defined as the the 'Bible of sports in South America' (Sánchez León 1998: 149).

A great deal of space was devoted to football, but other sports such as motor racing, polo, swimming and boxing, in which Argentinians had gained an international reputation, were also covered. At the outset, the magazine was a mouthpiece for the modernist ideology in vogue: it emphasized the importance of physical education for health, it introduced notions of hygiene, incorporated recommendations on the best diet to follow and how to avoid illnesses, stressed the importance of developing hobbies such as building model aircraft, emphasized the need to encourage women to participate in sport and, above all, persistently emphasized the moral and educational aspects of sport. According to *El Gráfico*, sport should be understood as the moral activity of the body, since it develops a strict code of conduct in those who play it, owing to the existence of rules, controls and sanctions. An activity of the

body which is the result of individual fantasy and creativity, and
not controlled by strict rules, is defined as a game, not a sport (*El
Gráfico* no. 394, 1927: 18).

El Gráfico is the middle-class sports weekly which has had, and
continues to have, the greatest influence in Argentina. The analysis
of the content of this magazine is, therefore, an analysis of the
construction of middle-class male imagery. Whether or not it was
hegemonic is debatable, but there is no doubt about its decisive
influence on the definition of the different areas of national and
masculine moral thought. The journalists of *El Gráfico*, excellent
writers in the main, think as members of the middle class but, at
the same time, give space to the expression and dissemination of
the voices, images and performances of football players and other
sportsmen of popular and working-class origin. The transformation
of the latter into 'heroes' or 'villains', into 'models' to be emulated
or not, and the careful analysis of their performances are examples
of the process of the symbolic construction of the 'national' through
an examination of sporting virtues. The term 'national' is used to
indicate that, in *El Gráfico*, voices, performances, successes or
failures of popular actors are combined with the intellectual reflections of middle-class writers and journalists. This confluence is less
apparent in specialist women's magazines or in the more political
or literary weeklies, where the dominant voices are those of the
upper or middle classes.

   In the context of the 1920s, when football was consolidated in
Argentina and became part of the global world of sport, *El Gráfico*
developed the theory of the two foundings of Argentinian football:
the first founding was British, the second was *criollo*.[4] One of the
arguments used refers to the ethnic origins of the players in the
most famous teams and also those playing for the national team.
In the era of the British founding – from 1887 to 1911, the date
when the hegemony of the Alumni, the 'glorious British team',
was broken – players of British origin predominated:

> The English who came to the River Plate were the first to play the
> sport and their sons continued to do so in English schools, where other
> sports like cricket are also played. Thus River Plate football had English
> origins in its first stages, and the first lessons in advanced technique
> came from Southampton and then Nottingham Forest, Everton,
> Tottenham Hotspur, etc. All completely English, as can be seen and
> appreciated in the famous stars of our football beginnings, who are
> called Brown, Weiss, Lett, Ratcliff, Buchanan, Moore, Mack, Watson

Hutton and so many others whose names are indistinguishable from football players in Fair Albion. (Own translation *El Gráfico* no. 470, 1928: 5)

The *criollo* founding began in 1913, when, as noted earlier, Racing Club, with only three marginal players of British origin – Wine, Loncan and Prince – won the championship for the first time. From that moment the 'British' clubs declined in importance, and their players disappeared from the national teams. According to *El Gráfico*, this change became possible because: 'when football began to spread, the stars with British names gave way to those with purely Latin, especially Italian and Spanish, surnames like García, Martínez, Ohaco, Olazar, Chiappe, Calomino, Laforia, Isola, etc. ' (no. 470, 1920: 5).

It is interesting to note that *lo criollo* is defined as having a predominance of Spanish and Italian surnames. *Lo criollo* is founded through the sons of Latin immigrants. The sons of 'English' immigrants were never conceived of as *criollos*, and could not become *criollo* by playing football. They remained English, playing an English sport and, in this way, keeping their English identity. How can these differences be explained? In the interpretation of *El Gráfico* genealogical reasons give way to reasons based on styles of play. These styles, in turn, are based on ethnic differences conceptualized as differences in character and in the form through which feelings and bodily movements are expressed. Once, from the middle of the first decade of the century, the sons of Latin immigrants had made football their own, *El Gráfico* explains:

it is logical as the years have gone by that all Anglo-Saxon influence in football has been disappearing, giving way to the less phlegmatic and more restless spirit of the Latin . . . Inspired in the same school as the British, the Latins soon began modifying the science of the game and fashioning one of their own, which is now widely recognized . . . it is different from the British in that it is less monochrome, less disciplined and methodical, because it does not sacrifice individualism for the honour of collective values. In British football a team is not important because of its separate members but because of the uniform action of the whole group. For that reason, British football is really powerful and has the regular and impulsive driving force of a machine, but it is monotonous because it is always uniformly the same. River Plate football, in contrast, does not sacrifice personal action entirely and makes more use of dribbling and generous personal effort, both in attack and defence, and for that reason is a more agile and attractive football. (Own translation *El Gráfico* no. 470, 1928: 15)

In the texts of *El Gráfico*, 'British' male virtues are identified with being phlegmatic, with discipline, method, the collective ideal, force and physical power. These virtues help to create a repetitive style like a 'machine'. The author recognizes that this style allows one to conceptualize British football as 'perfect' – that is, industrially perfect. The *criollo* male, thanks to the Latin influence, is exactly the opposite: restless, individualistic, less disciplined, based on personal effort, agility and skill. Owing to these characteristics, the author concludes, one can see River Plate football as being imperfect and, therefore, open to development once professionalism is established. Later, in the 1940s, the idea of the 'machine' is opposed to the idea of 'art' in the sense of artistic musical interpretation: Argentinians play football with the touch and virtuosity with which artists play the piano or the violin. For that reason, a great football team is like an orchestra made up of great individuals (*El Gráfico* no. 1124, 1941: 18). The most typical characteristic of Argentinian football would be the touch, which could be short, slow or quick according to the tactical requirements and the intensity of the game.

The notions of opposing British and *criollo* male physical virtues would remain, but become modified. The English physical virtues are associated with 'force and physical power', while the virtues of the *criollos* are those of agility and virtuoso movements. The metaphor of the 'machine' as opposed to individual creativity is a constant in Argentinian football imagery. 'Britishness' is associated with the industrial, the *criollo* with the pre-industrial social system. Faced with the machine, or the repetitive, the typical *criollo* response would be the dribble. Dribbling, which would later be called the *gambeta* (a word derived from gauchesque literature which describes the running motion of an ostrich), is eminently individual and cannot be programmed; it is the opposite of the industrial, collective game of the machine.

According to *El Gráfico*, by 1928 *lo criollo* had acquired its own characteristics. The 'founding' of the '*criollo* style' had to have a precise date, protagonist and event: this was fixed in 1913 when Racing Club deposed the champions Alumni, the major club power for many years, as we have seen above, and the representative not only of the British 'founding' of football but also of the 'British style'. It is interesting to note, as in any myth, that the historical reality does not coincide with the narrative. As we saw, Alumni abandoned competition in 1912 and not in 1913. They did not

participate in the championship of 1912, which was won by
Quilmes, another English team. Therefore, Racing did not win over
Alumni but over Quilmes. The two 'foundings' are, in many ways,
related to two clear historical hegemonies: Alumni dominated
organized football from 1900 to 1911, and Racing did the same
from 1913 to 1919. A concrete historical hegemony lies behind
the two 'mythological foundings'. More interesting is the genealogy
of the styles. One might conceive of a personal football-playing
style as something totally imaginary, but, in general, style develops
through comparison with other playing styles, as the texts quoted
above indicate. However, in the fifteen years between 1913 and
1928 the transformation from the British to the *criollo* style was a
gradual process. In this transformation the gaze of the 'distant
other', the Europeans, and the 'near other', the Uruguayans, would
be important.

El Gráfico argues at an early date that football will become the
fundamental sport in Argentina, since it allows a nation to express
itself through its national team (no. 190, 1923: 4). This, they
emphasize, could not happen through individualistic sports. To
play for the national team requires the players to have developed a
sense of the nation, since they have to put aside, for a time, their
private interests as players from different clubs. At the same time
the commentator observes that national differences, the differences
between styles, can be seen more clearly in a game of football than
in any other sporting competition.

The Uruguayan victory in the 1924 Olympic Games in Paris and
the successful tour in 1925 of Boca Juniors, a first-division side,
throughout many European countries would confirm the existence
of a 'River Plate' football, different from European and English
football.[5] Until the Boca tour, the Argentinians were more English
than the Uruguayans, even in the perception of the Uruguayan
players themselves (*El Gráfico* no. 190, 1923: 4, and no. 205, 1923:
15). The Europeans contributed to this change through their own
perception of the differences involved, through their definition of
a 'River Plate' football played by both Argentinians and Uruguayans.
The visit in 1926 of Real Deportivo Español, a Barcelona club, led
to the development of a theory of *criollo* football as something
distinct. Without a trace of modesty, *El Gráfico* wrote about the
visit of the Catalan team:

We feel that the quality of the football played in our country is very high – so high that we consider that only the football played by British professionals is superior to it – and it is thus within a very strict definition of technique that we respect the merits of our guests . . . and we conclude that football in Spain has made surprising progress that puts it almost on a par with our own. We say almost on a par since we are convinced that our own play is technically more proficient, quicker and more precise: it perhaps lacks effectiveness due to the individual actions of our great players, but the football that the Argentinians, and by extension the Uruguayans, play is more beautiful, more artistic, and more precise because approach work to the opposition penalty area is done not through long passes upfield, which are over in an instant, but through a series of short, precise and collective actions: skilful dribbling and very delicate passes. (Own translation No. 366, 1926: 17)

In *El Gráfico*'s perception, the Argentinian players' skill in dribbling would be one of the fundamental aspects of *criollo* style. Dribbling is an individual, not a collective, activity. The collective style would therefore come to depend on the qualities of the best players, those with highly developed dribbling skills. Dribbling would be the factor that enabled the transition from the 'founding' to the development of a style. Dribbling gave style a form. The gaze of the 'others', the Europeans, accelerated this process. At the same time, Argentinian and Uruguayans players who began to appear in Europe in the 1920s were great dribblers. The export of Argentinian players, mostly forwards, began in 1921 when the Italian club Torino bought Julio Libonatti, a very technical and enthusiastic centre forward who, during the 1920s, was a central player for the Italian national team (Brera 1975, vol. 1: 95–7). Interestingly enough the Italians decided to leave Libonatti in Italy during the Amsterdam Olympic Games in order to avoid the accusation that he was a professional player (Brera 1975: 97). This export of football players was strengthened in the 1920s and 1930s. In the process of the transformation of football into a 'universal sport', Argentina began to export performing bodies and to be identified with football and performing males.

El Gráfico develops the theory of the two 'foundings' in a new international context: Argentinians and Uruguayans dominated the South American championships in the 1910s and the 1920s as well as the Olympic Games of 1928. The final of the Amsterdam Olympic Games in 1928 saw the national teams of Argentina and Uruguay. The Uruguayans won their second consecutive gold medal. The football of 'River Plate' was defined as being a world power, no longer peripheral to European football. This was confirmed in 1924 by the visit of Plymouth Argyll, a rather marginal professional team playing in the Southern English league. They were defeated twice by the Argentinian national team: 3–0 and 1–0. *The Standard* commented on the first victory, presenting the national team as 'dashing', 'technical' and 'fast' and Plymouth as 'rather primitive' (30/6/1924: 2). In the second match, *The Standard* summarized the differences between the two teams, pointing out that the Argentinian forwards were both very good in dribbling and significantly more technical than their English counterparts (21/7/1924: 2). However, the 'charging tactics' of the professional English players were not understood by the Argentinians and, according to *The Standard*, the players were, in all matches, continuously shouted at by the public. In the farewell letter written by the captain of Plymouth and published in *The Standard* we can read that:

> it is evident that football lovers in the Argentine are not yet enamoured of shoulder charging, which in England is looked upon as perfectly clean and fair . . . the close results of our engagements permit me to emphasize the rapid development of Association football in South America and we are broad-minded enough to declare that the class of football shown by your best players is very little behind that of the strongest of the English League Clubs, and we beg you to accept our congratulations. (20/7/1924: 5)

In the same edition of *The Standard* the president of the Argentinian Football Association, Dr Tedin Uriburu, pointed out that: 'The visit of the Plymouth Argyll has been very successful and leaves us with great memories in our minds in that Argentine footballers, who in recent years were modest disciples and pupils of the great English sport, now can consider themselves worthy opponents of the best teams that come to this country from other countries' (20/7/1924: 5).

One of the best observers and judges of the changes occurring in Argentinian football was, without any doubt, Jorge Brown, the centre forward and mythical player of Alumni and the national team during the times of the British 'founding'. In 1921 he remarked nostalgically that:

The football I cultivated was a real demonstration of handiness and energy. A game more brusque, but virile, beautiful, vigorous. The modern football is weakened by an excess of passing close to the goal. It is a game that is more fine, perhaps more artistic, even apparently more intelligent, but it has lost its primitive enthusiasm. With the present style the scores are more modest compared with the results of the old style. It is important to keep in mind that football is not a delicate sport . . . It is a violent and strong game in which physical resistance and the muscles of the players are what is proved. This style has unfortunately disappeared . . . the 'kick and run' style is not practised, the style which produced so many invincible players. In our matches in the past there were more charges but always with strict legality and respect for the adversary. Today they believe that they play better because they escape from the physical contact, and, therefore, it is rare to experience the animated games of the past produced by the 'kick and run' style. It is impossible to watch the style consecrated in England and exported all over the world. I confess that I am a lover of tradition, and, I believe, expressing these ideas, that I am right. (Own translation *El Gráfico* no. 107, 1921: 11)

In 1921 Brown rejected the new style and defended the vanishing English tradition. Three years later, in 1924, he accepted the consolidation of the Argentinian style but explicitly demanded more hybridization in order to keep alive the English influence. He argued strongly for a mixture of styles with 'the aim that the Latin virtues had their complement in the perfection of the British technique' (*La Nación*, 10/6/1924: 5). In this way, Brown accepted in 1921 that the British style was part of the past, favouring in 1924 a return to the British in order to produce a more hybrid style. Brown was a man of his epoch. From his perspective the domination of the Latin style was negative, and a mixture with the British style would eventually produce a more accomplished style. We must not forget, if we believe *El Gráfico*, that as a real 'hero' of the British foundation of football he was always in search of perfection.

It is important to keep in mind that *El Gráfico*'s application of the term '*criollo* foundation' to a game transformed by the sons of first-generation immigrants should have been considered an insult by the nationalist writers of the time. The nationalists were against massive immigration, because it contaminated the 'national essence' and 'sullied the country' (Rock 1993: 41–2). In the world of football, however, the immigrants and their creativity allowed the national style to appear, strengthen and be reproduced over time. National identity in football belongs to the sons of non-British immigrants:

it is a cultural form created on the margins of the nationalists' *criollismo*. The narrative of *El Gráfico* is a homage to the mixing of sons of Latin Europeans with the local population and excluding, explicitly, the sons of the British. The exclusion of the sons of the British can be seen as a concession on the part of the writers of *El Gráfico* to the nationalists' 'anti-British imperialism' and to the dominant anti-Anglo-Saxon ideology of *arielismo* (Rodó 1994).[6] I think, however, that *El Gráfico* also contributed in its way, defining, in the field of sport, 'Britishness' as the relevant 'other' for the Argentinians. The magazine would even defend Argentinian players leaving to play abroad, even playing for national teams where they would be defined as 'native'. Italy made flagrant use of this, including four Argentinian players in the winning World Cup team of 1934. These players would be considered as ambassadors of *criollo* football. *El Gráfico* writes:

> We must not be egotistical. Orsi, Cesarini, Stábile and all those crossing frontiers in search of better horizons, on the way to countries that need them, should be seen in the way that old Spain watched its Advance Guard leave. They leave to conquer other lands. The country is now a little small for us, and a good football lesson given on one of our pitches no longer dazzles anyone. For many years we have held the Chair in dribbling and in scoring goals. For that reason, it is necessary to go outside; the good players that do us proud abroad are working patriotically. Stábile goes to Italy, not to defend football in the peninsula, but to defend *criollo* football, since he is a *criollo* player. (Own translation No. 589, 1930: 37)

It is timely to present and discuss the models explaining the growth of a *criollo* style in Argentina.

The *Criollo* Male Style: Undetermined Nature or Social Amalgamation?

As I mentioned before, the documentary film *Fútbol argentino*, based on the theory of the two foundings of Argentinian football, broadcast in 1990 to much acclaim, became a kind of 'master narrative' for younger generations of football enthusiasts. The majority of my informants saw it and accepted this historical presentation as a 'true story'. Matías, born in 1920 and the senior of all of them, remembered the importance of this 'theory' – according to his own words – in the 1940s, the 'golden age' of Argentinian football when the national team won almost every South American Cup and many clubs – after the Second World War – toured Europe with great success. He mentioned *El Gráfico* but also newspapers and radio programmes as the main sources of this 'theory'. Matías insisted on the importance of creating 'mythologies' and relating them to the need of having a 'national style'. He emphasized the competition with the Uruguayans:

> The Uruguayans won the two Olympic titles, in 1924 and 1928, and the first World Cup in 1930. Argentinians got two silver medals: in 1928 and 1930. We were second twice, and we created an understanding of the defeats based on an opposition between the force and effectiveness of the Uruguayans and the elegance of ourselves. It was like a *tour de force*: the Uruguayans were suddenly more British and we were exactly the opposite. You see, Uruguayans and Argentinians learned from the British, and abruptly we had good and bad pupils. We transformed the defeats into a victory: the consolidation of a different style.

Matías knew that the concept of *rioplatense* football, comprising Argentina and Uruguay, had existed during the 1920s. However, he believed that this concept was not only the product of some journalists of *El Gráfico* but was also imposed by the gaze of the Europeans. He maintained that, Argentina and Uruguay being in many respects important parts of the 'new world' in the first two decades of this century, it was obvious to put both together in a given style of playing football. I reminded him that in the film *Fútbol argentino* the *rioplatense* football was presented as something different and as a cultural export.

In spite of the fact that the genealogical narrative is presented as an ideological construct, Matías and many of my informants insisted on the differences of football style. Amilcar stated with characteristic clarity that 'without differences football will disappear; you cannot have thousands of teams playing the same way, because you have millions of different individuals playing differently'. Thus, everyone agreed upon variations; the question was how individual differences arose and how they developed into an imagined and 'real collective style'. Let me present the two interpretative models of *El Gráfico*.

Borocotó, a renowned journalist for decades, developed the idea of '*criollo* dribbling' in 1928 and elaborated it in 1950.[7] In his conceptualization the transformations permitting the development of the new style are open only to the descendants of Latin immigrants. His theory has two meanings: the original, in 1928, is based on the freedom of the *pibes criollos* (the '*criollo* boys') and the complementary, in 1950, on the absorption of substances. In the first theory the *pibes* learned to play spontaneously in the *potreros* (empty urban spaces of different sizes, usually small, with very uneven surfaces) without any teachers; this was unlike England where, according to Borocotó, football was integral to the school system (*El Gráfico* no. 480, 1928). Moreover, as we have seen above, the development of British football in Argentina was intimately related to the implementation and consolidation of the British educational system.[8] The great British clubs of the pioneer time sprang out from the British schools, and many headmasters played a crucial role in improving the standards of the game. Kanitkar (1994) has argued that the Imperial British created the image of the 'sporting boy'. The games recommended were team sports which required qualities of leadership, cooperation and loyalty. To be part of a team was conceived as being part of a perfect machine. The opposition between freedom – and creativity – and school – associated with discipline and pupil–teacher relations – therefore makes sense from a historical perspective. Borocotó recalls that Argentinian football has become known throughout the world through dribbling, and that the players leaving Argentina to play in Europe are the best dribblers. He argues emphatically that until now Argentina has been known throughout the world for exporting its valuable frozen beef and its quality cereals, 'non-popular products – in the sense that they came from the estates of the *pampa*-based landowning classes – and now it is important that it should become known for its 'popular products'. One of the high-quality 'popular products' is dribbling, and its exponents are the refined Argentinian football players. The practice of football permits the Argentinians – and the nation – to be 'seen' in the world, to be 'remembered' and, above all, to be 'prized'. To play in the finals of 1928 and 1930 is as important as to export footballers (*El Gráfico* no. 467, 1928: 16). Argentinians are 'global' through football, a bodily practice making it possible for many young athletes to take part in 'transnational connections', to paraphrase the title of Hannerz's book (1996) devoted to contemporary globality.

Chantecler, another of the great writers of *El Gráfico*, also contributed to the development of a theory of *lo criollo*. Dribbling, an expression of the body, would become a manifestation of the essential *criollo* character. Dribbling expresses the wily and crafty *criollo* as opposed to the artless British (*El Gráfico* no. 467, 1928: 16). To the central tenets of Borocotó's thesis – the pure imagination of the *pibe* and the congestion of players on the field – one more component is definitely added: wiliness. Without the existence of the qualities of craftiness and wiliness, dribbling could not emerge, and there would be no space for creative improvisation. Chantecler maintains that the British are cold and mathematical and, for that reason, play a 'learned' football. In contrast, the River Plate footballers, who are warm and improvisers, play an 'inspired' football. At the same time, he draws a distinction between the River Plate countries: the Argentinians play with the heart; they are faster and more aggressive; the Uruguayans play with the head; they are calmer and more romantic (*El Gráfico* no. 467, 1928: 16).

Chantecler would develop the theory of the 'melting-pot' and amalgamation, stressing a continuous process of *criollo*-ization. A *criollo* is not born but made; he is the product of a tradition that is altered by individual contribution. In an article entitled *Viveza criolla*. The Main Characteristics of our Game', he writes:

> When our immigrant country receives in its breast the great migrations of all races, it has assimilated qualities from each of them and has amalgamated them, giving them its own mark. This is the new race that European intellectuals talk about when they come to study the psychology of our people and cannot find a clear-cut defining characteristic because we have something from each civilization without belonging typically to any of them. (Own translation *El Gráfico* no. 654, 1932: 21)

Chantecler considers that, in the development of *criollo* 'craftiness', players from the British era, like Leonard, Brown, Buchanan and Arnold Watson Hutton, helped to change the coldness of the British. In a dictionary of *criollo* football Chantecler defined in a very precise way 'the products of *viveza criolla*: the feint, the 'bicycle' (a special type of dribbling), a fake attack, the *túnel* (to do a 'nutmeg'), the *marianela* and also what he calls 'disreputable cunning' (*El Gráfico* nos 652 and 653, 1932). *Viveza criolla* becomes not just a list of inventive plays but, rather, a quality that developed historically. Behind each one of these above-mentioned acts there is a creator, a *criollo* player who developed it. Chantecler begins with amalgamation, conceptualized as the process of blending all races in football, and adds aggregation, imagined as the product of individual creativity. Any style, following Strathern, is thus a combination of both societal processes.

Borocotó tried to develop a theory of national football by cleansing it of British influence, transforming it into something purely *criollo*. His *tour de force*, his modification of the theory of nationalist writers of the time, is to have linked *criollo* football with immigration and the city. He maintained that the Latin immigrants nationalize football because they become *criollos*, inheriting the characteristics of the 'authentic *criollos*'. There is no melting-pot; there is a transference of qualities through the absorption of fundamental substances. This perspective was fully developed in 1950. Let me present it briefly.

In the World Cup of 1950 in Brazil the final was played between two South American teams: Uruguay and Brazil. Argentina did not participate, continuing a boycott initiated in 1934. The fact that these two teams reached the final and dominated the tournament created a turmoil in Argentina. The victory of Uruguay was seen as a confirmation of the superiority of River Plate football. Borocotó took part in the public debate concerning the existence of different styles and defended an essentialist point of view. He emphasized the fact that Italians and Spaniards do not play like Argentinians in spite of having many Argentinian players of Italian or Spanish descent. He refused to accept a unilineal racial interpretation of the Argentinian style: the sons of immigrants had Italian or Spanish blood, but they were transformed by their contact with unique Argentinian substances. He defined the following substances as having transformative qualities: landscape – composed of earth and air, beef, barbecued meat (*asado*), *mate* – a local tea – and food in general. He insisted that these substances are not found in other places and that they defined Argentina as a different nation (*El Gráfico* no. 1618, 1950: 46–8). He reiterated that 'there is not a single way of playing football', and the existence of different styles is related to 'cultural traits'. He continued to use the argument presented in the 1920s: contact with the *pampa* and its culture transformed the immigrants. In this sense, something unique and untransferable becomes naturalized: the contact with nature allows the sons of immigrants – only some sons, of course – to be transformed. The style of play is thus derived from nature – it is a natural gift; a *criollo* player is born so, and cannot be made so. The 'natural', the *criollo*, appears as a barrier against cultural transference, against the importation of European styles, which was the main point of discussion in 1950. Borocotó finds a

symmetry between being and feeling: the natural has to do with
feelings, not with reason (*El Gráfico* no. 1618, 1950: 46). From this
perspective, the immigrants brought nothing of substance to help
this radical transformation: their sons, born in the pampas, become
criollos.

If Borocotó refuses to accept the idea of the melting-pot, Chantecler, on the contrary, acknowledges the importance of immigration
in the creation of a style in which there is even room for British
craftiness. Being *criollo* is not permanent; it develops over time
through a sort of successful melting-pot. What is common to both
theories is that the *criollo* has been divested of force and courage
by making supreme virtues of the art of dribbling – that is, a play
that avoids physical contact with the opposition – and cunning,
the ability to hide one's true intentions by turning life (the game)
into a series of continual pretences, making the opponent believe
the opposite of one's true intentions, turning deceit into victory
(see Archetti 1995a). The great icon of the British period, Brown,
agreed with Borocotó and Chantecler on the changes of style, as
we have seen above. The dominance of the British style had disappeared by the end of the 1920s, and the *criollo* style began to
travel in the world as a different way of interpreting the game.

By Way of Conclusion: the Criollo Male Style as a Mechanism of Exclusion and Inclusion

I presented my historical findings to some of my informants, and
we had several lively exchanges of ideas. Matías was clear in his
judgement: the ideology of *El Gráfico* was dominant at that time,
and it is still the 'standard explanation of the creation of a new
style'. He pointed out that in other leading newspapers, especially
La Nación and *Crítica*, the same arguments were presented. Amílcar
insisted on the 'middle-class and populist tone of the opposing ways
of playing football'. Roberto, a middle-aged bureaucrat, considered
Borocotó's model an effective mechanism for creating some kind
of solidarity and acceptance for the new immigrants. He insisted
that many of his arguments were 'opportunist' and a way of excluding the British, in a period of increasing nationalism.

The importance of landscape, food and blood in the creation of
the style was less acceptable to my informants. However, they
recognized that in order to conceive of the differences between

Argentinians born of Italian parents and Italians in the motherland some central properties of the new country must be taken into account. Roberto pointed out that, at that time, the importance of the *pampa* and the gaucho was substantial: 'the nationalist imagined a nation of gauchos'.[9] The *criollo* was conceptualized in relation to integration but also in terms of creativity. Hybridity is a mechanism of cultural creativity, a kind of selective creativity: in the world of football the descendants of British immigrants are less creative than the descendants of Italians and Spaniards.[10] The diversity of origins does not exclude processes of generalization in which a key factor is the continuous amalgamation of the new mixtures. The 'national' is a typical hybrid product, open but exclusive because the British are eliminated from the new style. The case of football analysed in this chapter illustrates the process of hybridization as the creation of a 'pure form' that did not exist in the past and is historically constituted as a new form and as a tradition. Applying the term '*criollo* foundation' to a game introduced by the sons of first-generation immigrants would have been considered an insult by the nationalist writers of the time. The nationalists were against the immigrants because they contaminated the fragile 'national essence'. In the world of football, however, the immigrants and their creativity allowed the national style to appear, strengthen and be reproduced over time. National identity in football belongs to the sons of immigrants; it is a cultural form created on the margins of the nationalist's *criollismo*. The narrative of *El Gráfico* is a homage to the sons of foreigners excluding, explicitly, the sons of the British. I think that *El Gráfico* contributed in its way to defining 'Britishness' as the relevant 'other' for the Argentinians in the field of sport. Hybridization thus does not produce the chaos imagined by some of the nationalist thinkers. The world of football gave rise to a positive image of the male immigrants, and the performances of the best players constituted important landmarks in imagining the complex relations between nationality and masculinities.

The virtues of the male hybrids produced in Argentinian football had a transgressive quality because they were able to subvert the dominant model based on English male virtues. The ideal of bodies in Argentinian football was not related to beauty as was the case according to Mosse (1996) in the ideological construction of modern masculinity in Europe. Team sport was regarded as education in individual freedom and creativity more than in collective discipline as the English ideology postulated. When beauty appears this is related to a way of playing, to the aesthetic of the game, and not as an achieved property of the body. Neither was will-power, which also according to Mosse was a quality of the image of modern man. He wrote:

> will-power was usually equated with courage, knowing how to face danger and pain. Steeling the body through sport was universally advocated as one of the best ways to accomplish this end. Angelo Mosso, a renowned Italian physiologist, in addition to praising gymnastics as a perfect way of perfecting the male body, also admired the manner in which English schools encouraged team sports. Sport, he held, develops individual energy, teaches the proper work habits as well as discipline, and in this manner completes the shaping of real men. (1996: 100)

Football in Argentina is seen in opposition to the discipline of school. The creolization process implied a change from the school to the street, and from the British to the new hybrids, products of the non-British immigration. In this direction, against the values of courage and will-power, the Argentinian football players represent almost the contrary; they were portrayed as sensitive, artistic and great improvisers. In the international landscape of football in the 1920s, the Argentinian players represented for the Europeans something different, as I have pointed out: the incarnation of dribbling and extreme individualism. The forged stereotype of the modern man was thus challenged by the hybrids of Argentina. The relationship between sport and modern masculinity is thus more intricate than Mosse imagined. The case of polo will permit me to return to the male virtues of courage and pain, and of ability and playfulness.

Notes

1. The Argentine Football Association (AFA) played a key role in the expansion of organized football in South America. By 1912, the most important leagues were affiliated with the AFA: the Uruguayan League, the Liga Rosarina, the Leagues from the northern provinces of Argentina (Salta, Santiago del Estero and Tucumán), the Liga del Sur (from the province of Buenos Aires) and the Brazilian Associations from São Paulo and Rio de Janeiro (*The Standard* 17/8/1912: 3).
2. Frydenberg's analysis is based on the reading of *La Argentina*, published twice a week from 1902 and transformed into a daily newspaper in

1907. The originality of *La Argentina* lies in the fact that the clubs not affiliated with the Association could use its pages for announcing their tournaments and results. A social world of real 'aficionado football' was thus created. It is worth noting that Frydenberg's findings are complementary to mine, based on the reading of *The Standard*, which represented official organized football and the British values of 'fair play'.

3. The confraternity dinner after important football matches was a common practice in Argentine during the 1900s – the so-called 'third half' (*tercer tiempo*). *The Standard* carefully described the dinners after international matches between Argentina and Uruguay or between the Argentinian teams and the British visitors. The menu of many dishes, the wines and the music played were carefully presented and commented on. The 'third halves' were social events. This practice disappeared from football in the 1910s. It has been kept in Rugby as a symbol of 'fair play' and gentlemanly values in a game characterized by physical violence. The 'third half' can be regarded as a representation of a class ideology which vanished from football when it became popular and was appropriated by the working classes.

4. It is important to point out that, although in terms of style the relevant 'other' is the 'British' style, *El Gráfico* knows that one can play against the national sides of Wales, Scotland, England and Northern Ireland. This is not something special to Argentina. According to Moorhouse, even in today's England 'Britishness' is either taken as equivalent to 'Englishness' or vaguely assumed to be a 'mixture' of all 'elements, with the "Celtic fringes" acting as sources of lovable, if eccentric, noble savages' (1996: 57). From the beginnings of Argentinian football, the main enemy, in the sense of an obstacle to be overcome before reaching maturity and a supposed universal recognition, is England. Not only had she invented modern football and its rules, but her players were professionals and, for that reason, did not mix with the amateurs at the Olympic Games. On innumerable occasions, *El Gráfico* not only compared different styles but also insisted on the need to follow the same road as the English and professionalize national football. This would not come until 1931, with the creation of the professional league. For decades Argentinians would dream of a victory over England. Reading *El Gráfico*, one always gets the impression that victories over other teams were less important. All my informants, without exception, would consider a victory against the English side as more important than a victory against Germany or Italy, the real European world-power countries in football.

5. Jules Rimet, the president of the Fédération Internationale de Football Association (FIFA), visited Argentina in 1924, after the Olympic Games. He observed that victory in a universal game like football, like that

achieved by Uruguay, was important for the new nations because they became known, gaining a prestige otherwise difficult to attain. He also lamented the absence of Argentina, because the world was deprived of a fantastic final between the two teams of the River Plate basin (*La Nación* 9/6/1924: 3). His premonition was right: the final of the next Olympic Games would be played by Argentina and Uruguay.

6. The *arielismo* was an ideology based on the famous book of Rodó *Ariel* published in 1900. Rodó followed Taine's theory of art, in which the complex relations between race, environment and historical events were supposed to create the 'genius' of different peoples and to determine their cultural identities. He identified the Anglo-Saxon tradition and genius, best illustrated by the North Americans, with utilitarianism and extreme materialism, while the Latin was profoundly humanist and artistic. If we read *El Gráfico* with this perspective we are not surprised that the Anglo- Saxon style was presented as industrial, mechanical and repetitive, while the Latin was sensitive, artistic and with a creativity based on improvisation. Borocotó's analysis, perhaps a result of being the good Uruguayan he was, distilled *arielismo*. On the importance of the press in the creation of national styles and sporting events see Oriard 1993; Leite Lopes and Faguer 1994; Pope 1997.

7. Borocotó – his real name was J. Lorenzo – became one of the most influential sports journalists in Argentina. Born in 1902 in Montevideo, Uruguay, he joined *El Gráfico* in 1927 and retired, as editor, in 1955. From 1927, he was active as a radio journalist. He was the author of many bestsellers and also had success in the film world. Alabarces considers Borocotó the best sports writer of this epoch because 'he understood that football was intimately related to the daily life of Argentinians, with their loves, their stories, their dreams' (1996:181). He wrote the script of one of the classics of Argentinian cinema, *Pelota de Trapo* (Rag Ball), made in 1948 (see Cechetto 1993), and in this way his fictional construction of Argentinian football mythology was transformed into 'reality' through the fictional power of film. The film describes with 'spontaneity and lyricism the world of children and their passion for football' (Maranghello 1984: 102). Alabarces maintains that *Pelota de trapo* can still be seen as the most important film on football made in contemporary Argentina (1996: 181). We shall address the film later in the book. On film and football see Alabarces (1996) and Romano (1998).

8. The practice of sports was seasonally limited: October–January for cricket; April–October for polo; and March–September for both football and Rugby. The combined intensive practice of football and Rugby was thus excluded. However, many Rugby and football players also played cricket. It was also common for polo players to play cricket and golf (*The Standard* , 29/10/1905: 6).

9. The nationalists accepted immigrants if they became a part of the nation. Roberto, a descendent of Russian Jews, is right in his observation and agrees with Shunway when he writes that 'Argentine nationalism is first and foremost nativistic, proud of the country's Hispanic heritage and its mixed ethnicity' (1991: 292). Given this ideological context and the influence of *arielismo*, the acceptance of Latin immigrants as the creators of a national style seems plausible, although controversial.

10. The history of Argentinian football with the 'two foundations' is comparable to the historical processes in Peru, Brazil and Uruguay. The historical development of football in Peru is similar, in many ways, to the Argentinian case: British and aristocratic at the beginning, but adopted very early in the twentieth century by the working classes of Lima and Callao (Deusta Carvallo *et al.* 1984). Mason (1995) has shown the central role of the British élite in the origins and early history in Argentina, Brazil and Uruguay. He, however, maintains that 'Britons were present at the birth of the game in Brazil . . . [but] other European migrants were important in football's early stages' (1995: 9). Leite Lopes (1997) has shown that in the development of Brazilian football the British élite was dominant. His analysis of the interconnections between football and cricket, and also rowing, is interesting. In the British clubs of Rio and São Paulo, the men practising football also played cricket, but some key clubs were organized around men's rowing. In spite of the refusal of some of the rowing clubs to admit the new sport because it was not perceived as a very masculine sport, football gradually became accepted. The poor whites, mestizos and blacks were incorporated in organized football in the 1920s. This process engendered a series of conflicts when Vasco da Gama, a non-élite club founded by Portuguese immigrants, won the championship in Rio in 1923. The next year Vasco da Gama was excluded from the league. The democratization of Brazilian football began in the 1930s (Caldas 1989; Leite Lopes 1997). Compared with Argentina and Uruguay, Brazil had a delay of almost twenty years. This explains the dominance of both countries in the early periods of South American football. In spite of the similarities in the South American countries, the mechanism of exclusion of the British from the formation of a national style is particular to Argentina. The same ideological developments have not been documented in the other societies at that time. In Brazil, and I imagine in Peru and perhaps Uruguay, in contrast to the Argentinian ideology of a *criollo* foundation, the idea of 'multiracialism' in sport – and in the building of a nation – became dominant in the 1930s (see Leite Lopes 1997). The important presence of the black population in the practice of football in Brazil and Peru – and to a lesser degree in Uruguay – conditioned national imaginaries. Sánchez León observes that in Peru the idols

in football are blacks or *cholos*, never white players (1993: 103). Therefore, it is possible, as a working hypothesis, to delineate 'black areas'
and 'European areas' in the consolidation of playing styles and
imageries in South America. The Argentinians never imagined that
they could play like Brazilians because they never had black players
on the most successful national teams.

CHAPTER THREE

Hybridization and Male Hybrids in the World of Polo

After several attempts, Enrique, a polo player with a handicap of 6 in the 1950s and 1960s – a six-goaler – found a space in his busy schedule to meet me. He, however, insisted that he had only one hour available that day. An important industrialist and landowner, belonging to a family of immigrants which earned a lot of money at the end of the nineteenth century before becoming 'aristocratic', Enrique in fact received me twice and 'gave' me more than six hours of his precious time. He helped me to find the paths of my historical research on polo. He emphasized the importance of rural origins, the transformations in the 1920s and 1930s when more people adopted the game and, above all, the importance of a style of playing which was identified with an Argentinian tradition. He said:

> We have the best players of the world because they have the best ponies and the best *petiseros* (grooms). The players today are professionals, and the best Argentinian teams are supported by international firms and eccentric foreign millionaires. The polo they play belongs to another planet; the best play in Argentina for four months, and when our Open is over in November they are transformed into nomads: they play in England, Australia, New Zealand, Borneo, you name it. Polo has became a more universal game than it was in my time as a player. However, there is a great continuity since 1936. In that year Argentinians became the best players of the world in high-handicap polo, winning the Olympic gold medal and the Copa de las Américas. This has not changed.

I asked him to elaborate on the factors explaining the international dominance of Argentinian polo and whether he could relate this situation to the existence of a national style. His answer was clear:

Horses and men, men and horses; there are few secrets in polo. You do not have a coach . . . well, like in football, a coach who is able to produce miracles like, for instance, you do not remember . . . [looking to me for help but without getting it] his name, he was so famous . . . [suddenly he remembered, showing great surprise] yes, Helenio Herrera in the 1960s, coaching Inter and gaining almost everything you could gain in football, I think he was called 'The Magician' . . . In polo there is no such magician: you need a lot of horses for a season, and you need to produce them as excellent players. Horses and men play; it is not only men. I would say that the horse is 70% and the rider the rest. The horses must be trained to play polo, and this takes a lot of years. We say that an ideal polo pony should have a lot of human traits: good temper, reflective, an extraordinary memory, intelligence, great courage and very stable emotionally. Well, if you judge the last quality, a polo pony is unlike human beings because you will accept that we are extremely unstable [this was said with great irony and he laughed loudly].

I also asked him how it was possible to develop these qualities, and he gave me a fascinating and unforgettable lecture. At the end, I felt myself knowledgeable and in a much better condition for watching polo games. Enrique put the emphasis on the role of the *petiseros*, the descendants of Argentinian historical gauchos, who, as he insisted many times, are responsible for taming, training and schooling the polo ponies. He said:

For the first two years the ponies must be treated with extreme care, they must not be scared, and a lot of small exercises should be repeated over and over. Taming begins when the horse is two years old and it is based on patience. The ponies must get what we call 'a good mouth' or ' a soft mouth', a great docility, and, at the same time, resistance. Speed is more genetically conditioned, but you must get with training what we call 'turn of speed'. You see, in addition to the psychological aspects of the horse that I just mentioned to you are physical attributes: mouth, a balanced body with well-rounded loins and a good length from the hip to the hock, strong neck and quarters, and legs, better 'clean legs'. The polo ponies are, after taming, trained and trained with the sticks, and they will not play their first serious games before they have enough experience, when they are ten or eleven years old. The player helps in this process but the main tasks are done by the *petiseros*. The quality of our *petiseros* is behind the great success of Argentinian polo. I must confess to you that many *petiseros* are better polo players than their employers. However, a good player, a high-goal player and even a low-goal player, must have permanent contact with his ponies. You are not a good player if you do not love your horses.

He then developed, his theory on the horse and the polo player:

Since the 1920s we have bred the best polo ponies in the entire world, because with the removal of the height limit, I think that this happened at the end of the First World War, Argentinian polo players began to produce 'small horses'. To have big and good-quality mares with a low-galloping ranch character was important. For Argentinian polo players, to produce a great number of 'small horses' was not difficult, because it was a spin-off from the business of ranching. This was and still is our advantage compared with other leading nations in this sport. Then, you need a player. Polo is not a gentle game. There are risk and danger involved. A polo player ought to be a man with great courage and physical resistance. Dedication and learning at an early age are important factors. In many cases it is a kind of family game: your father initiates you; then you play a lot with the *petiseros* and after you get brothers you will play with them and, of course, with your cousins. My father taught me, and I play with my brothers. We had a 'family team' like many of the best teams in Argentina in recent years. You must be an excellent rider, what I shall call an excellent natural rider, in order to cover the field, and above all you must have speed. Speed is very important, and this depends on you but especially on your ponies. Speed is central in polo. The Argentinian way of playing is based on the rare combination of speed and anticipation. These aspects are what I could call 'style'. Yes [and he repeated yes at least three or four times], style is speed and anticipation, and to this you add a 'natural rider' and you get style and horsemanship. This combination permits polo to be a beautiful game and Argentinian players to dominate the game.[1]

Frequently, we returned in our conversations to horses and men – players and *petiseros*, men and horses, performing bodies, Argentinian horses and polo players displaying their abilities in a game that became global in the same epoch as football. He reiterated the importance of polo: 'We ought to be proud of our ponies and our polo players and not only of Maradona.' I told him that my problem was related to the comparison of such diametrically opposed sports. Enrique gave me some important insights; he continually emphasized: that polo was a 'British sport' like football; his ideas on the quality of players; the importance of being a 'natural rider'; his concern with style and, above all, his perceptions on the attributes of good horses. I decided, at the end of my last interview with him, that national styles' and hybridity should be the keys from which to draw the main lines for comparison. When I phoned Enrique and confronted him with this idea, I felt that he did not like it. He was rather sceptical because, and he stressed it, 'These were such different sports', and different 'almost in every-thing'. He was also concerned with the fact that 'Social scientists will know nothing about polo, and they will be full of prejudices because it was an aristocratic sport.' I assumed that presenting polo is even more difficult than discussing football, because as a game it is rather unknown and in many countries is associated with Prince Charles and the British aristocracy. Some readers, perhaps, will relate polo to horses but nothing else. I feel, thus, the need briefly to introduce the reader to some of the main aspects of the game (see Watson 1986; Tocagni 1987).[2]

Polo is, perhaps, the fastest team competition in the world. It consists of two teams of four players competing with a long bamboo stick for the possession of a small ball, from the back of a galloping horse. The result is that the play twists and turns all the time in a rather chaotic flurry of sticks and stampede of ponies' hooves. It is a difficult game because there is much for the beginner to think about – controlling his pony, marking his opposite player, hitting and passing the ball, backing up his team-mates, anticipating the tactics and obeying the very stringent rules of the game – more than in any other sport. When polo is played by the best stars of the game it is certainly one of the most spectacular of all spectator sports.

The polo pitch is 300 yards long and 200 yards wide. The goal-posts are ten feet high, standing eight yards apart at the centre of each back line. The grounds are boarded at the sides to keep the ball in play. The winning side is the one that scores most goals. The game – divided into five to eight 8-minute chukkas or periods – lasts a little over an hour. Because polo is played at a continuous gallop, interspaced with sharp stops, twists and turns, it is extremely tiring for the ponies. They are therefore changed after each chukka, and, as a general rule, no pony is employed in more than two chukkas in any one match. Each team will need on average between 25 and 32 ponies for a match.

The players are numbered One and Two (forwards), Three and Four (back). The duties of Number One are: in defence, to ride off the opposing Number Four; in attack, to support the Number Two to score. The Number Two is usually the strongest of the two forwards and should be the driving force of an attack and the principal goal-scorer. Usually the Number Two is more cerebral and the Number One more aggressive. The Number Three, the key player in the team, is usually their best player; he will initiate the attacks and, at the same time, try to intercept attacks from the opposing team. The Number Four is the principal defender and the most reliable player. He is responsible for taking fouls and penalties.

Polo can be boring from the spectator's point of view due to the frequent interruption of play by the umpires owing to fouls. There is no offside rule but, owing to the use of sticks and fast movements, certain rules are severely enforced. Players cannot ride across another player's 'right of way'; they cannot misuse the stick, and they cannot bump into other horses or zigzag. Another infringement is the 'foul hook', that is to say, any attempt to interfere with an opponent's stick other than when he is in the act of sticking a ball. A player may not attempt to hook either across his opponent's pony or when his opponent's stick is above shoulder level. In all these cases penalties are taken.

Polo, like golf, is a handicap sport. Each player has a handicap, assessed by his national association but guided by international standards. A beginner starts his career at minus 2, the maximum is plus 10. Players performing in different countries can have different handicaps, for example 9 in England and 8 in Argentina. The majority of tournaments are played on a handicap basis, whereby in each match the team having the lower aggregate handicap receives a starting advantage in goals. The term 'high-goal polo' means that the aggregate handicap of a team entered for a given tournament is around 19 or even higher. In theory you can have a team with two players with a handicap of 10 and two with a handicap of 1. The quality of the tournaments is dependent on the aggregate handicap of the teams taking part in it. A normal high-goal polo tournament in Argentina nowadays will have eight teams with more than 35 of handicap and perhaps three of them with the maximum of 40. In contrast, in Europe a high-goal polo team may have as low as 17.

In terms of tactics polo is less complicated than other games. The team's objective will be to bring the ball within striking distance of the opposition goal. This is usually achieved by a combination of superior pace; fast ponies and hard galloping, sure and accurate hitting, coordinated team play, anticipation and perfect passing. Héctor, a 4-goal handicap player in the 1960s and a committed football *aficionado*, told me that the most important aspect of good polo is what he called *juego abierto* (open play).[3] Open play implies

an acceptance of the different roles assigned to the players. A good
Argentinian team, according to his description, will always organize
its attacks rapidly by diagonal and long passes to the side of the
ground, followed by accurate short shots to the centre. He insisted:
'In polo you play better if you combine long and short passes in
this order.' This remark is significant, and I shall return to it later
in the chapter. However, he explained me that one key feature of a
good team is the capacity of the players for interchanging positions.
And knowing my research on football he presented a pedagogical
argument: 'The Dutch team of 1974 played what was called "total
football"; you must understand that the Argentinians have played
"total polo", the best polo in the entire world, since 1936.' This
seems an accepted idea. Watson writes:

> Today Argentina boasts 150 clubs supporting more than 5,000 players
> thus rendering her – quite apart from her supremacy in terms of
> national team play – easily the most important polo country in the world.
> The vigorous grass roots of that nation's polo spring from her land-
> owning element, nearly all of whom base their prosperity on beef cattle;
> for which . . . much the same handy horses are needed as the game
> requires. While the majority of the tournaments are played off at the
> clubs, much polo is played, too, at the *estancias*, the ranches . . . Although
> Argentina took the Copa de las Américas from the United States in
> 1936, it was not until the Second World War – with which most of
> the other polo-playing countries, were deeply preoccupied – that
> Buenos Aires became the acknowledged centre of the polo world.
> (1986: 119–20)

Let me briefly present the origins of this story.

The Beginning of Polo

Polo, an old Asian equestrian sport, began to be played by the
British military officer corps in India in the 1860s. By 1865 the
game was established in Bengal, by 1867 in Madras and by 1870
throughout British India (Watson 1986: 26). However, the origin
of the game in Europe is not directly related to the military practice
of the British Army in India. The regiment of the Tenth Hussars
introduced the game in a cavalry mess at Aldershot in 1869. They
called the game 'hockey on horseback' and taught it to their friends,
officers in the Ninth Lancers. The first official polo match in

Britain was played between these two regiments at Hounslow Heath in 1869 (Watson 1986: 28; Holt 1989: 210). The first tournament for a championship cup in England took place in 1876. It was won by the Royal Horse Guards. In 1873 the Hurlingham Club, in London, decided to introduce polo, and the opening games were played that year. The popularity of polo increased the membership of the Hurlingham Club and more polo clubs were founded in London (Watson 1986: 32). By the end of the century polo was played all over Great Britain. The quality of the game played in Great Britain was highly dependent on the growth of polo in India, where it could be played the whole year round and, owing to the support given by the Army, the game – and especially the access to good ponies – was more generally open to all who were interested. Officers without significant economic means achieved high proficiency in India and were able to improve the standard of British polo on their return.

In 1876 polo was introduced in the United States by James Gordon Bennett Jr, son of the founder of the *New York Herald* and himself proprietor of that newspaper. He saw 'the cream of the British army: bronzed centaurs, hardened from years in the saddle, racing, foxhunting and troop duty' play the game at Hurlingham Club and was impressed by the game (Watson 1896: 40–1). He returned to New York with a large supply of sticks and balls, bought ponies in Texas, and staged a demonstration game. New clubs were created, and by 1879 it was an established sport in the New York area. The first public match was played in 1879, with 10,000 spectators watching the 'new English game'. Polo became a game for American millionaires. The Hurlingham team visited the United States in 1886, and they played for the first time against an American team for the Westchester cup. The English team won decisively the three matches played. The intense competition between England and the United States had just begun, and by the 1900s polo had become a fashionable and élite game in both countries, played by millionaires, aristocrats and cavalry officers. Watson rightly writes: 'Englishmen were the initiators and pioneers of modern polo; English sportsmen, more than any other people, were the harbingers of the game through the western world; and Englishmen first played it in the country which has been, since the 1930s, by general acclaim, the world's leading polo nation – Argentina' (1986: 60).

In 1875 the first polo matches were played in Argentina at the estancia El Negrete, owned by David Shennan, in Santa Rosa. All players were British (Laffaye 1989: 23). It is interesting to notice that some of the matches were played between teams called 'England', 'Scotland', 'City' and 'Countryside' (Ceballos 1969: 20–2). These names clearly indicate the origins of the players. In 1882 the first polo club was founded in Buenos Aires, the Flores Club. In 1884 the first public official match was played on the grounds of the Flores Club. One team represented the city of Bahia Blanca, province of Buenos Aires, and the other the newly established Buenos Aires Polo Club. *The Herald*, the daily competing with *The Standard*, wrote on that match:

> It is one of the most manly games ever invented, requiring great courage and dexterity and the finest horsemanship; the ponies also must be well trained, and then there is no doubt that they enter into the spirit of the game as fully as their riders. With two good teams at play, it is a most exciting scene for the onlookers as well as the players, and we are glad to see that this noble game has been introduced into this country by Englishmen. The Buenos Aires club proved victorious. The ponies of the other club had only arrived on the previous night and had been trained on sand and so were at a disadvantage on the turf. (Quoted in Graham-Yooll 1981: 194)

In 1888, the oldest existing polo club in Argentina was founded in Venado Tuerto by the British F. Hincliff, F. Thompson, J. Smythe, F. Bridger, C. Tetley and the Belgian Baron G. Peers. The initial years were described in the following way:

> At the beginning it was played only on Sundays. In the morning all the players arrived from their own estancias, which in many cases were far away. They ride on one horse and bring, all together, the ponies needed for the matches. The travel was exhausting, but they played six or seven chukkas. At the end of the game, and sometimes during the night, they returned the same way. They arrived home late, and they began to work early next morning on their farms . . . The original ground was just a *potrero* [an uneven piece of land]. The two good grounds were made in 1920, not before. (Own translation *Polo y Equitación* no. 58, 1930: 38)

By the 1890s, polo was mostly played in the provinces of Buenos Aires and Santa Fe, on estancias owned by landlords of British origin. However, polo was also played by British citizens in northern provinces like Santiago del Estero and Jujuy. Even on the first tour to England of an Argentinian team in 1891, two of the players,

R. M. Smyth and N. Smyth, played for the Santiago del Estero Polo Club. In 1892, delegates of the existing British clubs founded the Polo Association of the River Plate in Buenos Aires. The period of organized polo began in Argentina. Polo in the Army was introduced by Captain Oliveira Cezar in 1894 after watching what he called 'a game of crazy *gringos*'. He found that polo playing was an excellent exercise for army cavalry officers. The first official public match in the army was played in 1895. In 1908, a presidential decree declared polo obligatory in the cavalry regiments, and from that time until the 1950s it was a tradition to play an open tournament each year for teams representing cavalry regiments. By the 1910s polo was consolidated as a national sport in Argentina with the foundation of more clubs and the rapid expansion of polo in the Army. However, the original disparity of the players was never overcome: the civilian teams and players were much better than the military, and very few officers – rare exceptions that confirmed the rule – played in the best clubs and on the different Argentinian national teams (see Padilla 1969). Polo became a 'popular' sport among the landed British and Argentinian élite; they controlled the game, they raised the best ponies and produced the best players.

It is important to keep in mind that by the beginning of the twentieth century the rise of organized equestrian sport in the pampas followed, in many ways, the demise of the gaucho, and of his traditional contests and pastimes. The gauchos had a number of rugged and violent games, contests and pastimes ('crowding horses', *cinchadas, pechando*, the collective game of *pato*), which required a great deal of strength and courage in both man and horse and fantastic speed.[4] Accidents – even fatal ones – were common in these competitions. On the contrary, polo was defined as a civilized spectator sport and a sign of modern times. Its enthusiastic adoption by the landed aristocracy was seen as an expression of a well-achieved civilizing process (Slatta 1986). Moreover, through polo Argentinians could participate in a social world dominated by British and European aristocrats and American millionaires.

On the estancias the rural labourers became *petiseros* and adopted polo. The best proof is their participation on some of the winning teams at the beginning of the Argentinian Polo Open Championship. On the team of Las Petacas, winner of 1895 and 1896, the brothers Sixto (foreman) and José Martínez, and Francisco Benítez (the latter two *petiseros*) played together with Frank Kinchant. In

North Santa Fe, the great team of the brothers Traill with José
Gonzáles played in the winning team of 1906. In Western Camps,
winner in 1907 and 1909, the *petisero* Eduardo Lucero played with
Campbell, R. Leard and H. Drusdale (Asociación Argentina de Polo
1993: 16). The foremen and the rural labourers disappeared from
active practice in the official polo competition in 1910. The argument used for excluding them was that they were 'professional
players' because they received a wage while playing on the teams
of their employers (Ceballos 1969: 19; Laffaye 1989: 40).[5]

In the ideological construction of the *criollo* in the practice of polo
the team of Las Petacas holds a privileged position. Laffaye writes:

> Frank Kinchant . . . with the support of Jewell – owner of the estancia
> Las Petacas – decided to form a team pervaded by what we could call
> primitive force, because he chose three fantastic *criollo* riders: the
> foreman Sixto Martínez and the workers José Martínez and Francisco
> Benítez. Kinchant taught them how to use the stick, the rules of the
> game and nothing more, because those *criollos* had the rest. They were
> the preamble of the future hegemony of the Argentinians in the game
> of polo . . . Las Petacas, led by Kinchant as number Three, was the first
> great polo team, developing a style that was more open and whose
> players hit the ball on all sides of the horses (Own translation 1989:
> 32).[6]

The use of the category *criollo* has, in this context, an ethnic
content but also announces the historical, ideological constructions
related to hybridization and polo. We are confronted with *criollos*,
men of horses, great riders imbued with a gaucho tradition. The
condition of being great riders cannot, however, be an absolute
attribute of the *criollos*, because the British and their descendants
demonstrated in the practice of the sport that they also were
excellent riders. The ideological *tour de force* must be built up
around concrete mechanisms of inclusion and exclusion, as we have
seen in the case of football. In the case of polo, the descendants
of British immigrants dominated polo until the 1930s. Ceballos, a
former president of the Argentine Polo Association, describes the
adaptation of the English to the rural Argentinian tradition in the
following way:

> with a high degree of adaptation to the new environment, the English
> populated a great unexploited and uninhabited savannah. They founded
> estancias and more estancias, on which British and *criollos* lived together,

the *criollos* being foremen or simply working as rural workers. A cold milieu, with reciprocal consideration and respect, based on the fulfilment of duties, kept these men in contact. The *criollo* had a capital defect: he had no schooling . . . The greater culture among the English put them in a position of natural superiority with respect to our *criollos*, making it possible to assimilate all the good qualities of the natives and to continue, if possible, in the same rhythm of life to which they were used. This was a normal characteristic of the British: their fidelity to the tradition and customs of their parents. (Own translation 1969: 18)

What was perceived as being 'essentially good' among the natives was the riding style and their horses. Ceballos also comments that, from the first years of polo, the British in Argentina did not hesitate in thinking that polo would become a great sport in Argentina due to the fact that the country 'was a land of centaurs, where the fields are as even as chess-boards and the horses show exceptional characteristics and a predisposition for the struggle' (1969: 22). This ideology needs further exploration.

Playing Polo and Becoming *Criollos*

The history of the first two generations of Traills will help us to understand the role of the British in the cultural construction of a polo *criollo*.[7] The origins of the Traills, a family of nomads and entrepreneurs, are traced to a church in Austria, and from there they moved first to France and then to Scotland in the fourteenth century. Some of the Traills emigrated to Ireland in the 1600s, and during the nineteenth and twentieth centuries descendants crossed the oceans and settled in North and South America, Africa, New Zealand and Australia. The brothers Robert Walter and Edmund Bernard left Liverpool for Argentina by steamer in 1866. Upon arrival they discovered that they could not get land in the province of Buenos Aires, so they decided to go to the province of Santa Fe where they bought 12,000 hectares (45 square miles). They settled, bought cattle at a low price, and also horses and mares at much higher prices. Like every *estanciero* at that time the brothers bought land with every peso they could save but also borrow. By 1880 they owned 51,000 hectares. At that time, businesses went well, and some of the family moved back and forth from Argentina, leaving some of the children at boarding-schools in England.

It is possible to imagine the rigorousness of the life in the torrid clime of Santa Fe: the limitations of an 'uncivilized' nature with long grass, anthills and mosquitoes; the lack of roads and services; the absence of trees, and the absence of village life with pubs and entertainments. Robert had played cricket for Ireland, so he began to organize cricket games with other estancias. Willans comments that in this way 'began the Traill tradition of getting together at someone's estancia to play some sport' (1993: 14). Neither Robert nor Edmund was a good rider, but they became involved in local horse racing. The sport was popular in the area, and the stakes were large. Robert acquired Forrester, an English Thoroughbred stallion, for racing and for improving the quality of their local *criollo* horses. Johnny Traill, Robert's son, commented in his unpublished memoirs that by 1890: 'we had enough horses to ride when I tell you that the day before my eight birthday, our wild mares were rounded up from open camp and corralled, and with foals at foot they numbered over two thousand. Amongst them were some twenty-five quarterbred stallions bred from Forrester, and they were now running with the mares' (n.d.: 6).[8]

In 1896 Edmund bought Springjack, another English stallion, a six-year-old horse who had broken down as a three-year-old in the Derby. Willans describes him in the following way: 'A very dark bay, standing 14.3 hands, a good head carriage, deep girth, well sloping shoulders, a short back, good strong quarters and well let down hocks, the progeny from Springjack with the very inbred mares from Forrester were practically at the Thoroughbred level' (1993: 14). These ponies provided the first generation of Traills with a great advantage. According to Watson, 'the ponies got from . . . [Springjack] were among the first that marked the change between the old-fashioned Argentine and the blood pony of later days' (1986: 63). The Traills were, without any doubt, the first breeders in Argentina to play ponies bred by themselves for polo. Johnny Traill observed that Edmund's choice of this stallion was the best to breed polo ponies from: 'my father could not have found a better one than Springjack' (n.d.: 6).

As pointed out, Robert and Edmund were not good riders, and their race horses were ridden by local jockeys. However, their sons – and daughters – became excellent riders, 'accomplished gauchos'. During the 1890s Edmund set up a polo field in one of the estancias so the social life of the Traills was, to a great extent, organized around polo games. The polo tournaments played at different estancias were an occasion for competition and included other sports, like cricket and even Rugby on some occasions, social exchanges, and parties. *The Standard* used to present in its pages the estancia tournaments as important social events in the life of the British colony. I shall give two examples. In August 1905 a 'polo party' was organized at the estancia La Pastoril in Alberdi, province of Buenos Aires. The British-owned Pacific Railways set up a train for the players, families and ponies. The trip began in Retiro in Buenos Aires with various stops, including Hurlingham, close to Buenos Aires, where the main polo club was located. They arrived late during the night, and woke early next morning at the estancia station. The journey began with a 'heavy English breakfast'. The polo matches were played until 1.00 p.m., and 'a succulent *asado* [barbecue] in a pure *criollo* style was served in the main *galpon*'. After a break more chukkas were played. In the evening an elegant dinner was offered, and a dance exhibition was given by a 'dancing professor' from Buenos Aires (*The Standard* 22/8/1905: 5). A week later an entire page with photos of the event was published. In the second example, from 1912, we see the Traills in action. On that occasion the Central Railways scheduled a special train for North Santa Fe, the team of the Traills, and another English team, Los Dos Hermanos. The trip was of almost one thousand kilometres to the city of Concepción in the province of Tucumán, in northern Argentina. A polo tournament with other British teams, representing the sugar-mills polo clubs, and a team of the cavalry regiment of Tucumán was organized. The tournament lasted one week and was won by the North Santa Fe team.[9] In addition to polo other sports were played – cricket and tennis – and horse-races were run. The horse-races were socially divided into races for the polo players and races for the *petiseros*. The races for players were also won by the Traills. Different dancing parties were organized and cavalry officers of the local regiments were invited to all of them. On the last night a fancy dress ball culminated an intense week with success, because 'the men's costumes were designed and executed by the ladies' with great imagination (*The Standard* , 3 and 11/2/1912).

Polo was played by the Traills of the first generation, Joe, son of Edmund, and Robert, Ned and Johnny, sons of Robert, who formed the mythical team of North Santa Fe. Ned and Robert played on the team The Casuals, winning the Argentinian Open in 1898. They only played together on the winning teams of the Open in 1904

and 1908. Between 1900 and 1920, North Santa Fe won the Polo
Open Championship nine times – 1904, 1906, 1907, 1908, 1910,
1912, 1913, 1916 and 1917 – representing what was called 'the
true estancia polo' or 'countryside polo'. Hurlingham, a team
representing the urbanite British – Robson, Scott-Robson, Bennett,
Bedford and, later, Lacey – won five times. The polo played by the
Traills was different because their ponies were different and the
best. They played hard and with great speed, and they were part
of the origins of the 'Argentinian style'. Joe Traill was only seven-
teen when he won the open for the first time. Johnny was also
playing well at an early age, and he became the first 10-goaler
'Argentinian' in 1913 (Laffaye 1989: 269). He held this handicap
for twenty-four years without a break – an extraordinary achievement. Joe became a 9-goaler, Robert an eight and Ned a seven.
Johnny became a full-time polo player, playing in Argentina, England
and the United States, while the others were in charge of running
the estancias. He won the Argentinian Open ten times, a legendary
accomplishment – compared with the seven won by Lacey, the other
great player of his time. The careers of Johnny Traill and Lacey
can be regarded as paradigmatic of some of the dilemmas of the
British-Argentinian players: they were in some contexts defined as
Argentinians, when the style of playing and the quality of the ponies
were taken into consideration, and in others as British, when
citenzenship was stressed. Two situations clearly illustrate the
fundamental moral ambivalence of being, at the same time, Argentinian and British.

The Ambivalence of Being British

Since 1896 the British landowners and polo players living in Argentina took part in the big tournaments in England with great success.
Each participation implied an impressive mobilization of maritime
resources: five or six players, the labourers – *petiseros* – and between
twenty-five and thirty-five horses with all the fodder needed for
crossing the Atlantic Ocean. Usually they embarked in Buenos Aires
in February in order to be in good shape for the summer tournaments in Europe, which began in May. The team of 1897, led by
Scott-Robson and mounted entirely on their native-bred ponies,
won most of their matches, and gave England 'a foretaste of
how good Argentina was going to be' (Watson 1986: 62). It was the

usual case that the best players were the owners of the best horses, and gradually Argentinian polo ponies began to gain international fame. The great majority of British ponies were in Thoroughbred while the Argentinians had an important stock of *criollo* blood. A successful tour implied 'good business', because the best ponies could be sold to British players. In 1897 in the final of the Open of Hurlingham in England, Rugby, the winning team, used three Argentinian ponies in two chukkas (Laffaye 1989: 158). Moreover, an international circuit was begun, and the good players were invited to play in different countries with teams organized by British aristocrats and American millionaires.

In 1912 what was considered the most important tour to England was organized by Joe and Johnny Traill. They were accompanied by H. Swind and Lynch Stauton, who played with them at North Santa Fe. The team was called El Bagual. In England they were joined by John Argentine Campbell, who replaced Lynch Stauton, who was injured, in the first tournament. They won two important cups with handicap: the Social Club Cup and the Whitney Cup. Joe Traill, in a letter sent to the Polo River Plate Association, recounts that in the final of the Whitney Cup they met the team of Eaton Hall, led by the Duke of Westminster. Eaton Hall had a total handicap of 34 goals, against the 22 of El Bagual, and had the best English ponies, selected for a tour in the United States. Before the final, the polo journalist of *The Times* wrote that the Argentinian ponies had 'bad class' and were not as fast as the English ones. However, the team of the Traills won the final easily, with a difference of ten goals. Joe Traill commented that the journalist was wrong regarding the ponies, as the result had shown, and that the best ten ponies of the team were at least as good as the ten best of the Duke of Westminster. The best proof Traill gives is that after the match the Duke bought eight of their ponies, later selected to go on the tour of the United States (Ceballos 1969: 70).

In his book, Ceballos cites some of the comments of the English press. The *Morning Post* put special emphasis on the capacity of the players of El Bagual for riding with 'the power of a hurricane', and that their ponies, 'having no class when compared to the English', were, however, able to gallop in the games like 'wild creatures from the West'. The same journal stressed that the Argentinian players had their own way of playing, 'typically representative of the freedom of the countryside', implying that, while it was perhaps not sophisticated, it was a style at least. The words used for defining the style were 'power', 'enthusiasm', 'a great variety of hits', 'a profound knowledge of the game' and 'a great instinct'. *The Times* declared the 'Argentinian player Johnny Traill' a genius, and *The World* wrote that under the 'irresistible combination of the individual ability of the players and the power of the ponies, the handicaps of the London teams went down, like grass under the scythe' (Ceballos 1969: 70–1). *The Standard* in Buenos Aires reproduced some of these articles in which it was pointed out that the 'Argentinian back Johnny Traill' was the best ever seen in London since the times of Lord Wodehouse. The players of El Bagual were presented as 'good Argentinian sportsmen' (2 /7/ 1912: 4). Johnny Traill, the son of British parents and a British citizen himself, was defined by the English press as Argentinian, and – what will be more important later in the chapter – the ponies and the style of playing were also seen as 'different'.

The performances of the players and the ponies of El Bagual were central in the creation of an 'exotic' way of playing polo that was not English. In the Argentinian interpretation of the style displayed by Johnny Traill, the connection with the gaucho style of riding is made explicit. According to Balfour, one of the polo pioneers, Traill learned how to play polo from Sixto Martinez, a real gaucho and foreman of estancia Las Petacas, who played in the winning team of Las Petacas in the Argentinian Open of 1895 (Laffaye 1989: 72–3). However, according to Traill himself, he learnt from the gauchos in general, not from a single individual. He writes:

> All the horses had very good mouths and though the bits were severe, the *peons* (the gauchos) were extremely light handed. No force was needed and the merest check with one finger would stop the animal dead. I learnt to ride this way too, and soon found that if I pulled on the reins, the pony would stand still or run backwards. It was a case of loose reins or never leaving the mounting spot! (n.d.: 6)[10]

Traill confessed that in working with the gauchos he came to know and to respect a complex culture based on 'sayings and super-stitions' (n.d.: 36–7). The culture of the gauchos was more than a way of riding.

The British press saw something 'different', and this difference was codified as representing, in addition to individual abilities, a 'style'. In Argentina, the genealogical dimension was added: Johnny

Traill, who could not learn from his father, who was not a good rider, learned all the secrets of the game from a real gaucho. The gaucho spirit was reproduced through this accidental encounter with a tradition.

The model of hybridization as amalgamation is at work here. In relation to the way the English codified kinship, Strathern writes that:

> 'Tradition' is similar but not quite the same as and hence overlaps with the idea of 'continuity'; it is continuity seen from the point of view of what is regarded as characteristic or typical about something. The 'conventional' overlaps in turn with the idea of 'tradition'; it is tradition seen from the point of view of what is regarded as regulative in social life. (1992: 14)

In her perspective tradition comes before change. The gaucho style of riding existed as a tradition before it was transformed on the fields of polo. Thus, tradition can be seen as past style, and the Argentinian style of playing polo as present tradition (Strathern 1992: 29). But a present tradition needs to be reproduced in the future, and this happens with polo. This 'style' was cemented by the triumphant tour, in 1922, of the team composed of four 'anglos': L. Lacey, by that time with a 10-goal handicap, David and John Miles, and John Nelson.[11] They won the thirteen matches they played in different tournaments in England. An Argentinian winning style thus became part of the global imageries in the field of sport. In this particular context, as in football, the Argentinian 'culture' is manifested through style. The individual, Johnny Traill or L. Lacey, exists and is needed in this ideological framework. He synthesizes a style. Therefore, as an individual he is defined in reference to an existing whole – the gaucho tradition. Let me now present the second example.

Johnny Traill was in his way of playing defined as Argentinian; he was a product – and one of the main creators – of an Argentinian style, but, ironically enough, he never played for Argentina. As an international player he represented both England and Ireland. A key year in the history of polo in Argentina is 1924, because it was accepted as an Olympic discipline for the Games held in Paris that year. At that time, as we have seen in the case of football in the previous chapter, the Olympic Games were defined as 'world championships', and a gold medal implied acceptance as 'world champion'. Argentina sent a team composed of four '*anglos*' Nelson, Kenny, Brooke Naylor and John Miles, and one '*criollo*', Captain Padilla. The two best 'Argentinian' players, John Traill and Lacey – both with a 10-goal handicap – were called to play for England. They joined the training camp of the English team in May 1924 and were indisputably seen as the main players. According to Nelson himself (1969: 116), this situation created a problem for the Argentinian Polo Association, which was obliged to replace them, and insecurity among the Argentinian players selected. Miller, a well-known English international polo player, declared to the Argentinian journal *La Nación* that if Traill and Lacey played together neither the Argentinians nor the Americans could beat the English team (5/6/1924: 2). *La Nación* reports that the British Association of Polo had been in doubt about the designation of the team for Paris (6/5/1924: 1). The main problem behind the hesitations of the Association was revealed two days later: Lacey and Traill, the star players of the team, had officially announced that it was a source of pride for both of them to defend England, but, in case they were chosen for Paris, they would not play against the Argentinian team (*La Nación* ,12/6/1924: 2).

This decision and moral standpoint dramatically illustrate the dilemmas of two 'hybrid' persons. They were British citizens; they had played for England – and Lacey even fought in the First World War as an officer in a cavalry regiment, but they were key figures in the creation of a non-British style. They represented a 'polo tradition': the Argentinian. Suddenly, two individuals embodied a tradition which eventually, and paradoxically enough, could be defeated by them, by concrete individuals who were the product of a whole. It is, therefore, understandable what was at stake and why they could play against the powerful team of the United States but never against the Argentinians. The decision taken could easily be interpreted as a way of avoiding being accused of treason in Argentina and of being defined as traitors on their return to Buenos Aires. However, the situation of two hybrid persons complicates the analysis: they were at the same time British and Argentinians, and the question of 'borders' was exaggerated in June 1924. They were citizens of Great Britain, but also Argentinian players; they could play for England but not against Argentina – because this would be playing against a part of themselves. They were not pure. The result of their decision was positive for the Argentinian team, because the British Association decided to send to Paris a military

polo team that was much weaker than the civilian one led by Lacey and Traill. Nelson, the captain of the Argentinian team, opined that before this happened he was convinced of the superiority of the British team (*La Nación*, 25/6/1924: 2).
I have not found in Traill's memoirs a single comment on this event. We can imagine that this incident was not so important for him, and that the moral ambiguity was constructed by the journalists and, perhaps, by Nelson himself. It was an imagery that worked very well, however, for Lacey: Lacey left polo in 1937. That year the Argentinian Polo Association organized a public tribute at the aristocratic Alvear Palace Hotel in Buenos Aires. Ceballos, the president of the association from 1929 until 1934, mentioned in his speech that Lacey joined the national English team in 1922, but, he added, that he was 'pardoned by his Argentinian mates'. Ceballos emphasized the fact that he just fulfilled a patriotic duty because he was a British citizen, and for that he was praised. However, he refused to play in 1924, illustrating that he was also Argentinian. Ceballos stressed the fact that he learned polo in Argentina, and that his personality as a player was formed in Argentina, 'riding Argentinian ponies'. His closing words pointed out that his way of riding should be defined as '*criolla* and *argentina*, and that Argentinians were proud of him because he showed this style to the world' (*Polo y Campo* no. 48, 1937: 8, 36).[12]

The Consolidation of a Style: the Hybrids in the Olympic Games of 1924

The image of an original 'creole style' in the 1910s and 1920s was a product England sent to Argentina, and it confirmed, in many ways, the existing self-image. Argentinian players were not surprised by their victory in the Olympic Games; they were expecting this victory (*La Nación*, 6/6/1924: 1). Just before the finals, Major Sierra, a cavalry officer and a good player with a 4-goal handicap, elaborated a theory on the superiority of 'creole polo players':

> The [Argentinian] superiority is related to three factors: the stamina of the rider; the Argentinian way of riding; and the quality of the horses. The habit of equilibrium has been acquired – neither through advice nor through acceptance of the rules of riding-schools – in the usual and natural practice of riding in the countryside. The Argentinian on

a horse cannot be equalled by other riders . . . The way we take a rein
represents a great relief for the horse, which can feel much more
freedom than when it is ridden by an Englishman or a Yankee. We
have much more speed and slyness in the game and much more spirit
of sacrifice. We have much more temperament than they; we are real
fighters due, perhaps, to an atavistic gaucho instinct which is still in
our veins and is manifested in many of the things we do. I believe, in
sum, that Europeans will suffer a lot of defeats in the hands of the
savages (*salvajes*) . . . The English player has habits of moderation, being
conservative in all things he does. He is not the kind of man who will
take risks when he is in a difficult position, and, as you know, a polo
match contains plenty of such situations. When confronted with these
difficulties, the men of our idiosyncrasy will continue to fight. With
this, I mean that courage and resistance are traits of our players. (Own
translation *El Gráfico* no. 261, 1924: 19)

For Major Sierra, the Argentinian players of British origin who
represented the country in Paris are typically Argentinian or, better,
criollos, because they ride in a distinctive manner. However, to the
creole way of riding he added a number of masculine virtues. In
his perspective the creole polo players had inherited gaucho qualities,
and they are, so to speak, modern gauchos but still 'savages'.
Barbarism – an imagined definition of the other – is transformed
into a positive virtue because it is atavistic and, in many ways,
natural. Sierra reproduces the classic ideological antithesis of
barbarism-civilization which in the past – and in the 1920s – opposed
nationalists and liberal cosmopolitans. In this case civilization is
represented by the English and the Yankee riders. In this way of
reasoning, polo, a game with accepted universal rules, results in a
variety of styles under the influence of independent traditions –
the gaucho or the English. According to Sierra, the British descendants are 'transformed' when they enter into contact with the gaucho
tradition; they become hybrids, in which the gaucho qualities are
dominant. In the perspective chosen by Ceballos, presented above,
the British are perceived as moving between two traditions: the
one represented by gaucho culture and the other by their ancestors.
They are hybrids in the sense of combining the best traits of each
culture.

Polo is more than players. A good creole player needs a good
pony. The theoretical superiority of a player in polo is highly
dependent on the quality of the horses he rides. Argentinian
winning teams in international competitions knew that victories

were associated with business, with selling their ponies to the English aristocrats or the American millionaires. Sierra explains that the main difference between the Argentinian and foreign ponies is related to the following aspects:

> The main difference is that the foreign ponies do not enjoy, like ours, a strong and free life in an open landscape; they have been educated in an artificial environment, in small plots and inside boxes. In such conditions of captivity, the beast acquires a relative strength without developing his power, diminishing his flexibility and instinct for fighting. Do the British horses have at their disposal a place for a real run? No ... In the Argentinian polo horse, the bodily form has not been selected, as in the case of the *pur-sangs*, for a fantastic body, great velocity, but without resistance, because in case of an accident he will die; in the Argentinian pony, the creole blood has been kept; when pure-bloods have mixed with mares of our places, this blood is a heritage of freedom and of a brave existence in the desert ... The history of the heroism of the creole horse is well known, it is enough to say that his body is well-formed, that his organs are of steel and that he has benefited from the natural environment. (Own translation *El Gráfico* no. 216, 1924: 19)

Sierra enters into one of the great topics of discussion during the 1920s: the breeding of polo ponies. In the past, Ceballos, especially, and also prominent landlords and players were favourable to the utilization of pure creole horses, because they believed that docility and coarseness – values defining the creole horse – were central in polo (Ceballos 1969: 9–10). Even in the tours to England of 1897, organized by Balfour, the team leaving Buenos Aires had only creole horses. The results were excellent because out of twenty-three matches they lost only three (Laffaye 1989: 63–4). However, in 1924 the supporters of the creole horse had lost their battle and, of course, the early victories and dominance of the Traills had demonstrated the advantages of cross-breeding. They were crossing English thoroughbreds with the most promising of their ranch mares from the end of the nineteenth century. Ceballos recognized that in the aftermath of the First World War:

> The creole horse was displaced ... by horses with a high degree of cross-breeding ... The characteristics of the cross-breed pony gave a new physiognomy to the game, because the *pique* (rapid acceleration) of the creole horse was transformed by the continuous speed of the cross-breed horse, which will dominate in the new animal. The new

pony makes it possible to replace short dribbling, as a style, with rapid displacements along the field and by combinations which favour the best-mounted player or the best with the stick. (1969: 63)

In the generation of the new hybrid, in the conception of both Sierra and Ceballos, given qualities of the creole horses and mares are preserved. In Sierra the heritage of freedom, heroism and steel conditions – clearly military metaphors – are transformed, simply, in the *pique* of Ceballos. The pure creole ponies are unable to maintain high speed in the long displacements which will be dominant in modern polo strategy. This quality can only be obtained through cross-breeding with *pur-sang* or English thoroughbred stallions. According to Ceballos, the new ponies changed the style of short dribbling which characterized the old style of playing polo. If we now compare polo with football we get a clear asymmetry: the British style in football is associated with kick-and-run (the long balls), while the creole style utilizes short dribbling. In polo, the traditional style is related to short passing, while the new one, developed by players of British origin, is associated with long displacements. What is negative in football is transformed into positive in polo. The lack of creolization of the British in football is reinstated through polo.

In the model advanced by Sierra, the new hybrid pony is superior because it grows in freedom, a freedom provided by the *pampa*. It is the *pampa* – in addition to blood – that explains the qualities of the horse. The English horses, because they do not grow up enjoying liberty, will be less strong and more apathetic. The *pampa* is thought of as a whole transcending all the parts – the individuals. At the same time, the qualities of the *pampa* are possible to find in each individual, in each pony. The same logic of diversity and generalization is present when the different attributes of the crossed animals are imagined. The idea of fusion does not exclude the survival of the creole attributes. The loss of the creole components is, on some occasions, perceived as a threat to the pure creole horse. In 1926 *El Gráfico* refers to a polo tournament in Coronel Dorrego, in the province of Buenos Aires, in which a team using only pure creole horses won. The journalist is delighted because in such a way the creole pony, with his qualities of resistance, courage, rusticity and agility, will not disappear. It is stressed that these qualities were threatened by the advanced process of cross-breeding (*El Gráfico* no. 374, 1926: 5). Even a specialized magazine like *Polo y Equitación* in 1928 defended the importance of the creole horse in the constitution of the new pony. It is accepted that the majority of the good ponies had by that time 31/32 blood of *pur-sang*, and only 1/32 of creole blood. However, it is pointed out that cross-breeding over time and the use of creole mares permitted the consolidation of the Argentinian pony as something peculiar. Lacey, the great polo player, is quoted in the article as reinforcing this assertion when accepting that the creole blood was crucial in the creation of the new pony type. The qualities of the creole horse – presented above – are also mentioned in the article, but new ones are added. According to the anonymous author of the article, the creole horse has two extraordinary attributes: anticipation – he can read the game – and fantastic vision. He concluded by pointing out that these aspects are fundamental in any polo match in which the horses – and not only the players – ought to play (*Polo y Equitación* no. 34, 1928: 25).

Another argument used at that time was the fact that the method of training the ponies included a period of working with livestock on the estancias. The *petiseros*, who, in most cases were well-trained rural labourers, used to work with their horses in the managing of livestock. Miguel Martínez de Hoz, the president of the Argentinian Polo Association, explains the Argentinian victory in Paris without employing Major Sierra's military metaphors. For him the reasons were clear:

> The pony must have an appropriate conformation and a rapid acceleration and must be improved through the ranching activities carried out by the *petiseros* who educate them. Among these *petiseros* there are excellent players who, unfortunately, cannot play in the open tournaments. In addition the strategy is to breed *pur-sang* stallions with cross-breed mares. In the education of the ponies on the ranch the importance of rounding up other animals is very important. (Own translation *La Nación*, 13/7/1924: 1)

In his perception hybridity is also a product of education in the working activities of the estancias. The 'character' of the Argentina ponies is forged in work with livestock, which makes it possible for them, later, to play without fear. This is not the case of the English ponies. He also added with great conviction that the Argentinian players are the best in the world because they ride like true gauchos. He concluded by pointing out the importance of founding a new style of playing: 'the Argentinians have imposed in Europe the light polo . . . the practice of the long balls . . . and in this way the old belief that polo should be played slowly through short passings has been undermined . . . this style will disappear and the game will gain in vivacity and rapidity, and consequently acquire more beauty' (*La Nación* , 7/6/1924: 2).

As we have seen in the case of football, not only success is important in the recognition of a style. The gaze of the other will condition the outcome. Identity is a game made up of contrasting mirrors and gazes. The Argentinian polo style needed the explicit recognition of the Europeans after defeating the favourite teams of England and the United States. *L'Auto*, a French men's magazine combining automobile and sport news, described in 1924 the Argentinian victory in the following way:

> The Argentinian players try to stick to the saddle in such a way that the men and the horses constitute a single body. The thirty-five horses of the team are cross breed *pur-sangs* and Argentinian creoles, rather small . . . They have been selected among a great variety of types and trained in order to develop a great speed and resistance. Ridden with great gentleness, just with one rein, the horses make marvellous movements and incredible pirouettes, giving the impression that they enjoy complete freedom. The players control the horses like tennis players handling a racket . . . The Argentinians surprise us with their great ability in the use of the stick. Less strong than the Americans, they practise a way of playing that is much freer and more varied. Each player rides at a fantastic speed, giving the feeling that, at each moment, they know the position of each other in the field. (Own translation Quoted in Laffaye 1989: 96)

We must remember that the winning team included Captain Padilla as the only player with a Spanish name – the others Nelson, Kenny and Miles were *anglos*. *La Nación*, a newspaper considered to be the symbol of the Argentinian landlord class, saluted the victory of the Argentinian polo team as an expression of the unity between the civilian and the military forces and as a ratification of the quality of the new hybrids produced in Argentina – riders and horses. Concerning the new hybrids we can read:

> The [Argentinian] polo players are genuine representatives of the new race, strong and virile. The success that they have achieved . . . is an exploit that touches us and reveals how much the Argentinian effort is able to produce. The victory of these young athletes is, above all, a

victory of the will . . . and a moral example . . . The triumphs of the
Argentinian athletes show us and others that our race, by the extraordinary confluence of different ethnic streams, by the moral health
that infiltrates our blood, has a wealth of vitality and energy, and, last,
by the arrival of material and spirituals gifts that exalt the human
condition, have opened perspectives to all our dreams and hopes. (Own
translation *La Nación*, 13/6/1924: 1)

The optimistic tone of *La Nación* not only coincides with a given
victory. The 1920s had consolidated the image of Argentina as an
open country, a rich and emerging young nation. In the field of
sport, as well as in political history, unexpected victories are usually
explained as revolutionary moments, as dramatic events, as breaking
points, as the deployment of new cultural forms. The victorious
team was received in the harbour of Buenos Aires by thousands
and thousands of people: they had won against the two economic
world powers; they were champions of the world, and they had
amazed the sophisticated Parisians and the European aristocracy.
They were called 'the cavaliers of the South' or 'the big great men
of the South'.

In this euphoric scenario, Jack Nelson, the captain of the team,
imagined a better future for polo:

We shall undoubtedly realize a many years' dream: to transform polo
into the national sport of Argentina. Everything is given for such an
accomplishment: the characteristic of our country in which cattle-raising
is essential; the innate capacity of our riders; the education of the horses
in livestock activities in which they develop the fundamental attributes
for the practice of polo . . . The growth of the practice of polo in
Argentina will be secured if we can build more grounds and stadiums
around Buenos Aires so that the people who usually go on Sunday to
watch football will now go to watch polo. (Own translation *La Nación*,
16/6/1924: 2)

The Olympic Games of 1924 transformed polo into a 'popular'
sport, at least among the middle classes in Buenos Aires.[13] The
greater public hitherto were ignorant of the fact that Argentinians
(and British living in the country) were among the best players
of the world. The members of the Olympic team left Argentina
in 1924 without being noticed and were received back home as
national heroes. Polo transcended the rural frame of the estancias,
was recognized as 'national' by the popular press and the urban

public, but was rarely played by sons of the urban bourgeoisie and middle classes of European ancestry. Polo created and reproduced a pastoral imagery based on the importance of vernacularism, gaucho idealization and aristocratic standards. The private appropriation of the mythological pampas, populated in the past by the free gauchos, permitted the landed class to export grain and beef to the world market, to accumulate substantial wealth, to be in permanent contact with the descendants of the gauchos transformed into paid riders and rural labourers, to imagine a mimetic relation with the gaucho riding tradition, to produce marvellous horses and riders, to win against British aristocrats and American millionaires in prestigious polo tournaments, and to be fully accepted socially by them. They entered early into a global system of economic exchanges, and continued to accumulate wealth, trophies and glory.

The victory in polo in 1924 was followed by the successful European tour of the football club Boca Juniors in 1925, as mentioned in the previous chapter. Since the 1910s polo players had impressed Europeans, and Argentinian polo ponies were bought by Europeans and Americans. The first professional football player, Julio Libonatti, was bought by the Italian club Torino in 1921, and more players left the country during the 1920s. Argentinian bodies were seen by the others, and were recognized as representing something 'new' – the 'new and exotic races' from the South. The Italians and Spaniards mixed with 'Argentinian substances' were transformed into excellent football players, and the 'Anglo-Argentinian' or British born in Argentina, also mixed with some of these substances, were able to surpass, in the fields of polo, the playing ability of the authentic British. What happened in football and polo did not materialize in the other two important sports practised by the British colony at that time: cricket and Rugby.[14] Cricket remained British and died out in the 1930s, and Rugby was, internationally speaking, a sleeping sport until the 1960s. Argentinians were seen, paradoxically enough, through two disparate sports: the most popular one – football – and the most exclusive – polo.

Concluding Remarks: Contrasting Masculinities

I hope to have shown in this chapter – and in the previous one – how discourses and imageries of hybridization were channelled through sport, a practice that became global at the beginning of the twentieth century. The diversity of origins of its practioners did not exclude processes of generalization in which the dominant model was that of amalgamation. The original substance, *lo criollo* – in itself a hybrid – is supposed to exist, and its strength depends on its capacity to assimilate the characteristics of the strong ethnic groups: Italian, Spanish and British. *Lo criollo* is, sometimes, thought of as a pre-existing mixture with a stable identity – as a stable form – which, due to this condition, is able to absorb new influences. The process of absorption is designed as a double process: as a sexual and biological mixture and/or through an intimate contact with the symbols and practices of *lo criollo* – as in the case of the gauchos. In this context *lo criollo* is conceived in terms of given characteristics of the landscape, of the products of the earth, of the presence of individuals with powerful traditions – *petiseros* – or ways of riding, and the existence of given values and moral qualities. Thiesse, writing of the definition of places and identities in France, calls the combination of the logic of blood, races, ethnotypes and the presence of some people of genius with superior qualities 'la tautologie Montesquieu' (1997: 35–53). The tautological sin of Montesquieu is less French than imagined. My analysis demonstrates the role of repetition and redundancy in the construction of styles and traditions.[15]

The presence and the acceptance of new male hybrids in Argentina makes it possible to define these processes in terms of cultural creativity, in the sense that change is related to continuity. Without tradition change and creativity are unthinkable. The British playing polo are transformed into *criollos*; they create a style, even in developing new breeds of ponies that accept the importance of the original component of *criollo* mares. In the field of football, the British are seen as less creative – because in the imaginary construction they are not in contact with *lo criollo* – and are replaced by the descendants of Italians and Spaniards. The sons of these immigrant groups will produce a new style of playing football. My analysis has attempted to depict this logic of inclusion and exclusion. Behind these ideological models are both demographic and social class realities. Football very soon became a popular urban practice, while polo continued to be a sport practised by the privileged landlords of the pampas. The landlords, in most cases of British origin, expanded their properties and their economic endeavours, and, through intermarriages, were integrated into the dominant political class and into the cultural life of Argentina.

The cases discussed elucidate the difficulty of imagining rituals, the transformation of bodily practices and performances, into symbols of the 'new. In the case of football, in the dominant model represented by Borocotó, hybridization creates a new form that has nothing to do with the older one. Chantecler represents the melting-pot perspective because, in his analysis, even some British players contributed to the consolidation of the new style. In the case of polo, the model of fusion is clear when the qualities of rider and horses are taken into account.[16] However, in neither of the cases is the model of chaos, used to frighten by some of the nationalist writers, present. Nobody believed that hybridization could produce a radical heterogeneity in the field of sport.

The presence of social diversity does not exclude the continuous fabrication of a model in which a whole, perceived as composed of different hybrids, would not include all its parts. However, there are different degrees of alterity, and this fact transforms the national into something problematic, in need of being recreated again and again. An accomplished national imagery will attempt to integrate the different 'otherness' because it needs all the fragments, all the dislocated and mismatched identities, and it relies on the changing character of the groups who inhabit a given territory (see Masiello 1992: 165–200). Strathern has observed in this relation that:

> Over Englands's history, the displacement of royal dynasties, the rise and fall of classes of merchants and industrialists, the absortion of small groups such as Flemings and Hugenots – 'additions to an already infinite complexity' – all sustained the imagery of constant infusions of 'new blood'. The country's institutions were invigorated by cross-fertilisation. Each individual thereby contributed his/her unique portion without losing the characteristic of individuality: that was preserved in the singularity of 'the English' themselves. (1992: 36)

Argentina entered into modernity by producing a series of male identities and culturally contradictory tendencies that refused integration and containment in a single imagery. Cross-fertilization was accepted but only in relation to something defined as *criollo*. In the Argentinian case, once the model of transformation was open to all immigrants, ethnic identity was no longer accepted as public. 'Individuality', in the sense defined by Strathern, was private or, at least, limited. Moreover, my examples show that high and low culture, popular and élite, local and transnational visions were at work when Argentinian society entered into modernity. Another striking difference with Strathern's analysis of 'the English' is the fact that Argentinian masculine identity was highly dependent upon multiplicity, but also, at the same time, the presence of the British as the 'most relevant others'.[17]

The world of competition in polo shaped the ideas on male physical strength and an extraordinary sense of sacrifice as inner characteristics of Argentinian creole players. These qualities, especially in the way Sierra defined the Argentinian polo style, were related to fighting spirit and moral courage. 'Manly courage' and 'manly spirit' were not related to a standard of male beauty, as Mosse (1996) has postulated for the modern image of man. The Argentinian representation of the modern English polo players is associated with moderation, conservatism and lack of courage, because they do not take risks as the Argentinians do. It is clear that in the Argentinian rural imagery, based on the exaltation of gaucho traditions, chivalry and manly honour were transformed into physical toughness and even 'barbarism'. Mosse has also stated that the male body in modern times is seen as 'an example of virility, strength, and courage expressed through the proper posture and appearance' (1996: 23). In the Argentinian imagery it was the gaucho style of riding that was perceived as proper posture and appearance. The beauty of a style was more important than the bodily beauty of its practitioners.

I hope that the limitations of models based on an ideal typical notion of maleness have become clear for the reader through my comparison of football and polo. My findings suggests that 'nowhere is there only one version of masculinity and femininity operating within a single cultural context' (Lindisfarne 1994: 147). The focus on the contrasting characteristics of male hybrids in polo and football has also made it possible to present the models of transformation and the changing character of 'otherness'. Moreover, the masculinities defined in the previous two chapters enter into a kind of global scene through an explicit cross-cultural comparison done by the Argentinian themselves. In the next part of this book the existence of dislocated masculinities will be related to the field of moralities.

Notes

1. Enrique's judgements are not exceptional, and, in many ways, consti-
    tute standard truths. Watson (1986) reproduces in his book a short
    essay written by Juan Carlos Harriott, a 10-goal Argentinian player in
    the 1960s and 1970s, in which some of the key ideas of Enrique are
    presented. Harriott writes on: polo as a 'tough game' because there is
    'risk and danger'; the Argentinian 'tradition' and the importance of
    keeping it; 'dedication'; the need to play with 'hot blood and a cold
    head'; 'character' and the need to have the 'heart to fight back' (*garra*);
    'style and horsemanship'; the need 'to breed and make your own
    ponies'; how important it is to have speed and 'always remember that
    a well-hit ball travels faster than any pony'; and 'anticipation' (Watson
    1986: 14–20). As we shall see later in the chapter, Héctor, my other
    key informant, insisted on the importance of the *juego abierto* (open
    game) as defining the modern style of playing polo.
2. I have published two articles on polo in which I presented, in a more
    provisory manner, the main arguments of this chapter (see Archetti
    1995b, 1997). I can not count on the comparative perspective because
    the ethnography of polo is very limited, even more than in football.
    The two examples I found cover such distant places as the United
    States and Pakistan. Miller (1977) produced a Masters thesis based on
    research in an American polo club in 1976. He shows the importance
    of polo in the reproduction of a lifestyle restricted to the wealthy. He
    distinguished three groups in the club: the 'grooms', the 'professional
    players', and the 'owners'. These groups constituted a clear social
    hierarchy. The 'grooms' (*petiseros* in Argentina) take care of the horses,
    and the 'pros' are hired by the owners to play alongside them and to
    train the horses. The 'owners' are the men who pay the pros and
    grooms in order to play the game. In this development, which has
    been accelerated during the last two decades, Argentinian grooms and
    pros nowadays occupy a prominent place. Parkes (1996) has analysed
    the interplay between polo and politics in contemporary Pakistan. The
    polo-playing Pakistani élite accepted the changes of the rules of their
    traditional game by British officers in the nineteenth century. This
    civilized version of an equestrian tradition was imposed on local
    populations; a similar process occurred in Argentina, as we shall see
    later. In a once socially democratic game, the new rules, which also
    included the introduction of expensive Punjab ponies, produced a
    sharp distinction between the élite and rural villagers. Thus, according
    to Parkes, the historical transformation of indigenous polo in Pakistan
    makes possible an analysis of the politics of regional identity.
3. Watson believes that the essence of good polo is 'open play' (1986: 8).
    He admits that this style of playing is a kind of 'standard' which all
    players, in principle, aspire to reach. We shall see in this chapter that

the Argentinian players and teams played a central role in this process of 'standardization'. What, in the first two decades of the twentieth century, was defined as Argentinian style later became the standard of the game. However, the first revolution came from American polo. After the victory of the United States in the Westchester Cup of 1909, England was no longer the undisputed world leader in polo. This style of the game changed from the relatively slow form of play characterized by short, controlled hitting. American polo players used a long-hitting, fast-moving, 'wide-open style' that revolutionized the sport. In 1910 the Americans abandoned the offside rule that forbade players preceding the direction of the ball; this change made it possible to play even faster. What is called the 'Argentinian style' can be seen as a further development of the 'American revolution'.

4. The game of *pato* (duck) was a violent horse competition developed at the end of the eighteenth century in the province of Buenos Aires. Two teams competed for the possession of a living duck. The game has been described as cruel and accident-prone, provoking the death of horses, local disorders, drunkenness and knife duels among the participants. It was forbidden by General Rosas, Governor of the province of Buenos Aires, in 1822. In 1937 the Argentinian national government declared 10 November the Day of Tradition. On that occasion, and with a radical change of rules, the game of *pato* was declared legal. *Pato* is now played in the province of Buenos Aires and a Federation was created in 1947 (Somoza 1953). *Pato* is considered a regional game, not even national, and in many ways a form of primitive polo.

5. Johnny Traill tells in his memoirs that the Hurlingham Club grooms were more or less barred from taking part in tournaments in 1900 due to their extreme roughness in playing (n.d.: 27–8).

6. Johnny Traill remembered Las Petacas, Kinchant and the passion of polo in the following way:
   One of the best teams came from Las Petacas, belonging to Charles Jewell, whose mayordomo Frank Kinchant ran a team with three Argentine *peons* – the first man to play at Hurlingham with *peons* and the first to win the cup. Kinchant was a large, strong man weighing at least sixteen stone and who hit the longest ball of anyone I had ever seen. They often came to Chiru to play against us, but unfortunately the team came to grief. (n.d.: 12)
   Then Traill tells that the owner, Jewell, sent a telegraph to his mayordomo announcing his arrival on the Sunday train at two in the afternoon: the time when polo was played at his estancia. When he arrived at the station there was no one to meet him. Thus:
   He waited, fuming, but in the end had to hire a *coche* with a very broken down pair of old horses to drive the eighteen or so miles back to his *estancia*. When he got there, hot and uncomfortable, he found

them all hard at it in a polo game. And speaking from hearsay I believe it was the last polo they ever played there. Jewell was very hurt at the thought of his mayordomo playing polo and I think they all got the sack. (n.d.: 12)

This was the historical end of Las Petacas and the beginning of the mythology.

7. The historical background of the Traills is based on an unpublished manuscript written by Derek Willans (1993), the great-grandson of Robert Traill, which was generously given to me by the family. The saga of the Traills, so well documented in Willans's work, is scantily presented in this chapter.

8. The unpublished and unfinished memoirs of Johnny Traill were more than generously given to me by his descendants. They are fundamental for getting a clearer picture of his life, achievements, and his impact on Argentinian and world polo. They are written in a clear and natural prose. Reading it helped me to obtain an image of his activities in England and in Argentina through polo. Politics and society in Argentina are absent from his memoirs. The European context is present through the impacts made by the Spanish Civil War and the Second World War. He was a sportsman above all and an early world star of polo. We can say that he was cosmopolitan, and, paradoxically enough, the British product of an *estancia* in the Argentinian pampas – thus a cosmopolitan who was profoundly national and local.

9. Traill's comment on the success achieved in Tucumán was very short: 'we rather swept the board, winning all three tournaments' (n.d.: 37).

10. Johnny Traill could not join the British Army during the First World War due to a polo injury. He remained in England, hating 'being so useless'; when he heard that the Army was going to send to Argentina 'some remount men' to get horses for the war, he offered his services. They refused to let him take on the job. He ironically comments on this 'wise' decision:

An English vet and a major went over and I later heard that they had gone to a big *estancia* and bought thirty or forty very nice looking horses as riding horses. What they probably did not realise was that the animals had been tamed from below by the Argentine gauchos who had handled them well, riding them bareback with only a head-collar and lead rein; none of them had ever had a saddle on or a bit in their mouths. I can just imagine what they had been like with a bit of English corn in them and a saddle on for the first time. I knew only too well how a five-year-old could buck! (n.d.: 68)

Traill, a real gaucho, speaks to the ignorant British.

11. In the history of polo, this team is considered more important than El Bagual. In England they won the most important tournaments, and due to this success were invited to take part in the American Open. They embarked with their ponies and, leaving England, then

won all the cups they played in the United States, including the Open (Laffaye 1989: 79–92; *El Gráfico* no. 1207, 1942: 7).

12. My research on this 'incident' is not complete. Enrique told me that I could find a version of it in the polo magazine *Polo y Equitación*. He had read or perhaps heard the story of Lacey and Traill, but he could not confirm it. He even said 'you may not exclude the possibility that this incident is an invention, one of the many inventions in sport mythology'. I was, however, unable to find the entire collection of *Polo y Equitación*, a monthly magazine published for the first time in March 1925 and continuing until the end of 1932. A luxurious magazine, in both layout and paper quality, it was mostly devoted to equestrian sports, including polo. News of tournaments, in Argentina and abroad, were combined with historical presentations of all kind of equestrian sports, sports heroes, articles on horses, breeding and riding techniques, and an interesting section on cars, mechanics and car maintenance. In 1933 *Polo y Equitación* was replaced by *Polo y Campo*, which was published until 1938. Obtaining the complete collection of *Polo y Campo* proved an impossible task.

13. Polo was 'nationalized' in 1923 when the British Polo Association of the River Plate was replaced by the new Asociación de Polo de Argentina. For a while there were two associations but in the end the old association joined the 'new Argentinian'. Spanish then became the official language. We must remember that this change also happened in football in 1912. The list of players with handicap published by *Polo y Equitación* in 1930 indicates a process of 'nationalization' of the players: out of 974 players, 288 had British names (no. 57: 44–9).

14. King quotes Sir David Kelly, who complained in the 1920s that the British brought all sports to Argentina, but they were left with only cricket, the rest being absorbed by the Argentinians (1992: 164). *The Standard*, in a special issue of 1913 devoted to Argentina, placed special emphasis on the role of football and polo in the creation of sport enthusiasm in the country. Cricket and Rugby were not mentioned (1/1/1913: 23). It is worth noticing that cricket was practised by British merchants and financial people in Argentina from 1819, and that the first cricket club was founded in 1832 – the famous Buenos Aires Cricket Club (Olivera 1932: 16–20). It is interesting to observe that the role of football and polo in Argentina was fulfilled in former British colonies by cricket and Rugby. A comparative and systematic analysis of these differences is still lacking. It is also relevant to mention in this connection that the path followed by the United States was also different: they 'created' their own national sports – like baseball, American football and basketball – which were later also exported.

15. This process can be called semantic reification, in the sense that the
    actors interpret their reality with categories that, at the same time,
    are intrinsic properties of the same reality.
16. In the final of the Argentinian Polo Open of 1906, North Santa Fe
    played with José González, a *petisero* and gaucho, who replaced Ned
    Traill. The journalist commented that González played as well as Ned
    Traill. Moreover, he was like Ned Traill 'up to a point which compelled
    the admiration of every polo lover' (*The Standard*, 4/9/1906: 1). This
    idea of symbiosis in the imagery of the Argentinian style as a a hybrid
    is very important: Traill was González and González was Traill.
17. Of all the immigrant groups from Britain in Argentina the Irish were
    the most numerous and the ones who adapted most rapidly (Korol
    and Sábato 1981). Religion is perhaps the most important factor in
    explaining this process: they were Roman Catholics. Accepting and
    being accepted by the local population, they could marry natives more
    easily without entering into the complications of mixed marriages.
    This process was not easy for the other non-Catholic British (Hennessy
    1992: 16). The British, in the folk models and in this analysis, are
    associated with the English and the Scottish, non-Catholic immigrants.
    The Irish belong to another categorization. The Welsh immigration
    in Patagonia was also clearly distinguished from the British (see
    Williams 1991).

PART TWO

Masculine Moralities

CHAPTER FOUR

Locating Masculinities and Moralities

Dislocating Masculinities

Cornwall and Lindisfarne argue, with justification, that the different images and forms of behaviour contained in the notion of masculinity are not always coherent and can appear contradictory and indeterminate (1994: 12). In this sense it is important to try to capture the diversity of these signs and forms of behaviour by understanding that masculinity cannot be treated as something fixed and universal. The ability to negotiate these differences is a function of the power of the masculine imagery. Cornwall and Lindisfarne do not deny the existence of hegemonic masculinities, defining successful ways of 'being a man', but they refuse to accept that there is only one way of 'being a man' (1994: 3). In putting the emphasis on the study of a plurality of 'hegemonic masculinities' we are obliged to revise our research from concentrating on the exclusive domain of accepting the existence of a unique hegemonic model – and trying to find it (see Vale de Almeida 1996; Gutmann 1996).[1] This strategy has guided comparative cross-cultural research on manhood (Gilmore 1990) and influential historical analyses of the relations between nationalism and masculinity (Anderson 1983; Mosse 1985). Gilmore (1990) has emphasized the universality of values like toughness, aggressiveness, stoicism and heterosexuality in the definition of manliness and the manhood archetype. He has been criticized on two crucial methodological grounds: for looking exclusively at hegemonic discourses, excluding contradictions and fragmentation, and for focusing on those aspects of manhood that are supposedly perceived as positive and acceptable (Hart 1994: 51). Anderson's account (1983) of the growth and consolidation of nationalism can be seen as a history of active male nationalists (soldiers, generals, bureaucrats, writers, poets, politicians) trying to realize the destiny of fraternal communion. Nationalist writers like Lugones, Rojas and Galvez imagined Argentina in the sense described by Anderson: a community constituted by dominant men – and subordinated women. In this perspective nationality seems to have an aura of fatality, of moral obligation and disinterested solidarity, in which the role of some types of men is central.

The connections between class, sexuality, masculinity, morality and nationalism in modern Europe are made more explicit in the work of Mosse (1985). Mosse depicts the historical growth in the middle classes of a dominant discourse based on the importance of male virility, homo-social male bonding, passionate brotherhood, and, consequently, of homosexuality defined as a threat. Mosse writes that:

> Lesbians, like homosexuals, menaced the division between the sexes and thus struck at the very roots of society. Indeed, lesbians threatened society, if possible, to an even greater degree than homosexuals, given women's role as patron saints and mothers of the family and the nations. Motherhood was central to the image of women . . . Fatherhood, however, was not as important in the image of man, even though the father as head of the bourgeois family was also idealized. (1985: 105–6)

In his analysis motherhood became central and fatherhood less important. Virility was more important than fatherhood. The nation tried to remove middle-class woman from active life outside the home and keep her from facing a turbulent and dangerous age. The nationalist motto was: 'the more feminine women are, and the more masculine men, the more intimate the family life, the healthier the society and the state' (Mosse 1985: 144). In Mosse's analysis the ideology of the middle class is so pervasive that there are, again, neither contradictory discourses nor fragmented identities.

More recently, Mosse has developed the idea that modern 'man needs women to become conscious of his own masculinity, however rough-hewn it might be, but the woman who fulfils this essential function must remain truly feminine' (1996: 74). He also depicted the Romantics as idealizing woman as pure, chaste and tender, but, at the same time, as fascinated by the image of the *femme fatale*, 'who seduces men only to destroy them' (1996: 74). However, the dominant image of woman was associated with passivity. When

she was active and made demands upon man, they were thought
to strengthen his masculinity. In the presentation of the masculinities and moralities of the tango in the next chapter I shall come
back to some of Mosse's ideas.

It is not only an empirical question to decide which contexts
and arenas the anthropologist must explore in order to find the
plurality of hegemonic masculinities. We can define as central:
the study of relations at the workplace; local and religious notions
of hierarchy and power; forms of sociability and everyday interaction – like drinking and playing cards in coffee-houses or pubs;
the impact of school and the educational process; the gendered
labour division at home; the participation in politics and public
affairs; the notions of family, kinship, person and identity, or, as
in my research, taking part in sports, riding horses and dancing/
listening to the tango.[2] I shall not deny that my priorities, guided
by the advice of some of my best informants, can be seen as arbitrary, restricted and biased. In this respect, I willingly accept that
the 'total' – if possible – study of masculinities in Argentina should
include arenas like work, family, kinship, religion and politics – on
the condition that we ask the right questions.[3] The choice of
empirical fields is as important as the theoretical framework chosen.
Let me explore this more closely.

I agree with Cornwall and Lindisfarne (1994: 12) that the crucial
methodological – and theoretical – device is related to asking
questions that disrupt conventional understandings. The emphasis
must be put on the fact that men are differentiated from each other,
an area which has been neglected in anthropology, with important
exceptions in the analysis of homosexuality. Key questions in my
research were: how and when do 'boys' become 'men'? what makes
someone a 'man' in some settings and a 'boy' in others? how is
a man of honour defined and what is expected of him? how is
romantic love related to masculinity and femininity? what are
the male virtues associated with masculinities and how are these
commonalities constructed and used socially and symbolically? and,
finally, what are the moral contexts and criteria related to masculinities and femininities? My restricted empirical focus on certain
social arenas permits me to see how masculinity is produced
and reproduced differently. These arenas are constructed as both
complementary and opposed to the feminine, but there are also
contexts which are eminently masculine, where the relevant others
are men – different types of men. The tango makes possible the

study of cross-sex relations, while football – and polo in the first part of the book – confines my research to the realm of same-sex relations. My findings will expose the differing but mutual constitution of same-sex and cross-sex relations.[4]

In the analysis of masculinity as a system of creating differences it is crucial to consider discourses of agency, emotions, authenticity, freedom, happiness, personhood and identity. Then, to study masculinities – or, better, idealized masculinities – is not just to study men or relations between the sexes; rather it is a way of depicting a system for producing moral differences. In the words of Melhuus and Stølen concerning Latin America:

> On the one hand, we find a conflation, or mutual constitution, of issues of gender and issues of morality . . . discourses about gender may simultaneously transmit messages about morality. However . . . if the gender relation itself is ambiguously constituted, the moral messages will be equivocal too. On the other hand, we find that perceptions of gender inequalities (between men and women) and differences (between men and between women) serve as points of articulation or representations of ethnic relations, national identities or political rhetoric. (1996: 27)

My results are, somewhat, limited but, I think, relevant to understanding Argentinian imagery. What I have written in the introductory chapter is still valid: football, polo and the tango functioned historically as models and mirrors of identities; I shall postulate, with the support of my informants, that this is still the case today. These arenas make it possible to observe the confluence of ethnicity and hybridity, of national male identity and gender, and of local and global connections. In this sense, they constitute privileged fields for a reflection on the complex relations between masculinities and moralities.

Moralities

Durkheim distinguished a common morality, covering a given collectivity, and based on objective standards of judgement from a variety of subjective, individual and contrasting moralities (1966: 56–7). Assuming that the field of morality covers a vast area of actions and evaluations, it is difficult to imagine that we can attain the totality of moral codes and ideas without directing our concern to particular concrete activities. By doing this, we study morality, what is good or evil or right and wrong, through issues in which morality, presumably, is reflected (see Parkin 1983). We can analyse morality when we look at explanations of disease and misfortune, of fate, of gender relations, of marriage and family, of accepted games and so on. Actions and beliefs are key indicators not only of the moral code but also of contexts and actors (Rapport 1997: 74). But still, while doing so, anthropologists diverge in how to reflect the importance of society as a moral system. There is a tendency to perceive moral codes as the main support of social relations between groups and persons. It is expected that anthropologists will provide an ethnographic account of virtues, obligations, sanctions and feelings that make possible a detailed description of social moral values and modes of achieving them (see Edel and Edel 1959: 9). I do not intend to deny the importance of such an assumption, but personally I feel that we can gain new insights if we also consider the field of morality and moral analysis as a dynamic cultural code that informs, creates and gives meaning to social relations (see Melhuus 1996).

Lukes (1981: 410–34) has pointed out that Durkheim gradually deepened his view of morality as a social and cultural phenomenon, moving away from an exclusive concentration on moral rules and their obligatory character. Durkheim did not accept that a rational definition of duty, or a utilitarian respect for sanctions, is sufficient as a basis for moral commitment. Morality requires compassion, fervour and a sense of engagement. Thus, the later Durkheim (1966: 50–1) emphasized both the desirability aspect and the emotive character of morality. Criticizing Kant, to whom moral actions were reduced to obligation and to reason, Durkheim redefined the moral goals of society – and actors – as objects of desire, the only way, according to him, to reconcile reason and emotions in social analysis. Every moral action combines these two dimensions, and in some cases, defined as actions of 'moral heroism', the role of reason and obligation is minimal (1966: 65). To ask rationally what is right and wrong is not enough. We also need to focus our research on what is desirable or worthwhile for the actors. It is important to see that these are different questions; while perhaps something that is desirable to do is also something that one is obliged to do, it is still not the case that saying that something is worthwhile or desirable is the same as saying that one is obliged to do it.

If we accept the crucial role of desire in the constitution of the emotive character of morality, we must not necessarily eliminate from our analysis either the cognitive or the affective components. The cognitive component in Durkheim's consideration was related to the key role played by moral beliefs. Durkheim (1966: 58–9) rejected a sociological project reduced to the systematic examination of philosophical normative theories, and, correctly, emphasized the importance of finding moral ideals through the consultation of popular beliefs and people's reactions when such beliefs are contravened in practice. When one is holding true to moral judgements, the strong sense of the meaning of beliefs does not exclude an opening to examine other cognitive components like thoughts, apprehensions or imagination. Moreover, subjective affectivity, in the sense of expressing pity, fear, sympathy, admiration, love or tenderness, constitutes the basis of the relation between the individual and the society. Feelings fuse cognitive aspects with desires and sanctions, negative or positive, acting as moral indices (see Edel and Edel 1959: 188). In his study of religion as well as in the study of civic morals, Durkheim (1915: 207–8, 1992: 112) provides a theory of the emotive character of morality in terms of the importance of subjective affectivity.

I have stressed the role of imagery in the construction of social reality, and the same can be said about the construction of moralities. The cognitive component in the study of morals has been developed by Johnson (1993) in a ground-breaking book. Criticizing widely held conceptions of morality, Johnson argues for the recognition of the fundamental role of imagination in our moral reasoning. He writes:

> We human beings are imaginative creatures . . . Consequently, our moral understanding depends in large measure on various structures of imagination, such as images, image schemas, metaphors, narratives, and so forth. Moral reasoning is thus basically an imaginative activity, because it uses imaginatively structured concepts and requires imagination to discern what is morally relevant in situations, to understand empathetically how others experience things, and to envision the full range of possibilities open to us in a particular case. (1993: ix–x)

The field of morality is thus related to the contextual examination of desire, emotions and imagination – and reason. This implies a careful selection of concrete cases in order to apprehend better the variations and contradictions in the field of morality.

If we accept a perspective on morality that holds open the possibility of considering the construction of meanings as not completely given, as containing choices for the actors, our ethnographic account must deal with the type of arguments used, how discontent is expressed and accepted and how ambivalence and pluralism are tackled. This implies that there exists a division of normative ethical perspectives about what is intrinsically desirable in monistic and pluralistic theories. The existence of these different frameworks illustrates the point made by Evens (1982) that moral choices must be seen as conditioned by projects and reasons rather than by causes. This approach permits the consideration of moral choices and morality as a way in which actors construct meanings and imagine reality. Moral codes or fundamental values are not directly translated into behaviour; they are often mediated through moral choices.

Morality is not silent; it must be articulated in discourse and narratives. Man is essentially a story-telling animal. Johnson defines the central task of moral analysis as the understanding of how 'we narratively construct our lives and how our deliberations are framed by those narratives' (1993: 152). Partially following Johnson I shall put special emphasis on 'prototypical narratives', in which distinguishable patterns of narrating events, metaphorical production, and persons who serve as models are mixed. In this kind of narrative, stories are located in time and space, have a clear sequence and, almost always, are finished with a blatant moral conclusion. Many of my informants' accounts, as well as the poetics of the tango to be analysed in this book, are presented in such a way that personal identities are inextricably tied to the production of moral agency. Moral prototypical narratives have the power of evoking not only the experience of the narrator but also our own experiences, lived in daily life or easily imagined. The prototypical narratives are closely related to the narrative structure of the life of social actors (see Johnson 1993: 160-4). I hope to be able to show that moral reasonings and desires are connected to the structure of narratives. In the words of Johnson, 'morality is a matter of *how well or how poorly* we construct (i.e. live out) a narrative that solves our problem of living a meaningful and significant life' (1993: 180).

Narratives are not only voiced or written; they must, to a great extent, be public, since moral discourses include processes of guidance. In the everyday life of modern Western societies – and Argentina does not escape from this cage – we are barraged with a variety of moral claims and counter-claims: the moral arguments in support of them are diverse and conflicting (see Strathern 1997). Moral possibilities and choices could not exist without the prospect of relating projects and reasons to the existence of sound moral arguments. The elusive power of moral narratives and public discourses is commonly related to three general properties: the claim to objectivity; the claim to universality, based on relating an observed similarity of behaviour to a given context; and the concern for practicality, for action and for attitude-moulding. Beyond these claims, as Evens (1982) has argued, moral discourses constitute autonomous modes of discourses. Morality in society, no matter how carefully it is elaborated, can never become fully empirical. Actors cannot discover what they ought to do or what is desirable from a knowledge of non-moral facts alone, including the facts about human nature and conduct. As anthropologists we must try to find, empirically, the focus of the analysis of moralities. Howell has correctly situated our dilemmas when she writes:

> How we deal with the existence of apparently different moralities being operative according to context, or to the social personhood of the actors, within any one indigenously defined social group, becomes an important issue. Should we treat such multiplicities of meaning as pieces in a complex puzzle which may add up to some overall moral order, or should we be satisfied to explicate upon the apparent paradoxes? There can be no final answers, but I regard it as important to identify as many arenas as possible which may serve as 'pegs' for analysis for future anthropological studies of moralities. (1997: 5)

I hope my analysis of Argentinian tango and football can make a contribution on this important methodological problem. My preferences are for the elucidation of paradoxes and not for the attempt to depict, out of diversity and plurality, an overarching moral order.

Another important dimension of the analysis of moralities relates to the challenge of saying something about change. Durkheim (1966) developed some ideas on morality and change that have inspired my work. First, he located change in the critical and exceptional historical periods in which there is an intensification of public life and social contacts: new – and unknown for the individual – sentiments appear due to 'social effervescence' and 'physical friction'. Secondly, in those moments of effervescence individuals and societies are confronted with states of creation and renewal when new ideas and new relationships emerge out of crisis and conflicts (1966: 133–4). Thirdly, only in those situations can the ideal and the desired become real and individuals experience change as possible. Fourth, once the 'revolutionary' or 'the movements of enthusiasm' are over and society is back to normal, the change is ritualized, and the ideas that guided these social occasions are transformed into symbols (1966: 135–6). Collective ideals, Durkheim writes, 'can only become manifest and conscious by being concretely realized in objects that can be seen by all, understood by all and represented to all minds: figurative designs, emblems of all kinds, written or spoken formulas, animate or inanimate objects' (1966: 137). Things (emblems), places, days and dates, words and men (great men) become symbols of the changes experienced. In the presentation of my findings I will direct special attention to many of the symbols used in the narratives of the tango and football. In addition, and especially in the case of football, I shall articulate my reflection on the moral of the stories experienced by my informants as traumatic, and as marking changes. Memory – and time – constitutes the inner structure of narratives; it is always selective. In most cases, selection is intimately related to moments of effervescence and friction.

Tango and Football as Gendered Masculine and Moral Fields

A kind of historical flashback is needed before I present some of the key dimensions that guided my analysis. By the 1920s Buenos Aires is the exciting city of popular and bourgeois cultural life: bordellos and cabarets mix with dance halls; European opera and classical music with the tango; and movies and cinemas with sport spectacles, with football as the dominant sport. There is not a single other Argentinian city which is able to provide the same variety of leisure activities. Processes of popular creativity are not only related to politics, in a moment in which the masculine democracy is more or less consolidated; the women will get voting rights in 1947. Meanwhile the men, natives and immigrants, actively participate in building up modern political parties and trade unions. The choice of one's favourite tango orchestra as well as a football club defines taste, identities and territorial belonging.

Almost all *barrrios* have one or two football clubs playing in the first or second division. In this decade some amateur clubs like

San Telmo, Barracas Central, Defensores de Belgrano, Sportivo Barracas and Sportivo Dock Sud – all of them located in different *barrios* – are important and very competitive. In the 1930s, with the creation of the professional league, River Plate, Boca Juniors, San Lorenzo de Almagro, Racing Club and Independiente – called the 'five greats of Argentinian football' – together with Vélez Sarsfield, Huracán, Argentinos Juniors, Chacarita Juniors, Lanús, Quilmes, Atlanta – the Jewish club, Ferrocarril Oeste and Platense will strengthen the symbiosis between *barrio* and club identity. All these clubs were founded between 1901 and 1912. Each club will have its stadium, a particularity that Argentina inherited from the British, and its headquarters in which other sports, social and cultural activities are carried out. The clubs become civil – not commercial – societies in the field of leisure, and, in some cases, developed in the direction of 'total institutions' incorporating carnival, social feasts, theatre festivals, tango concerts and dancing.

As we have seen in Chapter 3, football integrated Buenos Aires – and Argentina – into a global network of performing male bodies. This was also the case with the tango. The tango arrived in Paris in the early 1900s. Argentinian aristocrats, musicians and dancers introduced it into different social circuits: private élite parties, cabarets and dance halls (see Cadícamo 1975; Gobello 1980; Salas 1986; Cooper 1995; Savigliano 1995). By 1913, the tango was well established in Paris and had travelled to the rest of Europe and North America. The tango was exported as music and dance, and adopted by Europeans and Americans as a display of a new kind of eroticism. Savigliano writes:

> Tango did not perform 'instinctive' sensuality (like the dances of the 'primitives'), rowdy excitement (like the dances of the peasants), or overt impropriety, cynicism, or defiant aggression toward the upper classes (like the dances of the urban marginals). Nor did it focus solely on the erotic powers of the female body, like other 'traditional' exotic dances. Tango's sexual politics were centered in the process of seduction. A fatal man and a femme fatale who, despite their proximity, kept their erotic impulses under control, measuring each other's powers. In its choreography, the tango resembled a game of chess where deadly contenders took turns moving invisible pieces with their dragging feet. Their mutual attraction and repulsion were prolonged into an unbearable, endless tension. And everything took place, apparently, under male control. (1995: 110)

Buenos Aires was, thus, seen as the city of football and the tango, the city of performing men and women, and the city of exporting performing bodies. Buenos Aires was, also, the city in which the tango was created. Borocotó, *El Gráfico*'s journalist, wrote a canonical piece in 1928 on the relations between the tango and football. He argued that football was the most modern of all spectacles because it had 'continuous action', 'passionate beauty' and 'improvisation'. It was transformed in Argentina into a national sport when 'the art of dribbling' was incorporated in its practice. In his approach, as we have seen in Chapter 3, the transformation of football in Argentina is closely related to creativity: the practice of football is re-created in Argentina. A British invention is locally appropriated, and, later, exported to the world. The tango, on the contrary, is an Argentinian invention. The practice of football and the tango constitute the popular social and symbolic worlds of Buenos Aires. According to him, in the field of football the aesthetic pleasures and local identities are mixed, while the tango speaks to sentiments and displays sensualities. Borocotó writes: 'Football is the collective sport of the *criollo*; the tango his music. How different are those predilections? The first constitutes an aesthetic pleasure associated with interested affections, the traditions of clubs and *barrios*; the other appeals to the sentimental side [of Argentinians] with some sensualism' (*El Gráfico* no. 467, 1928: 8).

Borocotó observed that the passion for football was not only masculine. The love and the practice of the tango was cross-sex, embracing both women and men, and this made it possible for women to be introduced by men into the world of football. They learned about the great players and they were introduced to the world of men, their clubs and their pleasures, besides the tango. He even maintained that the *milonguitas* – women who love to dance the tango – would come to realize that the men's steps in the tango are like the dribblings of the best players of the epoch. Borocotó, with a visionary style, wrote: 'the tango and football will be, for many years, in a privileged position, and perhaps for ever, this being the most expected outcome' (*El Gráfico* no. 467, 1928: 8). He added an additional argument in support of his optimism:

> Many years ago the tango was accepted in Paris. It was created in the *arrabales* [of Buenos Aires], in the same places where the football players were formed; it was introduced in the circles that rejected it, and later

the tango extended his kingdom to the City of Light. The tango can
say, with pride and as a parody of Carlos V of Spain: 'in my domains
the sun never sets'. To football was given the same destiny. To Europe
[football] brought something different from the British [play]. And
against the force of strong adversaries, the *criollo* dribbled and scored
goals. (Own translation *El Gráfico* no. 467, 1928: 8)

At the end of his article, and in a well-known style, Borocotó
enumerates what are considered typically Argentinian: gaucho and
pampa symbols – like the ombú, the typical tree of the plains; the
clothes; the music of the *cielitos*; the rebellious soul; the prodigious
landscape; the tango and the way of playing the tango. He conflates
the rural imagery with the cultural products of the city – of the
arrabales of Buenos Aires – in a kind of arbitrary collage, as in all
national imagery. The narrative of Borocotó is not exceptional for
that time, and the parallelism with the 'more cultivated' literary
attempts at fixing a national imagery is striking. Lack of space
hinders me from presenting results of my comparative analysis
presented elsewhere (see Archetti 1995a).[5]

My main hypothesis is that the fields of the tango and football
enable the investigation of the coalescing of moralities and masculinities, both in history and in the present.[6] My contemporary
ethnography meets history and memory. Through the analysis of
moral discourses in Argentinian tango and football I attempt to
depict an active and public process of understanding, evaluation
and argument about the following: What is a good society? Who is
a good person? Who is a good woman? How should good men
and good women act in private and in public? How is romantic
love defined and experienced? What are the key male virtues? How
important are values like honour and shame? How and when do
'boys' become 'men' or remain 'boys'? Is a man always the same
kind of 'man'? How important are traditions, roots and historical
continuities in defining identity at large and masculinity in particular? What are the meanings of styles and ways of playing football?
What are the main ideas, concerns and definitions of 'happiness'
and 'of feeling happy'?[7]

By discussing the moralities of the tango and football I attempt
to analyse how the historically available symbols and ideological
statements are re-created in new patterns of meaning. The moral
discourses of social actors create a scene in which available symbols
and historical narratives, new experiences related to given situations,

images and sports results, new questions, answers to these questions and judgements about the correctness of these answers are mixed together. Thus, normative discourses can be seen as general attempts to understand the nature of moral responsibilities and to persuade others that one's understandings and evaluations are 'correct'. The presentation of narratives will be guided by the theoretical arguments put forward in this chapter.

Notes

1. Gutmann (1996) has explored the multiple meanings of machismo in Mexico, and, assisted by good ethnography, challenged the notion that men, masculinity and male identity are homogeneous and provide uniform models of behaviour. It is quite interesting to observe that he does not quote Cornwall and Lindisfarne – two British anthropologists – who edited a volume on 'dislocating masculinities', two years before (1994), which today can be considered a classic. Also in 1994, the Norwegian anthropologists Melhuus and Stølen organized a workshop at the 48th International Congress of Americanists in Stockholm/ Uppsala, in which the participants were invited to question the accepted hegemonic images on masculinity and femininity. Some of the papers presented were later published in an important book edited by the conveners of the workshop (Melhuus and Stølen 1996). The rise of a new trend in American anthropology is illustrated by Gutmann, while the other works are representative of a parallel development in Europe. The 1990s were ripe for new ideas, new perspectives and more complex ethnography concerning gender and masculinity. The importance of this is illustrated by the publication of a book edited by Balderston and Guy (1997,) in which scholars from different disciplines – history, anthropology, cultural studies and literary criticism – present papers in which dominant views of sex and sexuality in Latin America are deconstructed and criticized. Melhuus (1998) has recently argued that the recognition of the possibility of a multiplicity of gendered positions within one society does not imply a limitless repertoire.

2. Important ethnographies on masculinity have been recently published. The work of Vale de Almeida (1996) in Portugal followed the route opened by the pioneering research of Herzfeld (1985) in a Cretan mountain village. The focus is on dominant models, with special emphasis on work, politics, masculine sociabilities and the 'poetics of emotions' and manhood. More unexpected empirical results are coming from the analysis of prostitution and male clients (Hart 1994; Nencel 1996), the investigation of masculinity and politics (Krohn-Hansen

1996) and the critical examination of homosexuality and transgendered prostitutes (Cornwall 1994; Prieur 1996; Kulick 1997). New topics
of research in Latin America and Argentina should include race,
ethnicity and class, as key contexts generating and conditioning the
complex relations between these dimensions of stratification, and
social hierarchies and gendered masculinities.

3. The ethnographic work of Stølen (1996) in Argentina, among descend-
    ants of Friulian immigrants in rural Santa Fe, has shown the importance
    of work, schooling and religion in the social and symbolic production
    of femininities and masculinities.

4. Melhuus and Stølen summarized the rich ethnographic findings of
    their edited volume in the following way:

> One aspect which seems to emerge from the material in this book, whose
> implications have yet to be fully explored, is the differing yet mutual constitu-
> tion of same-sex and cross-sex relations. It appears that there are different
> schemes of evaluation for men and women. Men are classified according
> to degrees of masculinity; women are discretely classified according to their
> moral character. Whereas masculinity appears to be continuous – you are
> more or less of a man – women are dichotomized: a women is either good
> (decent) or bad (indecent). These differing grounds of valuation for men
> and for women are perhaps at the core of the gender relation, making gender
> categorizations both complex and ambiguous. While same-sex relations have
> characteristics which are exclusive to each category, cross-sex relations appear
> to transcend this very exclusivity in their joint articulations. This is reflected,
> among other things, in the fertile field of imagery which can be evoked.
> (1996: 27)

My findings can be seen as a contribution to the 'differing yet mutual
constitution of same-sex and cross-sex relations'.

5. This list is almost identical with the way Borges in 1926 – two years
    before Borocotó, the most universal of Argentinian writers – imagined
    national territories and masculine heroes. In his list, the *pampa*, the
    gauchos, the *malevos* of the tango and the generosity of the *arrabal*
    were included. In an explicit way the centre of Buenos Aires, inhabited
    by recently arrived immigrants, was left out (Borges 1993: 24–5). Sarlo
    has emphasized the importance of the *arrabal* in the constitution of
    the poetic landscape of the work of Borges (Sarlo 1993: 21). Rural or
    liminal territories, neither rural nor urban – like the *arrabal* and the
    potrero in football – inhabited by 'marginal' people – like gauchos,
    malevos and *pibes* – have the power to generate a complex imagery
    and powerful narratives. The confluence of the intellectual preoccupa-
    tions of Borges and Borocotó shows that the envisioned radical
    dichotomy between cultivated and popular writers in Argentina is no
    longer acceptable. What really separates Borges from Borocotó is his

hatred of football, not the way he constructs and imagines national territories and men. But this is a minor detail.

6. My research concerning national imageries was centred around gendered masculinities, but it is an important task for the future to explore nationalism and femininities in the analysis of Argentinian narratives. The paths opened by Yuval-Davis and Anthias (1989) and Parker *et al.* (1992) must not be considered closed.

7. The tango is the music and dance of Buenos Aires which is perceived abroad as typically Argentinian. Argentinians will accept this judgement but will add that there are other Argentinian dances and music which are also considered typical but are defined as folkloric – and rural. Much of Argentinian folklore is still produced in provinces that have borders with other countries, and many tunes and dances are shared across borders (e.g. the *carnavalito* is played and danced in the province of Jujuy and in Bolivia and the *cueca* is as Chilean as it is Argentinian). The tango is not folklore; it is defined as 'popular urban music'. The logic of defining other music as 'folklore' and the tango as 'national' reflects the power of Buenos Aires. The same logic is found in other areas. For example, in the Argentinian cuisine the *asado* (a gargantuan barbecue), identified with the gaucho traditions, is national, and the cuisines of the provinces are defined as 'regional'. Added to the *asado* we find imports from Italy, Spain, France and the rest of Europe, which, in a kind of *tour de force* of hybridization, are placed at the centre of the national cuisine.

CHAPTER FIVE

Masculinities and Morality in the Poetics of the Argentinian Tango

Defining the Field

In the first chapter of the book I reproduced a discussion with one of my informants – Manuel eller Manucho, as he was, and preferred to be, called – on the importance of the tango in the construction of Argentinian national imagery. Manucho introduced me to the tango. He considered it his 'historical obligation' as a *porteño*, a citizen of Buenos Aires, and as a member of *la guardia vieja* (the old guard) – due to his age, almost sixty, and his love for the tango – to introduce a *santiagueño* to the secrets of the tango. In the first lesson he accepted my ignorance as normal because I was young – in my early forties – and because in my province we only created folk music ('folklore'): *chacareras* ('the music of the *santiagueños*' and, according to him, a contribution to the national folklore), *gatos*, *escondidos* and *zambas*. However, and as important evidence of the national character of the tango, he remembered that in the café where we sat, on the corner of Boedo and San Juan streets, one great *santiagueño*, Homero Manzi, wrote the lyrics of many tangos. He said:

> I consider Discépolo, Cadícamo and Manzi the three best classic poets of the tango. You must remember the classic poets. There are others, and very important ones, like La Pera, Castillo, García Jiménez, González Castillo, Romero, and Expósito, but those three are the best. All the others are *porteños* [later I checked this information, and Manucho was almost right; all were *porteños* with the exception of González Castillo, born in Rosario]. You see, Discépolo was a pure product of Buenos Aires, Cadícamo was born in the province of Buenos Aires, and Manzi in your province, in Santiago del Estero [this was also true: Cadícamo

was born in Luján and Manzi in Añatuya]. Two *provincianos* out of three, not a bad record [he repeated twice, almost to himself, with a soft voice showing great admiration, 'not a bad record']. Cadícamo and Manzi moved to Buenos Aires and wrote tangos. As far as I know Manzi never wrote a *chacarera* or Cadícamo a *triunfo* [this I also believe is true]. The *provincianos* were taking part in the construction of our national urban poetry, and when they did it, they did it very well. I cannot imagine a *porteño* writing *chacareras* or playing *chacareras* with the grace you *santiagueños* do [I mentioned other *provincianos* composing *chacareras*, and among them, Atahualpa Yupanqui, one of the greatest Argentinian folklorists, but Manucho rejected this proof: 'he was not *porteño*, they were not *porteños*']. The world of the tango was open, always in the making, always receiving newcomers: the immigrants, the sons of immigrants and the *provincianos*. It was like our country. You *provincianos* were, and perhaps are, more closed, always looking backward, thinking about the roots and the traditions. In Buenos Aires people were creating new roots, and for this a new music and poetry were needed. You must believe this is true, and not only in the poetics of the tango. You see, take music composers, musicians and singers of the tango, it is the same: it is full of *provincianos*. Even one of the greatest male singers of the sixties, Argentino Ledesma is from your province [this was true, and I imagine that the rest is too].[1]

He recommended that I read about the tango. He said: 'Football is everyday life in Buenos Aires and Argentina; you cannot escape it, but the tango is more subtle; you must find it; you must search for the places where it is still cultivated.' This was in 1988, and in the Buenos Aires of 1998, and many European capitals, the tango is again everywhere. Moreover, he mentioned the importance of football as a source of inspiration for tango composers and poets. Manucho, an avid supporter of San Lorenzo de Almagro, remembered four tangos written for his club: *San Lorenzo de Almagro* and *San Lorenzo* in the 1920s, and another *San Lorenzo* and *El Ciclón* in the 1930s. He also insisted on the existence of many other tangos written for other clubs and some, a few, dedicated to players.[2]

I followed Manucho's advice, and I began to read about the tango. I discovered that I knew very little, just the stereotypes of the tango. I could not dance it, but I could dance *chacareras*, *gatos* and *zambas*, folk-dances from my province. My time as a student in Paris resonated; for Frenchmen the associations 'tango and Argentina', 'Argentina and the tango', 'Argentina and football' were obvious ones, but for me the tango was always the past, the glorious past of the tango in Paris and Buenos Aires. I was always obliged to explain that, for me and my generation, the music of the 1970s was rock, as in France. Rock was not the music of Manucho, not even what in Argentina was, and still is, called *rock nacional*. I absorbed the books of tango lyrics – by Manzi, Castillo, Flores, Discépolo, Cadícamo, García Jiménez and Romero – edited by the publisher Torres Agüero, and I read Sarlo's (1985) analysis of romantic narratives in the Argentina of the 1920s, in which the partial analysis of the tango was, as a comparative device, important. Ulla's (1982) book on the analysis of the cultural meaning of the tango inspired me. However, I do not totally agree with some of her assumptions and conclusions. She distinguished different themes and topics in the lyrics, but they were not treated as ethno-semantic units that refer to different cognitive and moral universes. This did not allow her to find contradictions and oppositions in the tango narrative. In the meantime, I studied some of the data that Manucho provided me with, and I considered myself well prepared for the second lesson. I told him later that I checked some of the information he gave me, and he commented, laconically and with irony: 'You did the right thing; Buenos Aires is full of *chantas* (tricksters), we are not like you *provincianos*, so honests.'

Manucho invited two other good friends, who later became my informants: Jorge, a sixty-five-year-old retired taxi-driver, and Esteban, a sixty-four-year-old state employee. Manucho announced on the telephone: 'I shall come with *la guardia vieja completa*.' We sat for hours in Manzi's bar, and they literally designed my research. I accepted them as my 'exclusive academy of the tango', and they always laughed when I called them, after that day, 'academicians' (without knowing, at that time, that there was, in Buenos Aires, a National Academy of the Tango). They convinced me of many things. The first, and most important, was to concentrate my research on the poetics of the tango. Manucho had insisted on this aspect in one of the discussions we had on the complexities of national imagery (this has been partially reproduced in the first chapter). A synthesis of a dialogue will illustrate the richness of their reflections.

Manucho   The origins of the tango are music and dance, pure dance. I do not know exactly, but from 1880 until the 1920s, with the consolidation of the *tango-canción*, the tango was an Argentinian dance exported to the rest of the world.

Jorge   Everything was related to dance, to choreography. The most
                 important figures were the musicians and the dancers. The
                 tango was defined as exotic by Europeans [Manucho added
                 'and Latin Americans and Americans'].

Esteban   You must not forget, it was not only exotic, it was very erotic,
                 it was provocative, it permitted the flow of sexual fantasies
                 on the part of the dancers and the public in general. In
                 the 1910s the tango was unique.

Manucho   Yes, I agree with you Esteban. We must remember that the
                 tango was exported to Europe and came back to Buenos
                 Aires at the start of the World War. It came back as an
                 improved dance, as a dance that could be danced by the
                 porteño aristocracy and the bourgeoisie. It was refined in
                 Paris.

Jorge   Of course, we could not export the poetics of the tango.
                 The French, the English, I do not know, the Poles, they
                 could not understand Spanish. It was a perfect timing to
                 export something that was still only music and dance,
                 without texts.

Esteban   I believe that the acceptance in Europe is crucial for the
                 new period, when lyrics were written. We put the words,
                 and in doing this . . .

Manucho   Yes, in doing this, we redefined the tango as something
                 peculiar to us . . .

Esteban   Yes, not only sexual fantasies, like this image of the bed
                 that is still warm, but more complex sentiments, more
                 romanticism. In order to understand the new tango with
                 the special language of Buenos Aires, the Europeans and
                 the rest of the world were obliged to learn *porteño*, an
                 impossible task for millions of people.

Jorge   Exactly; Europe and Japan consumed the music and the
                 dance; the rest will belong to us. Yes, when it was written
                 the tango began to speak to the Argentinians, to the Argen-
                 tinian minds and hearts (*cabezas y corazones*), and became
                 more national.

Manucho   It is quite interesting to think that after the 1920s the tango
                 was more complete, and due to this development created
                 a difference in the audiences: those who could understand
                 the lyrics and the others.

Esteban   Yes, two tangos: one tango more silent, and the other with
                 the voice of the singer and the lyrics of the poets. This
                 tango dominated until the 1960s.

Manucho   This is true. At the beginning you could be a *tanguero* only
                 if you danced, but in the 1960s the tango was redefined as

music, music to be listened to. It was possible to organize
tango concerts of tango in big theatres or small *cafés-concerts*,
like concerts of classical music or jazz.

Jorge   It is the period marked by Astor Piazzola and the transformation of tango music. There is an irony in the destiny
of the tango: in the beginning was dance and music; later
dance, music and lyrics; and finally music, just music, a
music that was impossible to dance to in a traditional way.

Manucho   The revolution of Piazzola in the 1960s was a real revolution,
the only one in Argentina since the days of independence
from the Spaniards [this was said with a mixture of great
satisfaction and irony]. Piazzola began to write music for
intelligent listeners, mixing jazz and classic tones, but the
majority of the *tangueros* were sentimental, not educated
enough to understand what he was doing. Look at me; it
took me many, many years to listen to him, and I still have
problems with the more complex melodies.

Esteban   Still, I do not like Piazzola very much, with very few exceptions . . . like his melancholic tango *Adiós Nonino*, which is
now a kind of second national anthem.

Jorge   (*looking at me*) You must write on the poetics of tango,
because you can not write on music; you are not a musician,
and you cannot write on choreography, because you are
not a dancer . . .

Esteban   And it will take an eternity to learn how to dance. People
who dance do not like to talk about what they are doing
with their bodies and their feet. The texts are there; they
are still played, and we can sing for you, if you want, of
course, one tango after the other.

Manucho   I fully agree with you. We must not forget that with the
texts also began a period of making Argentinian films in
the 1930s and 1940s, in which the tango was essential. The
tango became more passive, if you permit me to use this
expression; we could watch dancing and singing in the
movies.

Jorge   A nice summary, Manucho: the tango goes from activity
to passivity, from dance to listening, and, now in the 1990s,
a new period of dance again with Europeans and Americans
coming, as in pilgrimages, to Buenos Aires in order to
improve their dancing abilities.

Manucho   The tango never stops; it will always surprise us. Yes, it is
now the rage in dancing, all over the world, as in the
1910s . . .

This dialogue is a clear illustration of the preferences inherent in the tango. The tango is a complex cultural product that offered – and still offers – different possibilities for identity construction through its different parts. Manucho, Jorge and Esteban need not be taught about this: they are conscious of the existence of discontinuities between lyrics, music, dance and performances, and the way the tango was historically produced. The survival – and constant renovation – of the tango is precisely related to the simple fact that in the tango there is an explosive fusion of imagery and bodily practice that permits integration of aesthetics with emotions and ethics in an innovative way.

The second lesson is, of course, related to the complexities of analyses opened up by the tango. The tango will never be just a set of lyrics. Therefore, my analysis will be partial and limited. I shall not try to interpret the meaning conveyed by the choreography of the tango or how this aspect can be related with the words of the songs. And I shall never attempt to make of the tango an important object of ethnomusicology. Moreover, my analysis of the lyrics will be limited to the period 1917–30 when the *tango-canción* or *la nueva guardia* or *período clásico* was consolidated; this was the same epoch of the consolidation of football and polo, as we have seen in the first part of the book (see Ferrer 1960; Cantón 1972: 21; Matamoro 1982). This chapter focuses on male sexual ideology and morality. I shall try to relate the discourse of the tango to moral choices and ambiguity. I intend to show that through textual analysis it is possible to depict a time of moral effervescence, in the sense of Durkheim, a period of creation and renewal when a set of moral rules and beliefs was contravened symbolically and, perhaps with less intensity, in practice. It is a time, and not only in Buenos Aires, when women were 'stepping out', going to cabarets and in the process creating a new night-life, a public social life outside the walls of home and work. Women were making choices and challenging conventional mores and moral standards. The tango reflects a male reaction to changes and permits us to analyse the transformation of the imagery of heterosexual relations. Borges imagined the poetics of the tango as creating the anonymous poetics of a nation, a kind of Iliad of modern Argentina. He wrote: 'the lyrics of tango will bring about, with time, a large civil poem, or will suggest to some ambitious writer the writing of such a poem' (1980: 93). I shall follow his literary intuition, treating the tango texts as a kind of 'large civil poem'. My main aim is to locate some ethnosemantic units – plots in narratives – that will permit me to say something about the double function of the tango as both a male discourse and a cultural code and mode of cognition of masculinities and gender relations. I shall not attempt to treat the particular poetic worlds of key tango writers. There are particular accents and visions in the texts of Cadícamo, Discépolo or Manzi, as well as in Castillo, Le Pera or Flores, that merit a careful analysis which lies beyond the scope of my research.

I left out, among others, two topics that, I fully accept, would have enriched my examination of the tango: the role of exotic eroticism in the acceptance of the tango in Europe and North America, and the process of hybridization in the historical development of its music. Savigliano's (1995) account of the tango covers, in a controversial way, these two dimensions. Her main hypothesis is that, in the modern global expansion of imperialism and colonialism, a political economy of passion had been occurring which was intertwined with the general political economy.[3] The capitalist expansion of the dominant imperial powers through the production and export of colonial administrators, goods, financial capital and machines was accompanied by the exotic peripheral world 'producing passion'. Thus, in the 1910s the tango entered the world market of passion and exoticism. Savigliano has shown that the tango, as music and dance, constituted an 'exotic raw material' that was transformed in Paris and London, and later in Tokyo. She demonstrates that the triumph of the tango in Paris was not an accident, because Paris 'hegemonized the power of expertise in love, passion, and all sorts of erotic affairs' (1995: 99). Savigliano's description of the transformation of tthe ango in Europe is fascinating. She presents with accurate and passionate literary vitality the development of two choreographies: the scandalous, erotic and voluptuous tango as performed by the artists of the French cabaret revue, and the stylized and tamed tango performed in the popular ballrooms. Parisians changed the 'original' dance because they perceived it as very rough and usually performed by 'primitive' gauchos in the pampas (1995: 119–20). Borges commented on this transformation, pointing out that, before the triumph of Paris, the tango was an 'orgiastic devilry' and, after it, just 'a way of walking' (1980: 89) – from sexual wildness into urban dance.

Hybridity in the tango is an old topic of discussion among tango historians and experts (see Martini Real 1976; Ferrer 1980, vol. 1; Salas 1986; Collier 1995). I shall give some examples as an indication of the kind of controversies that existed in Argentina in the first three decades of the twentieth century. Ibarguren, our nationalist writer, defined the issue in the following way:

> [the tango] . . . is an illegitimate product, which has neither the rural fragrance nor the natural grace of the land but the sensual pose of the suburb, has been all over the world . . . the tango has been defined by the world as Argentinian, giving it a false filiation. The tango is not proper Argentinian; it is a hybrid product, or mestizo, born in the *arrabales* and consisting of a mixture of tropical *habanera* and an artificial *milonga*. How distant the crude choreography of the tango from the noble and distinguished *cueca*, which is as aristocratic as the *pavana* or the *minuet*! (Own translation Quoted in de Lara and Roncetti de Panti 1981: 286–7).

To accept the tango as a hybrid implies, for Ibarguren, a denial of being Argentinian, or, at least, typical Argentinian. Lugones, the paladin of nationalists, called the tango 'this reptile from the brothel' (1961: 117) and denied its status as a music and dance representing the nation. Borges accepted the tango as a hybrid national music and dance, created in the brothels of *barrios* like Palermo, Chacarita and Boedo. He did not believe that it was created in the *arrabales* because, he argued, its original music and the use of other instruments than the guitar indicate a more sophisticated origin (1980: 87–9). The historical account of the process of hybridization in the creation of tango music and dance mixes gauchos, blacks and the newly arrived European immigrants. Cultural creativity, once again, is the complex product of mixings in which the African-Argentinian tradition of music and dance is integrated (Collier 1995: 45). Savigliano (1995) presents a similar historical account in her book, but hybridization is seen both as an integral part of the process of world eroticization and, at the same time, an endless search for origins in modern Argentinian national identity.

I could legitimately have included in the first part of my book a chapter on the process of hybridization of the tango, showing some of the main differences with football and polo. We have seen that the blacks of Buenos Aires, numbering 6,000 by the 1880s, are absent in the process of hybridization of football and polo but are fully incorporated in the origins of the tango – even for Ibarguren through the *habanera* tropical. The British immigrants did not introduce the tango, and they are not a relevant other in the imagery of the tango. The contribution of other European immigrants, mainly Italians and Spaniards, but also Jews and Germans, were central in the process of amalgamation of the tango. In the 1920s English choreographers, however, played a crucial role in the transformation of the tango as a competition dance, including it in the category of 'modern' – as opposed to 'Latin' – dancing and in exporting it to Japan, where the tango became an almost 'national' music and dance in the 1930s (Savigliano 1995: 130 and 170–90).

Let me now address the contextual introduction of tango narratives. I shall first give hints on the social and historical setting of the tango; then, out of this context of production, I shall depict the importance of tango lyrics in the wider background of Argentinian literature.

The Social and Historical Setting

We have seen that Buenos Aires, the city of the tango, was a huge, cosmopolitan and multicultural urban centre in the 1920s, with three million inhabitants in 1930, one-third of them being European immigrants. I have also pointed out that, as a consequence of these changes, the definition of nation and nationhood (*argentinidad*), in crisis since the end of the civil wars in the mid-nineteenth century, became even more problematic. Urban life in Buenos Aires was rapidly transformed: luxury hotels, restaurants, bistros, hundreds of cafés, a world- famous opera-house and theatres were built by European architects. This provoked changes in the use of leisure time and created a new environment outside the walls of privacy and home. The appearance of public arenas created new conditions for public participation and enjoyment where cultural life, sports and sexual concerns dominated. Four institutions, in particular, provided the public with new excitements and opportunities for the deployment of sexual fantasies: the modern legal brothel, the 'dancing academies' (*academias de baile*), the 'cafés with waitresses' (*cafés de camareras*) and the cabaret (see Cadícamo 1969). Since these various arenas were appropriated or dominated by men, the use of leisure time and the different activities involved were fundamental aspects in the construction of masculinity among the generation of urban and *porteño* men who came of age in the 1900s. These arenas also provided a space for women, albeit of a special kind. However, as I shall try to show, such women represented a new kind of femininity. Thus, the construction of images and models of masculinity were intimately related to the way men perceived, defined and imagined an idealized femininity. The tango narrative can be seen as a male discourse on gender relations and not as a solipsist tale.

The tango was directly related to these public contexts: in the last two decades of the nineteenth century, the brothels and the 'dancing academies' were the places where the original tango dance was created. Later, at the beginning of the twentieth century, the cabaret became a privileged public space for dancing and singing. It has been overstated that, originally, the tango was only music and was mostly danced by male couples. However, the importance of the 'dancing academies' and the 'cafés with waitresses' as meeting places for men and women, or couples, cannot be overlooked. Many of the most popular early tangos had obscene, almost pornographic, texts constituting what was called *la poesía rufianesca*, or the poetry of the pimps. These lyrics, in most cases anonymous, are very simple and consist of a presentation of a *rufián* or *malevo* (ruffian or evildoer), his ability to dance the tango and to control women and his courage and supreme skill in knife duels. This period, lasting from 1880 to 1920, has been called *la guardia vieja* (the old guard). Harp, flute, violin and guitar dominated the orchestra until the 1920s, when the piano and *bandoneon* were gradually introduced. Because the main objective was to produce music for dancing, the style of playing was oral, in the sense that musicians improvised all the time without performing real solos. The playing took the form of a kind of dialogue between the orchestra and the dancers, in which the musical improvisations were closely related to the rich and complex erotic choreography. At the beginning, then, the tango was for dancing and not for listening to. The few texts accompanying the music were direct, insolent, impudent, and, in many ways, reflected a kind of primitive male exhibitionism.

The 'new' tango, which constitutes the core of this chapter, developed after the 1920s and has been called the tango of *la nueva guardia* or *tango-canción* (Ferrer 1960: 31–6). Both the musical composition of this period and the new orchestras gave more freedom to the soloists, drastically reducing the degree of improvisation. The conductors became more concerned with details and nuances in the orchestration than with the performances of improvised solos. In this sense, the tango evolved in the opposite direction of jazz. The most important change, however, can be observed in the lyrics. The new authors of the tango tell concise, moving stories concerning characters and moral dilemmas that were easily understood and identifiable to a vast and heterogeneous audience. Thus, the tango shifted from being first and foremost a musical expression to being primarily a narrative interpreted by a plethora of extraordinary singers, both male and female. The real globalization of the tango took place during this period with the help of modern technology: radio, movies and records. The forceful combination of text and music gave the written, emotional stories a special dimension, because they were both sung and danced. During this period, and after the process of domestification in Europe, the dance lost the aggressivity of the first epoch, and many of the choreographic figures disappeared. As a dance the tango became impoverished, because, paradoxically enough, it could be danced by many more, and, in such a way, was converted into a dancehall activity.

Buenos Aires, like Barcelona, Berlin, Vienna, New York, Moscow and Zurich, imported cabaret-style entertainment from Paris. However, the cabaret of Buenos Aires is not typical European cabaret. Its music and dancing, primarily the tango and later jazz – sometimes accompanied by musical shows – lacked the experimental, revolutionary and artistic forms of the theatre, the arts, and the protest song that characterized the famous European cabarets (see Erenberg 1981; Siegel 1986; Brody 1987; Segel 1987; Jelavich 1990). Hence, the *porteño* cabaret was perceived as a threat to the bourgeois order only in so far as it represented a sophisticated space for erotic fantasies and excitement. The tango was a pivotal dance in the *porteño* cabaret as well as in Europe and New York. The role of Aristide Bruant (1924) in the cabarets of Paris, challenging the bourgeois morality with his music and narratives full of crime, alcoholism, deceit and moral decadence, can be seen as similar to the one played by the tango lyricists in Buenos Aires.

Between 1910 and 1930, more than twenty cabarets of elegant, even luxurious, style were established and flourished in the capital, which Argentinians believed was an emulation of Paris and the best cities of Europe (see Matamoro 1982: 96–8; Salas 1986: 126–7). It was during this period that the tango became the music of the cabaret. The cabaret provided an arena of entertainment, dancing, shows and informal social life that fundamentally changed the leisure habits of many men and women in Europe and elsewhere. For the first time in Buenos Aires, in an elegant and intimate atmosphere, men and women could enjoy informality in public. The cabaret as a public institution represented a challenge to the cult of domestic life, family feasts and celebrations, and formal balls. It was not a place for family entertainment as were, for instance, vaudevilles, the circus, theatres or movies. The cabaret became both a real and imagined arena for 'time out', and, for many women, for 'stepping out'. Women could escape from the order of home, from the routines and drudgery of family duties, and thereby be tempted by the excitements of the cabaret and night-life in the centre of Buenos Aires. Although the cabaret represented the possibility of 'stepping out', only a minority of women moved into this space. The cabaret was, therefore, both real – an existing physical space – and, at the same time and more powerfully, a dramatic fictional stage for many tango stories. The cabaret was represented in the tango lyrics as a key place for imagining stories, and it served, metaphorically, as a potent image in contrast to the home, the local bar and the *barrio*.

Tania, a great female tango singer of the 1920s who married the poet Discépolo, vividly depicts life in a *porteño* cabaret of this epoch. She writes that 'the span of my social life changed in the cabaret', because 'besides participation in the show, as artists we had the opportunities of a better social life than that of the performers playing and singing in popular theatres or cafés'. This change was possible due to the fact that 'the cabaret was a key social centre, with the fabulous force of the rich people squandering a lot of money' (Tania 1973: 28–9). Tania distinguishes three different types of women in the cabaret: the *artists*, like herself; the *milongueras*, who talk and exchange dances with the clients who were seeking 'love', even 'paid love', in a kind of 'slow and patient ceremony . . . where they drank together for days and days until an affair began'; and, finally, the *querida* or *mantenida* (mistress) (1973: 32–3). Tania comments that the bourgeois women of that time 'were very critical towards the mistresses but also envied them secretly'. According to her, the bourgeois man brought only his mistress to the cabaret but went to 'the theatre and the opera one day with his wife and the other with his lover' (1973: 33). Tania's description illustrates clearly that 'some' women moved definitely into the realm of cabaret and the imagery of the tango. These women – the *milongueras* or *milonguitas* and the *mantenidas* – represented the opposite of the bourgeois ideal of a domestic and acquiescent housewife. They were in many ways, and in spite of the latent 'moral condemnation' of Tania, like the artists themselves. They were seen as autonomous and hence dangerous women.[4]

In Buenos Aires the *milonguita* was, thus, a woman who worked in the cabaret, and her work consisted of dancing and entertaining the men. For this, she was paid a given percentage of the customer's consumption. However, if she went to bed with the clients once the cabaret was closed, she could earn additional money, get expensive gifts and, eventually, become a *mantenida*. It is interesting to notice that they were also called *alternadoras*, persons who could entertain, talk and dance with customers, and were never called *prostitutas* or *putas* (prostitutes or whores). It was even supposed that they had some kind of education and good manners. In tango lyrics two kinds of *milonguita* are depicted: the first type was the permanent lover of a rich man who brought her to the cabaret, and the second was the woman who worked in the cabaret. We can imagine that for many women the first solution was the best but, also, that most of them never achieved this goal of 'upward mobility'.

It is understandable that the nationalist writers like Ibarguren and Lugones reacted so strongly against the moralities depicted in the tango. Mosse has stressed that modern nationalism as ideology in Europe contains a strong idea of sexual respectability, in which normality, self-control, the sublimation of sensuality, the importance of domesticity and the key role of the nuclear family are key values (1985: 1–19). The world of cabaret contrasts with the importance of domesticity and family life as a warm retreat from the pressures and the attractions of the outside world. The modern bourgeois nation tried to remove middle-class woman from active life outside the home and protect her from having to face a turbulent age. In cabaret, on the contrary, temptations, fantasies and desires could be realized, a place for independent and dangerous women. Therefore, to imagine identities from the perspective given by the lyrics of the tango was to defy the accepted moral canons and the dominant values of nationalism in Argentina.

Argentinian Literature and the Interpretation of the Meaning of the Tango Lyrics

The musical and literary impact of the tango in Argentinian society was enormous. The rapid acceptance and expansion of compositions

and orchestras, and later lyrics and singers, created a universe for
native 'interpretations', 'readings' and analysis of various kinds:
panegyric essays, quasi-historical encyclopaedias and texts, auto-
biographies, popular academies of both the tango and *lunfardo* –
the *porteño* slang used in many tangos – and numerous biographies
of musicians, authors and singers. Only recently has the tango been
transformed into an 'academic' subject with some important contributions from what tango experts perhaps perceive as 'outsiders':
social scientists and professional historians (Cantón 1972; Ulla
1982; Collier 1986; Taylor 1987; Azzi 1991; Castro 1991; Vila 1991;
Savigliano 1995). Moreover, anthologies of classic tango lyrics are
periodically published and, in this process, the minor and outmoded
texts are filtered out, leaving only those that Argentinian popular
memory, or the editors, consider the most outstanding (Gobello
and Stilman 1966; Gobello and Bossio 1979; Vilariño 1981; Romano
1991). Romano's anthology is by far the most authoritative because
each tango text is accompanied by a careful history of recording –
the only way of knowing the real historical impact of the tango in
question. The tangos played by the best orchestras or sung by the
most popular singers in a given historical period are a guarantee
of historical survival. My later analysis of the lyrics has mainly been
based on Romano's anthology.

Among the natives' models of interpreting the meaning of the
tango, the ones produced by the most prominent Argentinian
writers are central because they enabled a 'cultivated' legitimization
of a popular cultural product. The first was Ricardo Güiraldes,
author of the classic of Argentinian literature *Don Segundo Sombra*
– mentioned in the first part of this book, who lived for long periods
in France; he was an eminent tango dancer and enjoyed the success
of the tango in the Paris of the 1910s. In 1911, he published a
poem simply called 'Tango'. In this Güiraldes placed the tango in
the *arrabal*, with the dominant elements of: 'tragedy', 'melody
played with a theme of fight', 'a dance that creates a virile vertigo',
'drinking', 'sadness', 'surrendered women and dominant males',
'blood and duelling', 'an ambience of uneducated women and
fighting men', 'the aroma of the brothel' and 'fatality, pride and
brutality' (see de Lara and Roncetti de Panti 1981: 271–2). The
tango is so remarkable in Argentinian culture that the most important writers of modern times, for example Borges and Cortázar –
and also other distinguished poets in addition to Güiraldes – have
written tango poetry and tango texts. In the context of modern

Latin American literature there are no parallel examples in other countries: Octavio Paz and Carlos Fuentes never wrote Mexican *corridos* or *boleros*; García Márquez has never produced a single *cumbia* in Colombia; Donoso a Chilean *cueca*: or Vargas Llosa a typical creole *walts* from Lima. Moreover, Argentinian writers, at different periods, have explored the relationship between this 'popular' literature and aspects of Argentinian reality and cultural identity. In doing this, they have moved into different lines of interpretation depicting distinct narratives, each one with his own cultural code and moral evaluation. They have transformed the popular literature of the tango into a privileged field of cultural analysis. Manucho insisted several times: 'the tango is literature; it is not popular literature; it is literature with music; it is more than romance literature'. He knew, as Jorge and Esteban did, that Borges was occupied with the tango and that some of his texts were produced as tangos with music composed by great composers like Piazzolla, Cosentino and Castiñeira de Dios. He was always very proud to point out that the most well-known Argentinian writer, to 'whom the stupid members of the Swedish Academy denied the Nobel Prize', loved the tango. Let me briefly illustrate this aspect with some examples.

I have mentioned Borges several times and pointed out that his famous essay on the history of the tango emphasized its fierce origins. For him, the tango of the initial period is an extreme, heroic, literary form because it presented and defended 'the conviction that fighting can be a real fiesta' (1980: 89). In this sense, the mission of the tango is 'to give Argentinians the inner certainty of having been brave, of having performed in accordance with the requirements of daring and honour' (1980: 91). Within this cultural logic, Borges argues, the aggressive man, the *compadre* or *compadrito* – one of the archetypical figures of tango lyrics, is imagined as a rebel denying the legitimacy of an abstract judicial system regulated and administered by the modern state. The social destiny of this rebellious man was thus based on a kind of ethic of 'the man who is alone and expects nothing from others' (Borges 1956: 8). Borges, a quiet and very cultivated man, prefers this kind of tango of the first period and emphatically dismisses the new forms developed after the 1920s. He observes that the lyrics move away from the themes of courage and virility to a kind of *comédie humaine* of the city of Buenos Aires. He accepted that the most well-known texts of the tangos were simple, and that the men depicted were perhaps stupid but, he adds, also brave. The poetics of the 1920s, in contrast, depict an unhappy man suffering his own misfortune, but, at the same time, obtaining some kind of emotional compensation through the suffering of others (Borges 1980: 94). Borges acknowledges the importance of popular poetics in influencing behaviour and attitudes, and, therefore, suggests that the new poetics may have had a 'harmful influence' on the Argentinians of the 1930s, when this essay was originally published.

Sábato (1963), in an essay which has also become a classic, tries to identify different issues and tensions coexisting in the tango lyrics. In the first place, he states that the sadness in the tango reflects a nostalgic love that cannot be fully lived through a carnal sexuality divorced from tenderness. He maintains that in this kind of poetics it is possible to find 'a resentful eroticism and a tortuous manifestation of the deep inferiority complex of the new Argentinian' (1963: 15). Secondly, the fear of making a fool of oneself is compensated by violent and aggressive behaviour (the famous *bronca argentina*). Thirdly, the tango as a literary and musical form reflects the building of a nation dominated by 'maladjustment, nostalgia, sadness, frustration, dramatic experiences, discontent, resentment and other problems' (1963: 19). Finally, for Sábato the tango is perhaps the first and most important 'metaphysical litera-ture' in Argentina, because it permits reflection on the elusiveness of life and the inexorable arrival of death.

From another perspective, Soriano more calmly reminds us that 'nobody could be a good Argentinian without a sense of real and profound failure, a complete frustration, so intense that it can evolve into an infinite sorrow', and adds, 'precisely of this the tango speaks' (1987: 140). This, he explains, leads to a cyclical relationship between Argentinians of the 1980s and the tango: in their youth they escape from it, but they return once they have lived and discovered that 'life is a cul-de-sac' (1987: 140). To expect light and joyful tangos, full of optimism and hope, therefore makes no sense for him. The same observation has been made by Cortázar, who writes that 'the tangos come back to us in a sardonic way each time we write sadness, when we are melancholic like a drizzly day, or when the bulb (*bombilla*) gets stuck in the middle of a mate' (the national tea) (1985: 69).

These summarized perspectives and interpretations of the tango confirm the existence of different ethnosemantic units and moral universes. But, above all, the tango, with the words and the cadence of its music, allows the deployment of a narrative in which stories, cases, events and places are embedded in a web of complex emotions and sentiments between men and women. The authors of the tango texts were important forces in the creation of a cultural universe mainly centred on gendered social relations, masculinities and imageries. Tango texts can therefore be seen as a key element in the charter of modern Argentinian 'mythology', in which the city of Buenos Aires is conflated with the nation. Perhaps more fundamentally, the analysis of the tango illustrates the argument advanced in the previous chapter that the language of morality is shaped by emotions, and that written discourses on emotions can be seen as commentaries on the practices of fundamental social relations (see Abu-Lughod and Lutz 1990). I shall try to show that the poetics of the tango relate not only to emotions like sadness, happiness, fear or anxiety but also to those of love, pride, guilt, shame and honour, which are fundamental in the articulation between individual identity, gender and moralities conceived as sociocultural processes. Manucho and many of my other informants insisted on the persistence of tango poetics because they appeal to 'permanent conditions and emotions'. In the words of Jorge: 'the tangos speak today to the emotional problems and dilemmas of any man or woman of Buenos Aires'. The tango, dispossessed of its history and particularities, has been transformed in Argentinian society of today into one among many public languages of gendered emotions and prototypical narratives.

Masculinity and the Morality of Romantic Love

The lyrics of the tango can be seen as a reflection of different types of love: love as duty, love as passion, love as a deep friendship and, finally, romantic love (see Luhmann 1985). This is transmitted through a peculiar language in which the authors try to achieve a balance between modern poetic forms and popular idiomatic expressions. Due to the fact that the tango is 'spoken' and 'sung', the slang of Buenos Aires, called *lunfardo*, is, as I have indicated above, profusely used in addition to orthographic and idiomatic modifications. The first modern *tango-canción* (tango-song) that we know of, entitled *Mi noche triste* (My sad night), was written by Pascual Contursi in 1917 (see Romano 1991: 30-1). This lyric inaugurates a new kind of narrative, in which a man tells, in an

intimate and confessional form, the story of a failed romance. He
writes:

> Beloved who abandoned me
> in the best moment of my life
> leaving me with a wounded soul
> and spines in my heart,
> knowing that I loved you,
> that you were my joy
> and my burning dream;
> to me there is no consolation
> and that's why I get drunk
> to forget your love.
> When I enter my room
> and I see it disordered,
> in sadness, abandoned,
> I feel like weeping,
> and I spend long moments
> in front of your picture
> to console myself.
> The guitar in the wardrobe
> is still in its place;
> nobody makes her string vibrate . . .
> And the lamp in my room
> has also felt your absence
> because its light has not wanted
> my sad night to illuminate.

The 'theme' of love as passion, as something almost impossible, is
a common one (see also the classics *La cumparsita* (1924), *Amurado*
(1927) and *Farolito de Papel* (1930) in Romano 1991: 64, 131, 186–
8). The men of these stories love with such an intensity that the
risk of not being requited is correspondingly overwhelming. At
the same time, there is a revalorization of sexuality, sexual relations
and 'sensual love'. A constant theme is the woman who abandons
the man. We are not told, at least not in these texts, but it seems
that it is rarely for another man. They portray a sad man remembering his lost happiness. In all cases the readers (listeners) are
confronted with a couple in consensual union, living together
without being married. They do not have children, and the woman
is always leaving the *casa* (house), the *bulín* or *cotorro* (one-room
apartment) or, simply, the *pieza* (room). In literal terms, she is going
out into the open world: metaphorically, she is 'steppin' out'. The

image of a lost man passing through an identity crisis, unable to
control the situation, is melancholically reiterated. The way he
speaks about sadness, nostalgia, the loss of happiness and the fear
of loneliness is sincere and passionate. García Jiménez writes in
Farolito de papel:

> A hundred flatteries I heard,
> a hundred promises I believed . . .
> That afternoon I found
> the sadness of farewell
> in the lips where yesterday
> the tenderness spoke of love.
> Little paper lantern,
> that illuminated my life
> and with a friendly and loyal light
> the love I now have lost.
> Elsewhere you illuminate today,
> to me you give no light.
> And in darkness I remain,
> lonely and poor as before . . .
> The promises, of paper.
> The flatteries, weak light.
> Nothing fragile stays erect.
> Only the virtue persists . . .
> Much smoke and scanty light,
> little paper lantern . . .
>
> (Romano 1991: 186)

In other classic texts, the world and locus of sentiments (and the
inevitable abandonment) occur in the cabaret. The women leave
the *casa*, the *bulín* and the *pieza*, in order to enter the fascinating
space of the cabaret (see *Flor de Fango* (1917); *Margot* (1919); *Mano
a mano* (1920); *Zorro gris* (1920); *El motivo* (1920); *Ivette* (1920);
Milonguita (1920): *Pompas de jabón* (1925); *Che Papusa, oí* (1927);
Muñeca brava (1928); *Milonguera* (1929); *Mano cruel* (1929); *Sos vos?*
(1930) in Romano 1991: 32, 34, 39, 36, 37, 40, 42, 84, 130, 134,
167, 164, 211). In this setting, the women are represented as
milonguitas or *milongueras*, one of the mythological prototypes of
the tango. The *milonguita* is young, unmarried, from a middle–
lower-class family and born in a *barrio*. She is sensual, very sensual,
egoistic and self-assured, with a self-confidence that emanates from
her beauty and elegance. The *milonguita* escapes from the *barrio*,
from poverty perhaps, and from a future as a housewife, to the

centre of Buenos Aires, to the life of excitement, luxury and pleasure that the best cabarets offer to young, ambitious and beautiful women. The lyrics portray this life as superficial from the man's perspective; they stress that the loss of chastity and pure sensuality lead to suffering and loneliness when youth vanishes, and, in the end, the women in these songs are abandoned by unreliable men – in some cases rich men – who only use and play with them. However, underpinning the texts is a recognition that the cabaret can provide a space of 'freedom' and material realization, if sensuality is coupled with 'authentic love'. Women's pure sensuality and their selfish interest in material security are portrayed in many tangos as being as destructive as passion. In *Mano cruel* Taggini writes:

> You were the spoiled girl
> of Pepirí street,
> the street I never forget,
> where I first met you . . .
> In this neighbourhood you learnt to seduce,
> and your charm made more than one boy sigh,
> but you did not find the ideal man
> who was able to conquer your heart.
> But in the darkness slinking
> the villainous thief
> who destroyed
> your youthful charm
> with a cruel hand,
> you surrendered to his words of passion,
> and never more your neighbourhood
> saw you return.
> Today, I have seen you at the door
> of a luxurious cabaret,
> in your afflicted face
> a deep sorrow I guessed.
> I know that you will offer
> even your soul
> for being what you have been,
> but you cannot be the same,
> the Spring of your life has abandoned you.

> (Romano 1991: 164)

Mano a mano, written in 1920 by one of the greatest tango poets, Celedonio Flores, opens up a new vision: that of the abandoned man who transforms his love into a deep friendship. The *milonguita* abandons him to become the mistress of a rich man, enjoying luxury, nightlife and the world of cabaret.

> Mad in my sadness
> I remember you today
> and I see that you have been
> in my poor pariah life
> merely a good woman . . .
> You were nice, consistent,
> and I know that you have loved me . . .
> Today your head is full of unhappy illusions,
> you were misled by untrustworthy men,
> friends, by a Don Juan . . .

The man accepts his destiny and even wishes her good luck and a 'rich lover with an everlasting fortune'. The tango concludes:

> and tomorrow, when you are
> an old piece of furniture falling into pieces
> without any hopes in your poor heart
> if you need some help and maybe advice
> you must remember this old friend
> who will help you in your need.

> (Romano 1991: 39)

He tries to understand her, he does not condemn her and, generously, he offers her true friendship and understanding.

The dramatic structure of these tangos is based on the comparison made by the narrator between himself, a virtuous and truly loving man, to the *milonguita* who is seduced by material gains and immediate pleasures, and to the *bacán* (rich man) who promises the earth and uses his money to seduce women. Luxurious living is condemned as superficial and extravagant, and contrasted to a world of authentic feelings and deep relationships. Through particular stories of *milonguitas*, they convey the idea that money or economic interest is, in the long run, a source of suffering, because it prevents the realization of romantic love, based on sexuality, friendship and mutual understanding, and it created the 'bad' man, with whom the innocent and pure cannot compete (see *Flor de fango* (1917); *Milonguita* (1920); *El motivo* (1920); *Pompas de jabón* (1925); *Mano cruel* (1929) and *Milonguera* (1929) in Romano 1991).[5]

In *Pompas de jabón* (Soap-bubbles), written by Cadícamo in 1938, the moral tone of the text is not related to the suburb and the authentic love that the women in the cabaret have lost. The main opposition is between the beauty and the success when they are young, when everything is easy, and the decadence that comes with age. Cadícamo writes:

> Young girl of my suburb, beautiful girl,
> that is showing off in a car with a rich man.
> Today your few Springs
> permits you to dream.
> You must think, poor young girl,
> that one day your beauty will vanish
> and that your poor illusions will die.
> When relentlessly age will come
> and with it your sadness
> you will realize that your madness
> was like soap-bubbles.
>   (Romano 1991: 84)

The tango clearly illustrates how the behaviour of women is judged to be morally good, bad or indifferent according to the happiness or misery of those involved. What makes many men and women unhappy and miserable is the rupture of given moral standards. The tango can also be seen as a discourse on human suffering and the negation of real and sincere happiness for both men and women. Happiness seems possible only if persons are guided in their behaviour by sincere and authentic love. The cabaret, almost by definition, is not a place for the realization of romanticism. The tangos, perhaps more than anything, defend a male morality by romanticizing a kind of subtle emotional control over women. In the action context offered by the cabaret, love is only exultation and pleasure. Only exceptionally are the choices of the *milonguita* justified. Maria Luisa Carnelli (1898-1987), the only woman who reached some status as a composer during the 1930s, and who wrote all her tangos with a male pseudonym – Mario Castro or Luis Mario – writes in *Se va la vida* (1929) (Vilariño 1981: 30-1):

> Life is fleeting,
> is fleeting and will never return.
> Listen to my advice:
> if a rich man promises you a good life,
> you must accept it.
> Life is fleeting, fleeting,

and not even God will stop it.
The best you can do
is to enjoy life and forget your sorrows and pains . . .
The days and the years elapse
and happiness is elusive.
You must not think
either of suffering or of virtue:
you must fully live your youth.

It is remarkable that Carnelli's advice refers precisely to suffering and virtue, the two values that men's texts perceived as lacking in *milonguita*'s behaviour. Carnelli's advice is radical: the women must forget suffering and virtue, values imposed by men and social circumstances, and pursue happiness – the good life offered by a rich man. The women of the tango have never been docile or passive objects of desire (see Savigliano 1995: 69). This text clearly shows the conflicts and tensions between gender and class.

Who is the narrator? What kind of man tells these stories and speaks complainingly to those around him? It seems: that the 'man of the tango' is middle-aged, single, lower-middle-class or, perhaps, just middle-class; that he has grown up in a *barrio* and is now living in the centre of Buenos Aires, enjoying leisure time with his friends (*la barra*) in a coffee-house which he visits daily (in many tangos called 'the home'); and that he has had 'great' love affairs or, at least, 'one' that has marked him profoundly. With the passage of time this man has developed a romantic and nostalgic view of the past. He has loved and desires to love again, but he is not looking for marriage and family life. The image of the ideal women he presents is no longer associated with virginity and chastity, as was the case of the traditional 'romantic novels' of the same period (Sarlo 1985). On the contrary, she takes care of her body, dresses elegantly and is extremely concerned with her appearance. However, she is also an ambivalent figure, because she is fascinated by money and a life of luxury. For such a figure love, as well as sexual relations, results in choice and an ability to listen to authentic feelings; he does not expect subordination and traditional respect from the woman. He is caught in the notion of romantic love where he expects that his feelings will be understood and that the women will love him with the same intensity as he loves her. Loyalty and fidelity are seen and experienced as the product of love and of precedence and authority. Nevertheless, modern urban life in a metropolis like Buenos Aires, shown in the life of the cabaret, is also portrayed with a kind of anxiety related to the transformation of sexual roles. The narrator of tango stories is depicting a process of social and cultural change in a historical context that affects traditional family patterns and places the responsibility for love on both men and women. The modernity of tango lyrics lies precisely in the fact of presenting the uncertainties related to the exercise of romantic choice as a problem.

To summarize: in this type of lyric the basic elements in the cultural construction of romantic love are intimacy, companionship (friendship), the existence of mutual empathy and the search for sexual pleasure. The distortion of one of these, such as too much emphasis on sexual pleasure, creates an emotional imbalance leading to unhappiness, loneliness and nostalgia. The universalization of romantic love in these texts is highly dependent on a definition of a 'self' that can choose in accordance with deep emotions and thus achieve a full realization of himself/herself, and they point to the dangers arising from the existence of a world dominated by *milonguitas* and *bacanes*. The poets of tango described the world of feelings and love with a mixture of realism and nostalgia; there is neither eternal happiness nor just tragedy. The poetic work with archetypes makes it possible to reunite a known feeling with a new imagery, inhabited by loving men and women.

The poetics of the romantic tangos depict a moral universe quite different from that presented in the romance literature of the 1920s, which was consumed weekly in Buenos Aires from 1917 to 1927 by hundreds of thousands (see Sarlo 1985). In the moral context of the tango, the ideal of happiness is no longer related to the constitution of a legitimate couple with descendants. The tango does not depict the felicity of the bourgeois family as the main value. On the contrary, in the romance literature:

> The engagement is the fundamental institution of this world of narratives. Everything that is interesting between a man and a woman is related to the definition of the kind of relation: engagement/mistress/ marriage. The engagement is the scene in which happiness or unhappiness is played, because from this a woman can be transformed into a mistress or wife. (Own translation Sarlo 1985: 111)

The engagement is, then, the scene in which the fate of a woman is challenged; it is quite different from the threatening world of the cabaret. The women of romance literature will never abandon the walls of the home and the security of the *barrio*, and they will never dare to undergo the risks taken by the *milonguita*. The men of tango will never attempt to renew a relation under the assumption or with the promise of marriage and the constitution of a happy family life. Fatherhood and children are not a male preoccupation in the cognitive and emotional context of tango.

Manucho, Jorge and Esteban accepted my interpretation concerning the importance of romantic love in the lyrics of the *tango-canción*. They pointed out that the cabaret is no longer important in the social life of Buenos Aires but that the problems associated with feelings, sexuality, independent women and loyal men are universal. While Jorge spoke of 'modern problems' (*problemas modernos'*), Manucho observed: 'in the past we had tangos; the texts of the tangos were a kind of therapy, a cheap therapy'. They remembered some of the cabarets: the Chantecler, inaugurated in the 1920s and closed in 1960; the Tabarís, one of the oldest, established in the 1910s and demolished in 1936 when the street Corrientes was transformed into an avenue; the Tabarín; the Armenonville, founded in 1910 and the most luxurious until the 1930s, and the Tibidabo, the most popular according to them, that has been associated with Anibal Troilo and his orchestra because, in the 1930s and 1940s, they played there. Esteban pointed out that 'the cabaret is gone and with it the *milonguitas* and the *bacanes*, and what is left is just love of normal people'. 'The tango speaks to all of us,' concluded Jorge, but there were other tangos that perhaps do not speak to the Argentinians today. Let me present some of them.

Masculinity and the World of Honour

Until now we have seen the world of tango populated by archetypes like the *milonguitas* and the *bacanes*, but the figure of the *compadrito* is also paradigmatic. I believe that the *problématique* of honour, shame and courage needs to go beyond the role of the traditional *compadrito*. Very few tangos of the 'old guard' period survived the classic works of the *tango-canción*; of these, two were texts still played in the 1930s and the 1940s presenting the *compadrito* as a social type (see *El porteñito* (1903) and *El taita* (1907) in Romano 1991: 22, 26). The characteristic traits of the *compadrito* are to dance the tango as a master and play the guitar. He is an elegant seducer whom no woman is able to resist; he has been in prison and is admired because of his courage, physical strength and capacity to cheat where necessary. The *compadrito* has a defiant and hostile attitude towards other men. These tangos explicitly relate honour to status achieved in a world where equals can and should compete for social recognition. In the code of honour defended by the *compadrito*, violence and fighting establish and reproduce social hierarchies. Here the idea of Borges, that 'for the *compadrito* fighting is a feast', makes sense.

The figure of the *compadrito* is quite different from the man in search of happiness through romantic love. He is very concerned with women's loyalty but in a context where what men expect from their women is obedience and submission. He is a character of the outskirts, not the centre of the city; he is not a man of the cabaret and most of the time he roams a local territory inhabited by other men like him. Many tangos between 1917 and 1930 present the figure of the *compadrito* in a deep identity crisis (see *La he visto con otro* (1926), *Malevaje* (1928) and *Bailarín comparito* (1929) in Romano 1991: 92, 151, 163)). In *La he visto con otro* (I have seen her with another man) the betrayed man will not kill her; while crying he will try to forget her. Pascual Contursi writes:

> I have seen her embraced
> with another man:
> my eyes cry
> of pain and sorrow:
> while in her face
> her glad black eyes
> smiled with love and happiness . . .
> There are nights that alone
> I stay in my room
> asking the Virgin
> to help me to forget her,
> and when I see her with another
> walking close to me
> instead of killing her
> I began to cry.

In *Bailarín compadrito* (*Compadrito* dancer), the *compadrito* abandons his suburb and becomes a well-known cabaret dancer. In this process, he transforms himself into the opposite of a *compadrito*, becoming a kind of bourgeois dandy hiding his social origin and past life. In *Malevaje* (Malevolent people), written by Discépolo in 1928, the *compadrito* surprisingly falls in love. A man offering himself to a woman is portrayed as one who has lost control and is, thus, in a weak position. In the world of the *compadrito*, relations between men and women are not based on equality and respect but on command and domination. The *compadrito* thinks that to love implies 'being in a cul-de-sac, lost, and a prisoner of the heart of a woman'. As a consequence of his feelings he has lost his 'hope, courage and wishes to be brave' and has abandoned his 'malevolent and ferocious past life'. Thus, love comes to be seen as having a real transformative capacity: the *compadrito* will avoid fighting and feels afraid of duelling because he can be killed or, if he kills, he suffers the consequences. The *compadrito*, in the last verse of the tango, begs the woman:

> please, by God, tell me what you gave me
> I am so transformed,
> I do not know who I am.

In this context of change, the *problématique* of honour and shame is mainly related to betrayed love. The knife duel between 'real' equals is no longer seen as the way to measure courage and to maintain male supremacy. In the tangos of the 'new guard' the *compadrito* vanishes and is replaced by a betrayed man who does not accept the logic of humiliation. The feeling of humiliation is replaced by emotional transformation; instead of being humiliated, the *compadrito* changes. However, some texts offer the extreme solution of killing the unfaithful woman and her new lover (see *Silbando* (1923) and *A la luz del candil* (1927) in Romano 1991: 58, 117; and *Fondín de Pedro Mendoza* (1928) and *Noche de Reyes* (1929), sung by Carlos Gardel, in Cantón 1972: 115,160]. The betrayed man is presented as honest, hard-working and decent, knowing that his code of honour is in flagrant contradiction to the new laws of the nation state. He knows the consequences of his action, but it is emphatically asserted that the most important value for a real man is to defend his worth before other men – and society at large – and not the state. In other tangos, the classic knife duel is chosen to defend outraged honour. In *El ciruja* (1926) the betrayed man kills the betrayer while in *Duelo criollo* (1928) both fight with a ferocious determination and are killed (see Romano 1991: 98, 142).

In these tangos male honour is dependent on the woman's sexual behaviour. In some cases the betrayal of the woman is punished by death, but in most the woman is described as weak, unable to resist temptation (see *Desdén* (1927) and *La gayola* (1929) in Cantón 1972: 84, 132). The 'other man' is guilty because he takes advantage of her moral fragility, and, consequently, he is punished. As I have pointed out above, in the romantic texts the betrayed man tries to understand and to forgive; he becomes a 'full moral person' because his actions are guided by authentic feelings and genuine passion. However, the women are not perceived as weak but rather as autonomous, and, in a way, very determined. In contrast to many of the texts on the moral discourse of honour and shame, the woman is portrayed as fragile and in need of protection. She can be treacherous. However, the women of the tango, in both ethno-semantic universes, are not by nature treacherous. The theme of treacherous women, which dominates in the Mexican *canción-ranchera*, for instance, is not dominant in the poetics of the tango (Peña 1991). Betrayal, then, can be seen and socially defined as a complex act where individual emotions are confronted with cultural and public moral expectations. The tango texts capture this tension while simultaneously elaborating various solutions that are acceptable for suffering individuals. In this process, the universe of honour and shame, which is central in the public domain, is confronted with that of individual moral and psychological choice, where there is room for a deep sense of guilt. Even in the classic text of *La gayola* (The prison) forgiveness is contrasted with vengeance. The killer admits that he has perhaps committed a terrible error in killing the man who was possibly loved by the woman who betrayed him. This position implies two things for our interpretation: that women can decide for themselves whom to love, and, in such cases, the chosen man is only responsible for himself and not for her decisions and feelings. Thus, this represents a break with traditional perceptions of women, reflecting a new way of constructing male identity.

The Limits and Dilemmas of Masculine Identity

The success and historical persistence of the tangos of the classic period illustrate the primordial place of a masculine narrative in the constitution of a national culture dominated by the metropolis, Buenos Aires.[6] We have seen that the tango became a global music, and in this process was defined by others and perceived by the

Argentinian themselves as expressing central aspects of their creativity and national character. The tango was also the music of
traditional Argentinian theatre (*sainetes*), of movies – almost one
hundred films were made in Argentina with tango as music from
1930 to 1945, of dancehalls, of *milongas*, and of cabarets. Of all
records sold in Argentina in the 1920s, 95% were tangos (see
Cantón 1972: 19). My analysis has shown that in the jungle of tango
texts there are a variety of 'men' with different voices and moral
and psychological dilemmas. They speak of moral issues and gender
relations in a context of change. On the one hand, in the world of
romantic love and personal dignity we find a man who narrates
love stories, and, on the other, in the epos of honour or shame we
find one that tells tales of vengeance and death. Guilt and forgiveness gradually replace the violence of duelling and killing. The
tango elaborates a series of paradoxical themes centred around
the sentimental education of mature urban men. Emphasis is put
on emotional control and, thereby, on the search for 'authentic'
and 'romantic' love. The analysis of tango texts is a crucial field
for understanding the complexity of male/female relationships in
contexts where new forms of conceptualizing love were developing.

Mosse has argued that modern masculinity tempered the aristocratic ideas of manhood dominated by medieval ideals based on
chivalry and institutions such as the duel (1996: 17). Modern
masculinity adjusted and transformed such aristocratic moral codes
to middle-class sensibilities. He observes that 'if the characteristics
of courage, sang-froid, and even compassion remained as ideals,
they were now changed, stripped of much of their remaining
violence, and embedded in moral imperatives' (1996: 19). The
analysis of the duality of moral codes in the lyrics of the tango in
Argentina clearly illustrates these adaptations. Moral attitudes
based on understanding the feelings of the 'other', uprightness,
honesty, loyalty and lack of extreme passion replace the primitive
reactions based on masculine bravery, vengeance and extreme
courage.

Moreover, the analysis of gender relations in changing contexts
cannot avoid the examination of conceptions of love. This exploration is usually lacking in the vast anthropological literature dealing
with codes of honour and shame in different societies and cultures.
The study of urban contexts, such as the city of Buenos Aires in
the 1930s or any large Mediterranean city in the 1960s or 1970s,
permits a much more subtle analysis of the existence of a complexity

of codes regulating gender relations.[7] The tango texts of the classic period are an important part of a complexity of contemporary writings where these topics were discussed: novels, essays, poems, short stories and, particularly, the romance literature, consumed by so many women in Buenos Aires. The tango appeared as 'subversive' compared with 'romantic novels'. The latter emphasized marriage as the only possible way to happiness: 'the *pax matrimonialis*, which presupposes economic tranquillity in the framework of dependency, decency and the virtuous reproduction of the species' (Sarlo 1985: 117). In the typical bourgeois novel happiness could only be achieved if the 'conventional moral world' could be changed. In the tango difficult romantic love is seen as an emotional arena in which it is still possible to be tender and forgiving, to be melancholic and to love again. In the Argentina of the 1920s, the socialists and the handful of feminists and suffragettes perceived romantic love as a kind of authentic rebellion against a conception of 'domestic love', based on the sacralization of the familiar space, and, at the same time, opposed 'human and achieved dignity' to the traditional codes of honour and shame (Ingenieros 1956: 115–36). The poets of the tango, expressing what Durkheim calls periods of effervescence, presented alternatives, dilemmas and some solutions.[8] The tango as literature and music wrote the ballads of a turbulent nation, disregarding laws and official moral codes. In the words of Manucho: 'the tango reflects a doubting masculinity, not machismo, and powerful women like we have plenty of in Argentina. You must remember that the romantic tangos have survived and will enter the next century, not the others; and saying this I will not deny that there is machismo in Argentina, but the world of *compadritos* has disappeared.'

Notes

1. With the exception of Homero Expósito, born in 1918, all the other poets mentioned by Manucho belonged to the generation that marked the classic period of the writing of tango lyrics. The oldest, González Castillo, was born in 1885 and the youngest, Homero Manzi, in 1907. As expected, the majority of them were born in Buenos Aires – with the exceptions of Cadícamo, Manzi and González Castillo. Cadícamo moved to Buenos Aires aged 21, and Manzi, born in Santiago del Estero, arrived in Buenos Aires at an earlier age. Manzi cannot be considered a typical *santiagueño* in spite of being claimed as such by

many *santiagueños*: he was the product of Buenos Aires. Many of them were prolific writers, combining tango texts with novels, journalism, script-writing and film-making. In the movie-making of the 1930s, with tango texts and music and tango scripts, Manuel Romero was the most creative. He made more than twenty films, among them the classics *La vida es un tango* (1939) and *Adios pampa mía* (1946). Cadícamo and Discépolo also experimented with film-making but without the success and continuity of Romero.

2. In the previous chapter we saw how Borocotó related football and the tango, but his analysis was partial. From 1911 tangos in tribute to football clubs and players were composed. Manucho mentioned the tangos written to San Lorenzo de Almagro, but there are also tangos to Racing Club – two, Independiente – two, Boca Juniors – five, Estudiantes de la Plata – two, Huracán – one, Banfield – one, and Gimnasia y Esgrima de La Plata – one. The first tango devoted to the tango, without lyrics, was composed in 1910 by Emilio Sassenus with the title *Football porteño*. In the 1920s, when Argentinian football appeared on the international scene, a series of tangos were composed both to great players – Botasso, Monti, Nolo Ferreira, Tarascone, Onzari, Varallo, Sastre, Bernabé Ferreyra and Orsi – and to great teams: *Bravo nuestros campeones*, to the winner of the South American Cup in 1927, and *Olímpicos*, to the team obtaining the silver medal in the Olympic Games of 1928 in Amsterdam. Most of these tangos are not played today. Ariel Obschatko has catalogued amore than one hundred tangos with football as a central theme (personal communication). These tangos were composed in the 1930s and 1940s, but only two tangos have survived the test of time and are still played today: *El sueño del pibe* (*Pibe*'s dream) from 1943, and *Desde el tablón* (From the pitch) composed in 1971. On *El sueño del pibe* more will be written in the next chapters.

3. Savigliano's book is very impressive. My only reservation, and, perhaps, a very important one, is her attempt to 'decolonize' the tango. I believe that the tango does not need a process of decolonization, because it was a historical product of Argentina. Argentinians could not control how it was appropriated and recodified in Paris or London or Helsinki. Argentinians are still the masters of their own creature: they have the best orchestras, the best composers, the best singers and, above all, the best dancers. They do not need to decolonize the tango; they are just simply 'doing the tango'. I prefer the framework that I presented in the first chapter, in which models and mirrors – colonial imagery and Argentinian creativity – are intermixed. Images, commodities, capital, persons, artists and cultural products were increasingly exchanged between Argentina, Europe and the rest of the world. In an open social and cultural global market, authenticity and national

identity are transformed into an enduring quest and unfulfilled search. Without this process there is no history, and the tango is, above all, history. We cannot deny the fact that it is quite an achievement to generate 'exportable' and 'permanent' artefacts and cultural practices that can travel for a long period of time beyond the cultural and political boundaries of Buenos Aires. This is, however, rare. Argentinians can proudly say that they participated in this rarity through the expansion, transformation and permanence of tango as music and dance. They reserved the poetics for themselves.

4. Guy (1991: 144) has correctly pointed out the crucial role of 'dangerous' sexual women, especially prostitutes, in the creation of gender anxiety in Buenos Aires. I agree with most of her historical analysis on the complex relations between the tango, gender and politics. I also accept that, in general, the lyrics of the tango did not convey a wholly positive image of independent and autonomous women. However, while she emphasizes a strong misogynist male view based on the dangerous woman, I attempt to depict models of masculinities in the plural, putting the accent on tensions, doubts, paradoxes and ambiguities. My focus is on masculinities and not on dangerous women. Judging and classifying different types of women can be seen as a cultural process creating an engendered masculinity. As a contrast, in the New York of the 1910s those who were dangerous were the seductive tango dancers of the cabarets of New York. They were called 'tango pirates' and defined as the men 'who trapped and tapped the sexuality of women. The master of such passion-inducing dances as the tango and one-step, the pirate held women in a spell they could not easily break. Tightening his arms around her, dipping her, holding her, and in the tango from which he got his name, bending her over backward in a perfect picture of sexual subjugation, the tango pirate was the master of all he surveyed' (Erenberg 1981: 83–4). In Buenos Aires the danger came from women, in New York from men: which society was more macho?

5. Parkin (1983: 6) emphasizes the importance of relating morality to a discussion on how happiness and misery are conceived in society. According to Wolfram, the only test of morality 'in the sense in which we seriously speak of moral right and wrong, is whether, discounting factual errors and idiocy, the judgements made of rules, acts, persons, that count as moral ones are in fact made on the basis of the principle it puts forward, that is according to the happiness or misery of those involved' (1982: 274). This principle can imply that empirically different groups conceive of happiness or misery as quite contrasting values. The consequences of such differences seem less important than the fact that actors are arguing about moral issues. In the tango the silent group is constituted by the women who have abandoned the traditional

morality – they were not very many but this is not the point. The men depict their lives as full of misery, but we do not know how they perceive themselves. It is obvious in my analysis that the life of the deceived men is not full of happiness. Therefore, the tango can be considered as having a highly moral discourse.

6. Most of the tangos analysed in this chapter are still central to the contemporary repertoire of some of the best singers and orchestras of Argentina. Other themes besides gender relations existed and developed in the 1940s and 1950s, but they were more marginal in the construction and representation of masculinities. Moreover, in the 1950s and 1960s the tango was challenged by traditional folklore and the impact of European rock (De Ipola 1985; Vila 1991). At the same time, as Manucho told us, a revolution inside the tango was taking place: Astor Piazzolla, the famous Argentinian *bandoneonist* and composer, produced a new tango, in which words and traditional rhythms were replaced by a complex and elaborate music (only incidentally accompanied by lyrics). My hypothesis is that the type of 'silent' tango created by Piazzolla was the only one able to challenge the classic tango but, at the same time and paradoxically, it confirmed the classicism of the latter. The classic tango is that of an existential masculine discourse related to a model of romantic love that perhaps still pervades Argentinian gender representations and relations. However, Piazzolla has, in the last three years, been transformed into a 'classic composer' played by classic interpreters like Barenboin, Yo Yo Ma, Kramer and Aix.

7. The Mediterranean construction has come under attack recently (Llobera 1986; Pina-Cabral 1989). However, the importance of gender relations and perceptions related to ideas about love, sexuality and marriage and their changes over time has not received adequate attention.

8. In the Buenos Aires of the 1920s and 1930s the practice of 'aristocratic and bourgeois duelling' survived the legal prohibition of such acts implemented at the beginning of the twentieth century (Viale 1937). It is interesting to notice that the division of the Socialist Party in 1915, the second largest in the city of Buenos Aires between 1904 and 1930, was provoked not by controversies concerning political principles or revolutionary tactics, but by disagreement regarding the morality and legitimacy of duelling. For many socialists of immigrant origin, the duel was a European aristocratic and feudal practice that ought to be abandoned. For many important and charismatic party figures of Argentinian 'aristocratic' origin, on the contrary, to enter into contests of honour was unavoidable. They were irremediably duellists (see Walter 1977: 113–34; García Costa 1986: 7–56).

CHAPTER SIX

Masculine National Virtues and Moralities in Football

Introduction

While talking about the importance of football in the daily life of so many *porteños*, Carlos, who in 1988 was in his early forties, said: '*Los argentinos somos de raza futbolística*' ('We Argentinians are of the football breed') and added, anticipating my answer, 'Yes, I know, women are not of the same breed, although they accompany us; they tolerate us, and there are men who do not agree with the majority of us.'[1] He continued:

> You know what I mean. We must learn to think as a united people, as a society. Argentinians are very individualistic, with little national feeling . . . except when the national football team plays. Then our patriotism emerges, including many of the people who feel that football is not important. We enjoy being well represented, that the national team plays well, and we like to win. In many senses it is a demonstration of what we are.

In some ways I thought he was right, and he expressed an argument that I had heard many times before, but many of my informants could contradict him. Manucho, Tomás and Manuel, for instance, always insisted on the fact that Argentinians (male) are very nationalistic – *patrioteros* according to Manucho. Manuel said to me once that 'our *patrioterismo*, our chauvinism reaches a climax in the field of football; we always expect to win'. Manucho emphasized this need for victories as something negative, 'an indication of our insecurity', and contrasted the need with the tango: 'you do not need to win in the tango'. I remembered my answer: 'but in the tango we do not have competition'. I did not find Manucho's answer in my notes because he, perhaps, agreed with me, and there was no answer.

Working on football narratives and national male imageries was, sometimes, difficult. My informants were supporters of different clubs, and, as can be imagined, they were more chauvinistic – and in many cases 'racists' – in relation to their clubs than to the national team. Juan José, supporter of Boca Juniors, confessed to me that he did not care about the results of the national team during the last three years; this was because the coach – Passarella – was an emblematic figure of River Plate, the historical enemy of his club, and always preferred River Plate's players. He even said that he enjoyed the defeat of the national team in 1995 against Brazil because Passarella replaced Maradona with a mediocre River Plate player. He considered Passarella's attitude a 'joke' and his decision 'an offence to Argentinian football'. Fortunately, Juan José was joined by only three of my other informants in his refusal to talk about national teams and national styles.

Euphemistically, Argentinians call the national team *la selección*, 'the selection', in the sense of the pick of the best, while the players are called *los seleccionados*, 'the selected', the chosen. One of the favourite pastimes of many of my informants was to imagine an all-time best selection, 'the eternal selection', made up of players who had played on the national team during different historical periods with unequalled success. They relied on their experience or on the selections made by the experts, radio or television journalists. Since 1928, when Argentina reached the final of the Olympic Games in Amsterdam, generations of Argentinian men have heard on the radio, read in the newspapers and sport magazines and seen in television presentations of their national football teams and footballers playing all over the world. It is quite interesting to note that Argentinians are very proud that their players are playing well and gaining admiration in Europe. Still, Europe remains the place where the fame of Argentinian players must be recognized. The gaze of the relevant other creates meaning. This archive of memories has been considerably increased by the massive production of videotapes on football in the last decade. The different *selecciones* and the most successful players have been perceived as models and mirrors of what Carlos described for me: an expression of the Argentinian breed and a display of national male virtues and qualities. In this chapter I shall concentrate on the historical, social and cultural meaning of the national team. In connection with this I shall touch superficially upon the variations of identities related to the history of the great clubs of Buenos Aires and the impact that these have had in the process of producing a national imagery.

The Masculinities and Moralities of Football

In the presentation of my findings I shall place special emphasis on the way morality is constituted as a discursive practice when Argentinians reflect on the historical achievements and defeats of the national team. I shall show, following some of the ideas advanced in a previous chapter, that at moments of crisis morality is presented and experienced in terms of moral choices. This perspective renders possible an analysis of the plurality of male identities and moralities as constructed public narratives in Argentina. I hope to be able to show that, while it is crucial to get to know what is defined as good in itself, it is also crucial to determine what is perceived by the different social actors as worthwhile and desirable.

After an unforgettable match in the South American Cup between Independiente from Argentina and Olimpia from Paraguay one Wednesday night during the very cold winter of 1984, I was sitting with 29-year-old Héctor, a devoted fan of Independiente, in an old café on the main plaza of Avellaneda, an industrial neighbourhood of Buenos Aires. We had decided to escape from the crowd fighting to get into the buses going to the centre of Buenos Aires. While waiting for the cappuccino and the traditional glass of Bols geneva, Héctor insisted on telling me a story which, according to him, was a beautiful synthesis of the philosophy of football as a game: the contradiction between elegance and force. He began:

> When I was a child, in the 1960s, my father slowly introduced me to the history of Independiente. He would say that it is not possible to experience every situation in life at a football arena, but he repeated again and again that a vast number of situations and ceremonies of life are part of the game. The heroes and villains, who were always players, were transformed into victims, orators, judges, killers, jugglers, workers, bureaucrats, usurers, impostors, criminals, mercenaries, magicians and survivors. My father insisted that, under the influence of the passion and the involvement of the game, different types of men coexist – expressing generosity, misery, enthusiasm, tragedy, comedy, magic and hope. He told me a very beautiful story, one that he believed represented

the contradictions of football. He remembered that in the 1920s Independiente had a good team, with an excellent right insider – Lalin, a juggler – and a very effective killer – the centre forward Seoane, called The Pig. The episode happened in a match against Estudiantes de la Plata. During the first half Lalin kept the ball for himself, all the time, danced and dribbled with it. 'Can you picture, my son,' my father asked me, 'when you play football with an orange until it softens and you see the juice? Well, Lalin transformed the ball into an orange; in each match the ball was transformed into an orange. Seoane did not like it at all. His job was to produce goals and to win. You know, to make goals is indeed the most dramatic moment of football. Lalin was postponing the moment when winners and losers are divided and joy and disappointment are experienced. Seoane did not like it. In the break, Seoane insisted on getting the ball: "Lalin, if you can give me the ball, just one cross-ball, and that is what we need. If give you my guarantee, one cross-ball, one goal." At the beginning of the second half', my father said, doubting for a moment, 'I think it was in the second minute, Lalin sent a cross-ball, a perfect cross-ball, and Seoane, like the goal-machine he was, volleyed it into the goal. Goal! what a nice score', my father added. 'Seoane, very happy, ran to embrace and to thank Lalin and said: "You see, if we play like this we shall win; we shall always win." Lalin answered laconically: "Yes, I am sure we can always win, but if we play in this way I do not enjoy the game."'

I remembered this story and each time I met Héctor during 1984, and again in 1988, we agreed on the ambivalent meaning of joy, of happiness and of feeling happy expressed in the story told by his father. For Lalin, we imagined, to feel happy was not ultimately related to victory, which was the real meaning of football according to Seoane. For Lalin the pleasure of the game was not to inflict moral pain on the losers; in his world, there was no compelling place for efficient and determined centre forwards. Lalin knew that in football the loser has an opaque destiny of forgetfulness. In my discussion with Héctor, he mentioned that his father used this story in order to counterpoise 'the romantic figure of the juggler to the cold and metallic role played by the killer'.

Several years later, during my stay in Buenos Aires in 1993, I understood that the story of Héctor's father was, in a way, part of an Argentinian historical narrative in which the oral sources are mixed with heterogeneous authoritative texts (see Humphrey 1997). Borocotó, the journalist known from previous chapters, writing with his real name referred to the event in a short article. All the theatrical elements in Héctor's father's story are present, but the end is different. Lalin's replay to Seoane states the importance of victory: 'Yes, but I do not enjoy myself. Is football to mean just goals? How horrible!' (Lorenzo 1946: 47).

Ernesto Sábato, the great Argentinian novelist who reflected on the tango and who is a supporter of Estudiantes de la Plata – and because of this he obviously knew the story – incorporated the event into his classical novel *Sobre héroes y tumbas* (Sábato 1961: 86–7). The setting here is located in a bar in Parque Lezama, a neighbourhood of Buenos Aires. Some friends, drinking the traditional afternoon vermouth, exchange ideas about the negative changes in modern football which have brought about an extreme aggressivity among the players, only interested in winning and less and less in the creation of beauty. One of them refers to the Lalin–Seoane story in order to illustrate the overriding importance of goals. In this story, the reply of Lalin is: 'Yes, but I am not enjoying myself,' and the narrator concludes: 'You see, if you like, here lies the problem of Argentinian football' (Sábato 1961: 87). The conflict of Argentinian football is, then, the abandonment of elegance and beauty and the consolidation of a way of feeling the game based on the cult of efficiency and results. The narrative indicates a profound and irrevocable change in which the ethos represented by Lalin can be seen only as an anachronism, belonging to the time of amateur football.[2]

In 1986, in a long interview just before the World Cup in Mexico, Jorge Valdano, a player with Real Madrid in Spain and a striker on the Argentinian national team, remembered the story of *Sobre héroes y tumbas*. In his narrative the names of Lalin and Seoane had disappeared as main actors; nevertheless the roles that they played were retained. The setting was moved from a football stadium to a *potrero* – the mythological space where the national style of playing was modelled, as we have seen earlier. Interestingly enough, Seoane is transformed into 'a practical player' and Lalin into 'a crack'. At the end of the story, the practical player, after scoring, says, 'You see; you passed me the ball, and I scored', and the crack answers, 'Yes, I see, but I enjoyed myself much more than you.' Valdano explains: 'For Sábato, this was the problem of football, but for me this is its great secret, nothing more or less. The struggle between two kinds of apparently incompatible bodily practices, elegance and force, determine at the end the popularity of the game' (*El Gráfico* no. 3479, 1986: 11). Thus, according to Valdano, the main contradiction of football implies that the pre-eminence of ability over force or vice versa must be understood as a permanent feature of the contradictory character of Argentinian football. Male individual virtues are transformed into contrasting styles and moral attitudes, as I have shown in the first part of this book. Lalin and Seoane represent different, contradictory and competing male styles. The competing masculinities are thought of as either problematic or enigmatic. Through the performance of football players this contradiction is transformed into a public concern. In Valdano's interpretation, masculine styles in football are multiple and permanent.[3] The story illustrates how meaning is dependent on who is performing or speaking (see Cornwall and Lindisfarne 1994: 12). The original 'juggler' in Héctor's tale was converted into a 'crack', representing virtues such as ability, dribbling, elegance and beauty, while the 'killer' was seen as expressing force, efficiency, determination and practicality. Héctor always insisted that these styles were moral choices. He suggested that searching for and realizing different football styles convey information concerning 'our and their beliefs about how we see what the world is like' (*nuestras creencias en el fútbol, y las de otros diferentes, indican cómo vemos el mundo*). He told me:

> You see, I feel a strong sympathy; I can identify with players like Lalin, and this is not purely irrational. Even I can recognize that players like Seoane are needed, but they must never take over the game. My feelings are reasonable; I am choosing what I think is right for keeping the essence of the game. This is my truth.

Héctor gave me some 'reasons' for his moral considerations and his knowledge of football in a way that showed that he accepted a possible disagreement. He added: 'I know very well what I prefer and I know what kind of players and games and styles will affect my basic attitudes.'

I discussed the relationship between ability and force in relation to male moral choices and the Argentinian style of playing with many of my informants. Juan, or Juancho, in his late forties, introduced a dichotomy based on *serio* (serious) and *alegre* (joyful), which I also later found when reading the sports magazine *El Gráfico* of the 1920s and 1930s, but he rejected its validity for understanding the history of Argentinian football.[4] He argued:

> You see, many people believe that Argentinian football, as represented by the national team, has moved like a pendulum between seriousness and joyfulness. Joyful football has been identified with creativity,

imagination, dribbling, doing things in an unexpected way, and serious football exactly the opposite, like total tedium (*el tedio total*). I do not agree. For me, being serious means to play with engagement, with discipline and with a real will to achieve victory. To play well always implies creativity and imagination. It is possible to be serious and to play well. You see, in Argentina, seriousness has been identified with the cult of force and masculine courage, with the myth of the Uruguayan Indian grip (*la garra charrúa*). Courage will never replace imagination. The Uruguayans defeated us in two finals, at the Olympic final of 1928 and in the World Cup of 1930, because, we were told by many, they were more macho than us. You see this way of explaining these two dramatic defeats confirmed the myth of the ability of Argentinian players and their lack of strength.

Juancho refers to the traumatic defeats, accepting, in a way, the myth of the generosity of Argentinian football as opposed to the systematic use of tactical considerations that could guarantee a victory. The history of the final at the Olympics in Amsterdam in 1928, when the Uruguayans defeated the Argentinian team, 2–1, was repeated in 1930. The written accounts tell that in the final of the World Cup in 1930, which was played in Montevideo, the capital city of Uruguay, the Argentinians controlled the match due to their technical superiority and were leading by 2–1 at half-time. The Uruguayans then 'humiliated' the Argentinians, winning 4–2. Bayer, in his history of Argentinian football, which, as we have seen in previous chapters, was used as the basis of a script of a popular movie in 1990 and watch by millions of Argentinians including Héctor, Juancho and Tomás, commented on the two defeats:

> The River Plate [an expression that included Buenos Aires and Montevideo, the two cities of the River Plate] placed the two finalists in Amsterdam. And again the Uruguayan Indian grip (*la garra charrúa*) wins. Two to one. An indisputable triumph. The Argentinians play well but the Uruguayans show more personality; they are not intimidated; they stand up (*mejor parados*). In order to gain some consolation, the Buenos Aires newspapers write: 'The River Plate football (*el fútbol rioplatense*) has won'. Argentinians must wait two years for vindication . . . For the final of the (first) World Cup thousands and thousands of Argentinians take the boat to Montevideo . . . In Buenos Aires thousands and thousands listen to the radio transmission in front of the newspaper buildings of *Crítica* and *La Prensa* . . . In the stadium, a real climate of war predominates. The Uruguayans must not win, as they did in Amsterdam. The Argentinians would like to be rid of the

complex of paternity. Luis Monti, the Argentinian centre half, has received thousands of threatening letters telling him that, if the Argentinians win, he will be killed. The Uruguayan supporters knew Monti very well: he is a great player but fragile and unstable. In spite of the tremendous pressure, Argentina lead 2–1 at the end of the first half. Forty-five more minutes and Argentina will be World Champions. The Uruguayans do not surrender but, on the contrary, play with more stamina. Using violence in a couple of situations, and insulting Monti when the referee cannot see them, is enough. Monti crumbles . . . The Argentinians show signs of physical weakness, and the defence is a sieve. The Uruguayans score three times, and that is that. They became the first World Champions of football. Argentinians will continue to be their sons. (Own translation Bayer 1990: 34–5)

As in the story about Lalin and Seoane, we can see that victory in decisive situations is intimately associated with the deployment of some male virtues: courage, physical strength, tactical rational planning and moral endurance. In addition, these virtues are seen by Bayer as constitutive of paternity and the relations of father and son. Before the match, equality was recognized and accepted, but the defeat transformed Argentinians into sons and Uruguayans into fathers. Bayer (1990: 35) contrasts the figure of the Argentinian Monti, 'good player but fragile and unstable', with the great Uruguayan 'heroes': Nasazzi, a man of great energy; Fernández, a centre half covering all the ground with his physical strength; Scarone, the technical player; and Gestido a 'real male' who always stands up. The fragility of Monti was perceived by the press and the fans as the main reason for the Argentinian defeat. Monti was called 'double breadth'. His nickname was an indication of his impressive physical figure, and he was a very strong athlete, a technical but rather aggressive player, even violent; his style of playing contributed to the public recognition of 'The Cyclone' as the *nom de guerre* of his club, San Lorenzo de Almagro.

The defeat of 1930 was so traumatic that Argentina sent a third-class team from the amateur league to the World Cup in 1934; this was a disguised protest against the purchase of their players by European clubs, and they refused to participate again until 1958. Juancho told me:

I will not deny our fascination with technical ability and the cult of dribbling. This is our tradition, what we usually call *la nuestra* (our style), but it has always been under threat. You see, you can have a nice style of playing, fantastic individual players, players with success in great international club teams, but you need victories, international victories by the national team. Without victories, I mean important victories, you cannot have a tradition in football. To get a tradition you have to be known. Others have to accept your way of feeling for the game; other teams have to respect you and even be afraid of playing against you. A tradition in football is related to a certain aesthetics and to criteria for defining a correct style. It is again *la nuestra*. We failed in the two finals of 1928 and 1930, and we decided not to expose ourselves; we decided not to take risks. We sent hundreds and hundreds of individual players to Europe, to South America. In a way we exported quality. I will give you an example: in the winning Italian team of the World Cup in 1934, there were four Argentinian players, almost half of the team. Well . . . it was much more than half because they were one inside forward, the centre half and the two wings. We stayed in South America; we won the South American tournament many times, and we defined ourselves as 'the best of the world'. For many, many years it was enough to defeat Uruguay and Brazil. But we knew that the power, the international recognition and the consolidation of a tradition really happens in the World Cup. My father always said that winning the South American tournament was like playing in the patio of a house – the patio of a house in a *barrio* – while playing in the World Cup was like playing in the shop-window of an important department store on Florida Street, in the centre of Buenos Aires.

I insisted on discussing why Argentinians, including the players, football authorities and, of course, supporters, perceived themselves, despite the evidence to the contrary, as belonging to a 'football tradition' that was 'the best in the world'. Juancho, without hesitating, answered me in the following way:

You must remember that Argentina had problems in being identified by others as an important nation. Football made it possible for us to be recognized as something in the world [I thought that perhaps he exaggerated, leaving apart the tango and polo]. An authentic masculine passion was developed, and, for many men, the majority of men, football becomes a part of what I will call an internalized national identity which includes the sense of football. We thought: well, at least, we play good football and we export football players . . . Because of this the defeats and the failures are particularly painful for us. When the national team is defeated in very important matches it affects me and many, many others like me. Sometimes I ask myself, why is this so important to me? Perhaps it is childish, but in each defeat there is more than football. It is our prestige and self-esteem that is at stake. You see, each time we lose an important match, we asked ourselves why. How was it possible? And we hope that it will never occur again, never again. The failures showed our fragility and our weakness. At the time, when the football authorities, supported by the government – especially under the government of Perón in the 1940s and 1950s – decided not to take part in the World Cup, not only were we exporting players, but the best club teams dominated in South America and played with brilliance in Europe during their tours. We were 'the best'. We truly believed that the best football in the world was played every Sunday in Argentina, but we were never really convinced that we were invincible. The myth of invincibility was a creation of the Uruguayans after they won the World Cup in 1950, defeating Brazil in the Mecca of football: the Maracaná Stadium in Rio de Janeiro. You see, we had not participated in the World Cup after 1930, and when we decided to participate again in 1958 we had created an image of ourselves that we were the best . . . Too many expectations, great, great expectations . . . we were defeated in the first round by Czechoslovakia. This we had never imagined. We always considered England, Italy and Germany as the great powers – but Czechoslovakia? Never! Unthinkable . . . Well, we were defeated by the devastating score of 6–1. What a shame! You must understand that this was the end of the world. The crisis of our tradition. A moral crisis. From that time, for many, many years we could not distinguish right from wrong.

Juancho is touching upon one of the dark chapters, perhaps the darkest, in the history of Argentinian football: the débâcle with Czechoslovakia in the World Cup of 1958. Juancho is not exaggerating. In their recently published dictionary on Argentinian football, Fontanarrosa and Sanz (1994: 17) define Argentina as 'the country where until 1958 everyone believed that they had invented football'. Juancho is telling us that, through the world of football, Argentinians created a powerful imagery, producing a collective memory based on selected images and stories referring to a beautiful style of playing. He also talks about this style as *la nuestra*, which literally means 'ours' – but implying 'our way of playing' – and the defeat is seen as provoking 'the crisis of our tradition'. His narrative is prototypical concerning the importance of 'a national tradition' in which there is a description of the constitution of identity in opposition to difference, and inside against outside; the superiority of the inside (*la nuestra*) is assumed as a requirement to resist the possible invasion of other forms, others styles of playing football. Thus, the sudden superiority of the outside, of outsiders, needs an explanation, especially when it is perceived as a 'moral crisis', as the crisis of 'our tradition'. It is important to keep in mind that for Juancho the sign of crisis is associated with a state of confusion: Argentinians could not distinguish 'right from wrong'. Juancho expanded his arguments on the Argentinian tradition and the style of *la nuestra* in the following way:

> Our style, *la nuestra*, is related to the football played in the *potrero*, a small field where twenty play against twenty. There, if you get the ball you must keep it; you must hide it; you must treat it with love; you must protect it; you must flatten it; you must not give it away because if this happens you will never get it back. *La nuestra* is the cult of dribbling . . . the ball should be kept on the ground, never in the air. Our style is neither English nor Brazilian. They like to have the ball in the air: the English like to get into the penalty area as quickly as possible, and the Brazilians are known for performing the ballet they are used to. *La nuestra* is not natural; is not atavistic; it is the product of two historical circumstances: the ideology of the *potrero*, and the development over time of a certain taste (*el desarrollo de un cierto gusto*).

I observed to Juancho that what he said to me was developed many years ago by the best journalists of *El Gráfico*. He replied that 'the history belongs to all of us, and the *potrero* is a common belief in Argentina', and he added, 'I doubt if you will find someone in disagreement with the importance of the *potrero* and of taste.' Then, I asked him whether – accepting *la nuestra* as historic and related to given circumstances – changes were possible. Juancho replied:

> Of course. This happened after our defeat in Sweden in 1958. We imported what we called 'the European tradition' (*la tradición europea*), a kind of football based on physical strength and planning, collective planning with no possibility of being ourselves. No more freedom; no more creativity. The most important aspect of football was not to play but to win. We got confused, and we did get good results in the following World Cups. We must never forget our roots.

I again mentioned *El Gráfico* and the historical opposition between the creole style and the English. He remembered moments of the film of Bayer, because that opposition is presented in it, and concluded: 'Yes, we developed our style in opposition to the English, and, after all, they are Europeans.'

As I mentioned before, Durkheim insisted on the importance of taking into account moments of crisis for the analysis of moralities. Juancho is explicitly relating the crisis of a tradition to a moment of effervescence in the history of Argentinian football. He also accepts the possibility of another football morality based on other principles. He is not an essentialist; he is just traditionalist in the sense that tradition provides roots, continuity and identity. He gives morally derived interpretation based on history in the sense that choosing what is right or wrong is open. Styles of playing as a means of producing and/or reproducing identities can be seen as possibilities, as moral choices. He recognizes the existence of *la nuestra* in contrast with a style called *la tradición europea*. *La tradición europea* remains as an alternative. Thus, for Juancho, a certain football practice is a moral selection (see Evens 1993: 111–13). In his analysis, the Argentinian style, *la nuestra*, is fragile and its reproduction uncertain. He insists on *la nuestra* being an authentic style – in a typical Borocotian way of reasoning, as the social product of a collective practice in the *potrero* and as a consequence of the existence of a certain 'taste', as something that, perhaps, for many Argentinians is not fully conscious (see Evens 1993: 111). Obviously, the same could be said of others choosing *la tradición europea*.

Juancho is not alone. He presents a socially accepted narrative of the events, Bayer writes:

> The greatest shame of Argentinian football was Czechoslovakia's 6–1 victory . . . The front pages of the newspapers expressed disappointment and anger: 'Even crippled, they (the Europeans) run more than the Argentinian players', 'Argentinian football remained in the past; it exists in pre-history'. And as a reaction against the justificatory arguments of the players, a newspaper wrote: 'You must not cry as women for what you did not defend as men.' Openly, many newspapers accused the Argentinian players of lack of maleness. When they arrived at the airport of Buenos Aires they were received by a shower of coins and insults. Hundreds of fans waited with the intention of attacking them. By order of the political authorities, the tax officers confiscated all the gifts that the players had bought for their families during their stay in Europe. (Own translation 1990: 85– 6)

Bayer adds: 'the 1960s provoked a total mess in Argentinian football. They tried to change it, to modernize it, imitating the Brazilians . . . But the result was the formula of "every player back, every player a defender". Defence gained priority to the detriment of offensive football' (1990: 89).

Lázaro, in an interesting essay on the ethical and political language in Argentinian football, also comments on the events of 1958:

> We were prepared to show to the entire world our daring stamp, our childlike tenderness, our innocent wiliness, and we were quite sure that when they saw us they would love us. We thought to sow in the sons of school discipline, in the sad kids of the cold European countries, the joy of the *potrero* and the feast of abundance. In this spirit our players, the coach and the happy and optimistic journalists, guardians of the purity of the doctrine (*la nuestra*) and the doctrine of purity, left Argentina . . . The disaster in Sweden is the origin of the maelstrom of Argentinian thought. More than a maelstrom, it will be a whirlwind. The old chain of virtues that distinguished the Argentinian creole will break into halves. One half will softly whisper about the 'past times' when it was a great pleasure to watch Argentinians play football. The other half will always find arguments for demanding a radical change of mentality. This bifocal ethic will sweep across the world of football transforming it into a fertile field for ethical and political debates. (Own translation 1993: 31)[5]

With Juancho as well as with Lázaro some common key arguments are at work: the importance of the *potrero*; the style of *la nuestra* as an expression of virtues related to childhood; innocence, creativity, tenderness and the picaresque; the acceptance of the quality of football as an innocent game will vanish if maturity, speculation and planning replace the childish spirit that every man has inside; the concern for the purity of a doctrine (*la nuestra*); the relevance of keeping a tradition in order to avoid intellectual and moral confusion. The *potrero* as a perceived space of freedom is related to childhood. We can say that football, like other games, is opposed to work, duties and family obligations. It is interesting to note that in Argentina many of the great players are defined as *pibes*.[6] They also agree, like Bayer, on the historical impact of the débâcle in Sweden because, since then, two moralities have coexisted in Argentinian football.

It is interesting to notice that in this narrative the image of a 'child' (without a father) is seen as very positive, as a potent image of freedom and creativity, while being a 'son' (with a 'father') is defined as negative, as an indication of subordination and control. Creativity in Argentinian football has often been related to players being imagined as 'children' who will never reach maturity, as we shall see also in the next chapter. As I pointed out before, these

narratives confront us with a plurality of male identities and moralities as created and transformed in the culture of football. [7]

In one of my latest conversations, Juancho continued to elaborate
on this problematical issue:

> We tried and tried to play like the Europeans but we lost and lost and,
> at the same time, we continued to export talented, skilful players to the
> best European clubs. It was terrible; we were without moral strength
> until Menotti was appointed coach of the national team at the end of
> 1974. With him we entered into a period . . . well, I am not afraid of
> perhaps exaggerating, we entered a period of moral regeneration.
> Menotti insisted on playing *la nuestra*, our style, while accepting that in
> order to beat Europeans what was needed was to equal them physically
> . . . I always say that with Menotti we remarried our past, our tradition . . .
> You see, this marriage was successful. With him as coach we won the
> two World Cups of 1978: first, with the senior players in Buenos Aires
> and with the junior players in Tokyo, a year later.

Juancho is right: Menotti presented himself as a kind of crusader
and his victories transformed him into a successful prophet, a very
influential and powerful prophet. He summarized his success as
coach of the national teams in the following way:

> It was necessary to find a path pooling together all our efforts in search
> of one identity. I thought that this was the secret: we had lost our
> identity; we lived running behind the 'last word' in football, trying to
> catch the last system or recipe that lay behind the last success, and in
> this way we forgot what our idiosyncrasy was. (Own translation Menotti
> 1980: 15)[8]

And more recently he has added:

> Who will put in doubt the existence of an Argentinian football style?
> An authentic national football exists, in the same way as an Argentinian
> way of life exists, and it was modelled since the origins of our nationality
> with passion, with sacrifice, with patience and with rebelliousness . . .
> Once I heard somebody say that 'there is no national football because
> football is universal'. I would say that man is universal, but that the
> best way to reach universality in any activity is 'to paint one's own
> village'. And the Argentinian football players who left the country, from
> Julio Libonatti to Diego Maradona, became well-known because they
> painted the village with the magic of the Argentinian dribbling, which
> is bantering, different, with a hallmark of identity. I dare to say that

I could recognize in any pitch of the entire world an Argentii
player . . . In our past the way of playing was intimately related to oui
sentiments . . . This made possible the survival of a line, of a style,
modelling *la nuestra.* It was the acceptance of the good taste that was
not only present in football but also in the way of clothing, in the music,
in the dance, in the customs . . . Football must also be measured with
aesthetic criteria). . Happily, the aesthetics and the good taste of
Argentinians are unchanged, and they believe more and more in our
style, in *la nuestra.* (Own translation Menotti 1994a: 51)

On the day of the victory of the Argentinian team in 1978 in the
finals against Holland, Menotti coined a phrase that has since
become installed in the collective memory of Argentinian football
lovers: 'our victory is a tribute to the old and glorious Argentinian
football' (Bayer 1990: 113).

The crucial defeats are not seen only as acts of treason. Tomás,
in his late forties, always insisted on pointing out the fact that these
kinds of defeats are critical because they bring about unhappiness
in the way that victories obtained with beauty and elegance bring
about happiness. In our conversations Tomás consistently presented
non-controversial assumptions related to the importance of cona-
tive–emotional dispositions for the analysis of morality in football.
He insisted on the importance for a football lover to allow himself
to become emotionally aroused by various types of situations experienced in a football stadium (for example, being ready to feel shame
or indignation if beauty was lacking, or becoming happy when it
was manifested). I believe that he is a convinced relativist: he
accepted the existence of different values, exemplified by the
successful coaches Menotti and Bilardo, which represented the
contrasting values of *la nuestra* and of discipline and tactical organi-
ization; he also acknowledged the fact that these differences are
fundamental for achieving a proper understanding of Argentinian
football history. He contended that these disagreements could not
be eliminated, since they were important for maintaining ethical
diversity. He said to me several times: 'it is important for Argentinians to agree on the issues that divide us'. He made an important
distinction between 'being happy' and 'feeling happy'.[9] He explicitly
denied that football will bring about a well-balanced psychological
state in which one's total life pattern and the general circumstances
permitting 'being happy' are matched. For him, 'feeling happy' at
the terraces was related to certain emotions. Happiness in this way
is associated to a species of joy in regard to one's partial situation.

ιat, in this sense, football can function as a
ɔne's negative total situation, but 'this is not my
ly told me.

.sion

In this chapter I have presented an ethnographic account of some
of the complex relations between masculinities and moralities in
Argentinian football. The presentation of findings followed four
empirical fields:

1. Male virtues.
2. The importance of traditions, roots and historical continuity.
3. The meaning of styles and ways of playing football.
4. Ideas, concerns and definitions of 'happiness' and 'feeling
   happy'.

In considering the process of hybridization in football the first
three fields were also treated. It is obvious that many possible topics
could have been taken into account, particularly those pertaining
to the field of rules and sanctions governing the game (see Nilsson
1993). One of my main theoretical aims has been to show that the
analysis of moralities needs to combine the aspect of desire and
the emotive character of male morality in concrete ritual practice.
Football is, and I hope that this has been made clear to the reader,
a very privileged arena in a country like Argentina.

The narratives of Argentinian football are presented by my
informants in a prototypical form, using common discursive symbols
and producing a plurality of moral meanings (see Rapport 1997).
The actors themselves, through their narratives, bring time and
history into the fabric of their lives and vivid experiences. Johnson
(1993: 152) argues that a central task for any moral theory must
be to explain how actors narratively construct their lives and how
their deliberations are framed by those narratives. In this chapter
the focus is on the moral discourses and concerns of mature football 'aficionados'. From this perspective the Durkheimian moments
of effervescence, which make possible critical moral reflections,
will vary for different social actors who represent different generations and class. To my informants 1930, 1958 and 1974 – the defeat
by Holland in the World Cup in Germany – were key years; these

were the years of shame and humiliation for Argentinian national football – and, as a consequence, for male Argentinians' national self-esteem. For the young supporters the year of 1993 has been, and, I am quite sure, will be in the future, a year of shame and confusion. In October 1993, in a qualifying match for the World Cup in 1994, Colombia defeated Argentina 5–0 in Buenos Aires.[10] Juancho expresses what many Argentinians felt when he said:

> In the future, even for us old people, the defeat by Colombia will be seen as perhaps more important than the other setbacks. You see, Argentinians taught Colombians to play football; they were, for years and years, our son; they respected and admired us, and now they humiliate us. I feel bad, not only because of the five goals but mostly because they play our way; they play *la nuestra*, and we play nothing.

I was at the stadium of River Plate that night, and I think that what I, together with seventy thousand supporters, experienced was quite special. I agree with Juancho that Colombians played our way; the public applauded them, and as it did so the Argentinian national team was morally punished. During long periods in the second half, the crowd did not support the national team; it just cried: 'Maradooo . . . Maradooo . . . Maradooo . . . Maradooo', demanding his comeback – which he did after the match, announcing that he was going to save the national team from this disaster.

The story of Lalin and Seoane and the confrontations on the meaning of different male virtues, styles of playing and ways of achieving happiness illustrate the 'painful coexistence', as one informant put it to me, of contrasting moralities in Argentinian football. Social actors are exposed to contradictions and paradoxes in the construction of moral meanings. Thus identity, *la nuestra*, can be seen as atavistic or as a product of choice. Tomás, with his relativistic position, accepting and tolerating contradictory moral standpoints, is a clear example of the dynamics of moral choice.

The histories of Argentinian football have been written about in popular books and are continuously written, every day and every week, in journals and sport magazines. Moreover, in a regular fashion its visual history is displayed on television or can be bought via the extremely large collection of football videos that now exist in the Argentinian market. My main argument in this chapter has been the following: the present moral discourses of social actors are embedded in history; the actors use history and their own life stories, or, better perhaps, they construct historical representations of football and themselves as supporters in order to find meaning and to argue about what is correct and what is wrong or what are the ways of feeling happy. I believe that by using the voices of Héctor, Juancho, Juan José and Tomás this argument has been made clear. This chapter can be seen as an example of the imaginative synthesizing power of moral narratives. The importance of Maradona in the epos of Argentinian football will be analysed in the next chapter.

Notes

1. Large sections of this chapter have been published elsewhere (Archetti 1997a). The structure of argument has been maintained, although changes have been introduced.
2. There is an important emotional dimension in this story. Lalin, the most celebrated insider in the late 1920s, was supposed to play in the World Cup of 1930. He was injured in 1929 and, after an unsuccessful operation, was obliged to retire from football at the age of 23. Seoane, on the contrary, played on the Argentinian team without great success. It is my firm belief that the dramatic end of Lalin's carrier was important in the creation and reproduction of the story. We shall see in the next chapter, moreover, that Lalin, being so young and technical, belonged to the plethora of *pibes* (young players), whom Argentinians admire the most.
3. Valdano was a successful player who, after leaving Argentina at the age of 19, triumphed in the Spanish teams of Alavés, Zaragoza and Real Madrid. He played for the World Cup winning national team of Argentina in 1986 in Mexico. Retired, he began a new career as a journalist and writer. Valdano's writings on football are of excellent literary quality (1997), and he has edited a beautiful book in which well-known 'serious' South American and Spanish contemporary writers write on football (1995).
4. The dichotomy *serio* and *alegre* was related to the style of different first-division teams (see *El Gráfico* 1949, 1549: 8–12). We can see that the Lalin–Seoane contradiction is reproduced at the collective level, creating contradictory styles. If we accept this historical reconstruction which was also related to the 'taste' of the supporters, Argentinian football, since its beginning, was divided into different club identities and styles (see *El Gráfico* no. 636, 1931: 13). *El Gráfico* was obliged to find in the 'joyful style' the expression of the Argentinian style, of *la nuestra*. In the essentialist perspective of *El Gráfico* the 'national style' must be a product of a superior and more authentic tradition.

5. Behind the pseudonym 'Lázaro' hides a prestigious Argentinian professional philosopher educated at La Sorbonne.

6. For example, Diego Maradona is called *el pibe de oro* (the golden young boy). To be a *pibe* is related to freshness, authenticity of feelings and extreme creativity. In Argentina, a football aficionado usually expects to see 'real football' when it is played by the *pibes* and the *fútbol-pibe* is opposed to 'normal football' (see *El Clarín Deportivo*, 2/5/1994: 4). The calculating and conservative style of playing is always associated with maturity, with losing freshness (*perder la frescura*). This will be explored in more detail in the next chapter.

7. The Argentinians have always enjoyed the victories of the national under-21 junior teams. The junior teams have played four World Cup finals and won three, while the senior teams, playing the same number of finals, won only two. The last two junior World Cup was won by the Argentinians.

8. Dante Panzeri, a brilliant writer and sports journalist of *El Gráfico*, defended the Argentinian style, *la nuestra*, in the 1950s and 1960s against the imposition of European systems and tactical discipline. For Panzeri the essence of football beauty was expressed in the unexpected, in the improvising and creative capacity of individual players. He believed that 'systems' kill fantasy. His concise definition of *la nuestra*, as a matter of 'Argentinian taste', is, for me, the best: 'our taste regarding good football implies a way of playing with short passes, low balls, penetrating, subtle, from the backs to the strikers' (*El Gráfico* no. 2020, 1958: 39).

9. Menotti has elaborated on the meaning of 'happiness' in football (see Menotti 1993, 1994b). He has constantly repeated the formula: 'Football was always a beautiful pretext for being happy' (*el fútbol fue siempre una hermosa excusa para ser feliz*).

10. Since the 1930s Colombia was a 'land of mission' for Argentinian coaches and players. This was made evident in the late 1940s when some of the most important players of the Argentinian professional league emigrated *en masse* to Colombia after a long strike for better wages and contracts (see Pedernera 1993: 72-6). In 1941, Fernando Paternoster, a mythological full back of Racing Club and the national team which played the World Cup finals in 1930, emphasized the importance of Argentinian football as both a model and an ideal for Colombian youth (*El Gráfico* 1941, 1123: 9; see also Giordano 1955: 533). Also Colombians from very early on adopted and adored the tango. The mythical Argentinian tango singer Carlos Gardel died in 1935 in an aeroplane crash in Medellin, Colombia.

CHAPTER SEVEN

The Masculine Imagery of Freedom: the World of *Pibes* and Maradona

Introduction: the *Pibe* and the *Potrero*

The first part of the book presented, in great detail, *El Gráfico*'s ideological construct of a national style of playing football, opposed to that of the English. In this context, and with this accepted view of a collective style, Borocotó developed the theory of '*criollo* dribbling' in 1928 (*El Gráfico* no. 470, 1928). The creation of this style is not only *criollo*, but, more concretely, is the product of the *pibes criollos*, of the young boys playing football. This theory is based on the personal qualities of the *pibes* and their relation to the social and spatial contexts that allowed them to develop these qualities. In the first place, the *pibe criollo* realized, when he saw how the English played, that this style of play left no room for improvisation, for 'imagination'. Secondly, the *pibes* played football spontaneously in the *potreros* – the empty and uneven urban spaces – without any teachers, unlike in England where, according to Borocotó, football was integral to the school system. In the *potreros*, with so many other players in such a confined space, the only way to keep control of the ball for some time was by becoming an inveterate dribbler. Thirdly, Borocotó recalls that Argentinian football has become known because of dribbling, and that the players leaving Argentina to play in Europe are the best dribblers. He argues emphatically that until 1928 Argentina had been known throughout the world for exporting its valuable frozen beef and its quality cereals, 'non-popular products' – in the sense that they came from the estates of the *pampa* – owned by landowning classes; now it is important that Argentina should become known for its 'popular products'.

One of the high-quality 'popular products' is dribbling, and its exponents are the exquisite Argentinian football players.

In this theory the *pibe* (the boy), without any form of teaching, is clearly the inventor of the *criollo* style in the *potrero*. This image of Borocotó emphasizes not only that there was an infantile beginning, as in every game, but also the importance of the freshness, spontaneity and freedom which are associated with childhood and usually lost with the advent of maturity and its resulting responsibilities. Borocotó proposes that Argentina should raise a monument in 'any walkway' to the inventor of dribbling. This monument would have to be:

> A *pibe* with a dirty face, a mane of hair rebelling against the comb; with intelligent, roving, trickster and persuasive eyes and a sparkling gaze that seem to hint a picaresque laugh that does not quite manage to form on his mouth, full of small teeth that might be worn down through eating 'yesterday's bread'. His trousers are a few roughly sewn patches; his vest with Argentinian stripes, with a very low neck and with many holes eaten out by the invisible mice of use. A strip of material tied to his waist and crossing over his chest like a sash serves as braces. His knees covered with the scabs of wounds disinfected by fate; barefoot or with shoes whose holes in the toes suggest that they have been made through so much shooting. His stance must be characteristic; it must seem as if he is dribbling with a rag ball. That is important: the ball cannot be any other. A rag ball and preferably bound by an old sock. If this monument is raised one day, there will be many of us who will take off our hat to it, as we do in church. (Own translation *El Gráfico* no. 470, 1928: 15)

In the canonical narrative of *El Gráfico* the privileged image of the ideal player is the *pibe*: the authentic Argentinian player will never stop being a child. Football allows a man to go on playing and remain a *pibe*. One could say that the imaginary world of football reflects the power of freedom and creativity in the face of discipline, order and hierarchy. *Pibes* are liminal figures and *potreros* are territories where freedom and creativity are experienced. In the account of *El Gráfico* – and of my informants as will be clear in the next section – the Argentinian style is seen in the mirror offered by the liminal figures of the *pibes*. Let me now present how these ideas persist in contemporary Argentina.

Maradona: the Saga of the *Pibe de Oro*

Maradona is, without doubt, the most famous contemporary Argentinian football star. He has been world champion twice, once with the junior national team, and for several years he played for the best sides in Europe.[1] Maradona is still called *el pibe de oro* (the golden young boy); hence the other great *pibes* of the history of Argentinian football are metaphorically made of silver or bronze, less prestigious metals. Moreover, Maradona was discovered as a prodigious player at the age of 10, and, by the age of 12, the media declared that Argentinian football had never had such a talent. At 15 he played his first league match for Argentinos Juniors in the first division. At 16 he was admired by the people as a precious gift to the nation. At 17 he played his first international match with the national team. At 18, as captain, he won the first gold medal for Argentina in the Junior World Cup in Tokyo. At 26, as captain, he won the second goal medal for Argentina in the World Cup in Mexico City. His precocity and, of course, his ability were a confirmation of his quality as a *pibe*.

Tomás explained to me that:

> To be a *pibe* is not only to be liberated from several responsibilities. To be a *pibe* is to feel pressure from the authority of the family, the parents, the school. But also to be a *pibe* implies that it is easier to see the positive aspects and to forgive the imperfections. It is common to say in Argentina, and perhaps in a lot of places too, 'but he is a *pibe*, just a *pibe*; let him be a *pibe*'. Maradona is a *pibe* and will remain a *pibe*. He represents this state of perfection and freedom when we disregard the most negative traits of an individual. Spontaneity, to be fresh and to do things just right away without thinking of the negative consequences are qualities that we appreciate. A great football player must have these qualities.

Tomás is, in many ways, less idealist than Borocotó: to be a *pibe* is to feel the pressure coming from the family and the society at large and to be imperfect. The imperfections, in his interpretation, are related to what is expected from a mature person. Maradona, a real *pibe*, is not perfect as a man but he is perfect as a player. His perfection is attained, and kept, because he is still a *pibe*. He, like the case of Peucelle in the first part, has the *potrero* in his heart.

For many years, and without any doubt for most of my informants, Maradona looked like a *pibe*. They would say that he really looked like a happy *pibe* when he received the World Cup trophy in Mexico City in 1986. This image is perhaps the most perfect symbol of his achievements and global fame. Moreover, he seemed like a 'naughty child' and, for that reason, he had not yet lost his freshness. This paradox, a mature young man at the top of his career being defined as a *pibe*, is significant: an important virtue for the best Argentinian players is to preserve as far as possible, this pure, childlike style. Through this image football is conveyed as a game and, as such, can only be fully enjoyed when one has total freedom. Football is ideally perceived as a perfect game for children.

Another forceful image emerged in the memory of my informants. Sergio, a man in his late twenties and a devoted follower of Maradona's exploits, remembered well a 'historical television programme with Maradona, a real *pibe* at that time'. He told me that, when Maradona was 12 years old, Pipo Mancera, at that time a famous television entertainer, showed Maradona juggling with a ball, doing incredible things that even a worshipped professional player would have enormous difficulty imitating. After a minute of juggling, 'a minute that was eternal due to its beauty' according to Sergio, Mancera asked Maradona what his dreams, as a football player, were; without hesitation he answered that he had three dreams: to play in the first-division league, to wear the shirt of the Argentinian national team in a World Cup and to win it. Sergio explained to me:

> It was like in the famous tango *El sueño del pibe* [The *pibe*'s dream], do you remember? But Maradona was more aspiring and conscious of his capacity. Well, the lyrics narrate the story of a talented *pibe* who, while crying for joy, shows to his mother a letter from his club telling him that he has been accepted as a player in the junior team. During that night he dreams that, like so many crack Argentinian players, he will reach the First Division and that in his début he will score the winning goal. Look, in this tango the *pibe* is a forward, and he scores after dribbling past all the defenders. Defenders ought to look and to perform like real men, not forwards or midfielders.

This image has been used hundred of times in Argentina and international television programmes devoted to the life of Maradona. The perfect synchronicity of the performance, the age of the performer and his future career parallel real life with the flavour and melodrama of a soap opera. Maradona has the benefit of the shape of his body. It is easy to associate his status of *pibe* with his

height, his roundness, his tendency to be fat, his sudden acceleration, his theatrical exaggeration, his way of walking with short
movements, and his constant struggle against rude and aggressive
defenders. In long periods of his career Maradona has looked
casual, unkempt and unfit and, in many ways, inelegant.

The meaning of the *pibe* is related to a cluster of features that
promote and limit the social construction of the stereotype. One
such feature is the small body, particularly in terms of height. In
addition to body shape, the content of bodily performances seems
to be another important feature. The image of a typical *pibe* player
is based on an exuberance of skill, cunning, individual creativity,
artistic feeling, vulnerability and improvisation. In this sense it is
easy to understand that the image of a powerful, disciplined and
perfect athletic body is absent. A third, related feature is the kind
of daily life *pibes* lead. In the case of a *pibe*, a lot of disorder is
expected. Chaotic behaviour is the norm. There is a tendency to
disregard boundaries, to play games even in private life – life is
experienced as a permanent game, or gamble. There is a capacity:
to recompense, penalize or forgive others in an exaggerated way;
to convey arbitrary judgments and choices; to display stupid and
irrational heroism; to 'die' – by being, as in the case of Maradona,
imprisoned and a drugg addict – and to be resurrected; to have a
special talent in critical games to make the unexpected move,
ensuring victory for the team. Maradona left football three times,
and he came back three times – one of them as the leader of the
team in the World Cup of 1990. Thus, a perfect *pibe* is creative,
free of strong feelings of guilt, self-destructive and, eventually, a
bad moral example to other players. Knowing this, Maradona
always argued that he was not a moral example for other players
or for children. In the global moral evaluation of this kind of player,
the ultimate criterion is the creativity of their bodies. My informants, and I imagine supporters in general, tend to forgive the lack
of moral and social responsibility of the *pibes*. In this sense, Maradona
is not alone. Explicitly, the amount of joy given by the *pibes* is more
important than any consistent moral evaluation.

As I have pointed out we can classify the *pibes* as liminal, as being
on a threshold, in a Turnerian state of 'betwixt and between', a
kind of transformative period (Turner 1969). The *pibes* are perhaps
the most typical products of the 'free zones' of cultural creativity
that I have discussed in previous chapters. My informants, however,
put stress on the fact that, in football, 'once a *pibe*, always a *pibe*'. I

hope that it has been made clear that the category of *pibe* is marked by ambiguity, ambivalence and contradictions, because the model of interpretation is based on potential disorder: *pibes* will not become mature men. The recognition of liminal attributes makes possible the differentiation of players and of particular bodies and performances. The image of the *pibe*'s body, as we have seen above, is the image of imperfection. Liminal individuals provide an object of identification that appeals to the subjects who are establishing the differences. Identifying a typical *pibe* in the cultural construction of football has the power of evocation. My informants recognize the 'eternal *pibe*' condition in some men – even among themselves – through identification with players like Maradona. This process involves the differentiation of qualities proper to an established dominant model of masculinity, based on reason and responsibility, from those alien to it. The *pibes* serve as mirrors and, at the same time, operate as models defining a style, a way of playing. The image of Maradona contains these two aspects.

Maradona as a *pibe* is defined as the archetype, as defining the boundaries with adult players. In the world of freedom of the *pibes* there is no room for disciplined, powerful and cynical men. Maradona helps to fix the fundamental line separating the two categories. Maradona is perceived by my informants as a key figure in a rite that consecrates the crucial difference between kinds of players (see Bourdieu 1991: 117). He is thought of as the more pure product of a 'natural nature'. Maradona as a *pibe* is a natural product and is the mythical – albeit historical – fulfilment of an idea of football based on the naturalization of some playing qualities – what we can call Borocotian logic. He becomes the living statue of the *pibe* imagined by Borocotó forty years before. Tomás enunciated this in the following way:

> Maradona is like a gift from God, or from nature if you are not a believer. In Argentina there is a mythical style of playing football that has at last been realized in the body and the performances of Maradona. Thus, to be a *pibe* is something that cannot be explained; it is like this, and that is all. We must accept it.

What Tomás is telling us is that a *pibe* is a *pibe*, a natural condition that must be known and recognized by himself and the rest of us. The first consequence is that in the presence of the *pibes* we must be indulgent. We, adult men – and women – must transform our

conduct; we must adapt to them. The second consequence is that
the *pibes* are themselves obliged to behave in a subtle way that
reproduces this representation; Maradona, the real and ideal *pibe*,
is neither reasonable nor responsible in real life, and it is not
expected that he will be different. Maradona creates himself as
potently as others create him.

Does Maradona, being defined – and dreamed of – as a *pibe*,
abandon his true nature? If for a moment we imagine that he did,
how would his supporters react? In the dramatic theatre of football,
mirrors and models are created and reproduced. In this process,
social and personal identifications fuse in a pervasive and, perhaps,
perverse way. Maradona is himself a concrete individual, and, at
the same time, a kind of archetypical person representing a style
and a mythical condition. Tomás clearly expressed this idea:

> You imagine the *pibes* as the best players, as being a part of our style,
> our way of playing; then, suddenly, the most perfect one appears. It is
> perfect. It is the movies; it is a videotape. You have been dreaming
> along with thousands and thousands of football fanatics, and one day
> your dream is transformed into a reality.

The assurance of Tomás and other informants, without one single
exception, made me feel that an entire nation had been waiting
for this occasion to materialize. The figure and the performance
of Maradona can be seen not only as the continuation of *el mito
del pibe* (the myth of the *pibe*) but also as its most perfect mythical
realization.

To be and to remain a *pibe* is a powerful image, because in football
the most creative period of some players is associated with imma-
turity. My informants do not deny the role of experience and the
passing of the years (*el paso de los años*) in the development of
physical automatization and tactical sense. These qualities are
considered important for expected performances. But a *pibe* is by
definition an unpredictable player, finding unexpected solutions
in the most difficult moments of a game. The magic of Maradona
is always understood as a performing skill, for it produces inexplic-
able effects and illusions, paralysing opposing players and charming
his audience. This is defined as a powerful, bewitching quality.

The imagery of Maradona is even more complete because he is
the product of one of the poorest neighbourhoods of Buenos Aires,
where *potreros* still exist. He was born in Villa Fiorito in 1960, and

one could write that 'everything started in Villa Fiorito, a forever forgotten neighbourhood where prosperity never arrived, on a remote day . . . in a humble house' (Casas and Chacón 1996: 5). It is easy to presume that in Villa Fiorito the streets were without asphalt and there was a plethora of *potreros*. The most original Argentinian player comes from the *potrero* of Fiorito which is now used as a mythical name, as the essence of the *potrero* (see Fontanarrosa and Sanz 1994: 53–4). We are not told to which school Maradona went (this is not important), and we get to know that when he joined his first serious club he was already an outstanding player (Gilbert 1996: 17). What has not been learnt in the *potrero* cannot be taught elsewhere. Carlos explained to me:

> Maradona is pure *potrero*, even when he is not playing football. Well, I can put it this way: he still lacks civilized manners, and he has obvious problems in accepting boundaries and control. In the *potrero* life you learn how to be free and to improvise. Later in life you realize that this situation is temporary, then you change and adapt to society. This even happens in a football club, and this is the role of managers and trainers. In addition, trainers will try hard to teach players new tricks, to be better technically and to think in tactical terms. Thus, you will hear some players saying that they are thankful to a given coach because he taught them many things or because they became accomplished players due to his knowledge and advice. Well, you never heard that Maradona said that someone taught him anything. I believe this is true. His knowledge and capacity for inventing new tricks are something that is impossible to learn from a coach. On the contrary, I will postulate that his creativity is a victory against discipline and training. You can write, if you want, that his accomplishment is the victory of the *potrero*. I assure you that I am not exaggerating .

Carlos said it in an elegant way: 'the victory of the *potrero*', and this sentence synthesizes decades of Argentinian imagery construction, and, at the same time, historical realization. The reproduction of a prima facie arbitrary imagery needs some kind of historical outstanding marks. Maradona has permitted myth and history to reunite for the Argentinian masculine imagery.

This was clear in many of my conversations. My informants insisted on the importance of situating Carlos's arguments historically. Special emphasis was put on the fact that Maradona appeared as a player at a moment when national and international football was dominated by ideas of the superiority of elaborated tactical systems, based on an integrated, machine-like team. The international dominance of Dutch and German football in the 1970s was related to these aspects. Franz Beckenbauer and Johan Cruyff were perceived as emblematic players, but they were great because they had the quality to intensify the performance of their team-mates. In other words, their influence upon their teams surpassed their own ability. They were the main components in complex and well-lubricated engines. Maradona, however, always impregnated the teams for which he played with his solitary and unique style. Sergio used the metaphor of the aroma of the *potrero*:

> The teams which Diego, the *pibe*, played for were transformed by his aroma. His aroma was in a way the aroma of the *potrero* of Villa Fiorito. I mean, an aroma that you cannot resist and that will follow him all his life. I do not like it when people say that he has the *potrero* in his blood. Well, this is perhaps true, but I prefer to imagine the *potrero* and its aroma.[2]

By Way of Conclusion

My informants did not read Borocotó, but some had seen the film *Pelota de trapo* (1948). In this film the world of children and their passion for football reaches 'cosmological dimension', according to Manucho. They were not really astonished when I presented, in great detail, Borocotó's ideas on the role of *pibes* and *potreros* in the creation of a football mythology. They perceived themselves as part of a 'national narrative', as Carlos said, and they remembered articles in *El Gráfico*, in other magazines, in *Clarín*, the largest Argentinian newspaper, and discussions on television where the importance of belonging to a territory (the *potrero*) was crucial in the definition of a football style. We agreed that Maradona transformed a myth into reality and automatically reproduced it. Sergio said: 'now our problem is that we have had Maradona, and we will always expect to get another one'. This illustrates the power of mythical accounts. We concluded by agreeing that new Maradonas would appear only in the world of *pibes* and *potreros*. We were full of optimism and completely utopian.

In a global scene the production of local territories and identities is supposedly difficult because the life worlds of local subjects – at least it is stated all the time in anthropology and in the media –

tend to become deterritorialized, diasporic and transnational; Argentinians have framed the opposite view. The tango has been produced in Buenos Aires and placed partially in the life of cabarets. The best polo players from the Argentinian pampas permitted a reunification of the past and the present through the powerful imagery of the gauchos. It is unthinkable to conceive of a possible contradiction between the *potrero* and the *pibe* and a mode of belonging to the imagery of a national style. It should by now be clear that the *potrero*, the *pibe*, the gaucho-like polo player, as well as the *milonguita*, the *compadrito* and the *bacán* pertain to a mythical account which reproduces a tradition and a multiple and complex masculine world. In this world there is no room for the family, work and fatherhood. This national male imagery is not the official one. All these liminal figures become signs of the nation because they are, in many and dissimilar ways, ambivalent and ambiguous, and they threaten well-established moral codes. Manucho, as always, expressed it in a poetic and synthetic way: 'We Argentinians like to imagine ourselves as active, free, without many obligations, with a lot of free time, because only in this state can one be creative; and who is not interested in being creative and perceived by others as such?'

Notes

1. I have published an ethnographic account of the cult of Maradona in Argentina (see Archetti 1997c). On the complex symbolic relations between Maradona and national identity and politics in Argentina see Rodríguez (1996, 1998).
2. Maradona has refused to be identified with a national tradition. His talent is an individual and 'divine gift'. He has often declared that he is touched by the magic of God and not by the power of his Argentinian football ancestors (see *Corriere della Sera* 11 November 1985: 1). However, he usually accepts that he learned everything as a *pibe* in the Argentinian *potreros*. In his lecture at the Oxford Union Debating Chamber on 6 November 1995 he clearly stated that he is a *pibe*, a pure product of *potreros* (John King, personal communication). Maradona's account, at this level, is empirical and entirely related to his lived experience. My Argentinian informants move further, making the connection between individual cases and a football tradition thereby partaking in the production – and reproduction – of an ideological account.

Epilogue

I am conscious that to read about football, polo and the tango has not been an easy task. The reader has been obliged to change subject on several occasions, and, of course, a genuine interest in the history and ethnography of football does not necessarily presuppose the acceptance that polo or the tango are important clues for getting a better understanding of Argentinian masculinities or masculinities at all. I am also aware of the fact that the rules and the meaning of polo, being a minority sport practised by Argentinian landlords and their sons, by British aristocrats, American millionaires and exotic princes of distant places like Borneo or Malaysia, is not a part of the standard knowledge of social scientists. I expected, therefore, the goodwill of the reader, and I counted on the contemporary global popularity of football and the tango.

I did not want to leave my conclusions to the last chapter, and the reader, therefore, has been obliged to follow the complex interaction between the theoretical and the empirical findings in the different parts of this book. Moreover, I do not know how successful my strategy has been for putting together different histories, fields and bodily practices in a comparative perspective guided by the scrutiny of selected same-sex and cross-sex relations in Argentinian history and society. I hope that I have been able to show that while same-sex relations in football and polo have traits that are exclusive to men, cross-sex relations, as in the case of the tango, make it possible to transcend this exclusivity. Images of men need images of women as well as of 'other' men. The technical ability and individualism of the Argentinian football player called for the contrasting image of the disciplined and collectively orientated English player. The physical strength and moral courage of the Argentinian polo player required the conservative and restrained figure of the English rider. The romanticism and fidelity of the man displayed in the tango asked to be accompanied by the image of a free woman – a kind of local *femme fatale*, the *milonguita*, leaving the social and emotional roots of the *barrio* and home for the excitement of cabaret. My findings indicate that once the differences between same-sex and cross-sex relations are taken into account, the complexities of masculinities – and gender – as an empirical field of investigation become evident. I hope my book can be seen as a contribution to this field of enquiry and debate, in which the works of Mosse opened new paths for historical and sociological comparisons.

Performing Bodies in Latin America: a Comparative Perspective on Sport, Music and Dance

In the prologue I mentioned the importance of the anthropological research on football and dance in Brazil inspired by the early publications of DaMatta (1978, 1982). DaMatta problematized the 'national' through the analysis of carnival, a central ritual in Brazilian society, and the construction of popular heroes – the villains. This paved the way to an examination of football. Since the 1930s Brazilians of all races and mixtures have achieved great success and worldwide recognition of their excellence in this sport. Brazil, according to DaMatta, is a society articulated by the sharp division between the 'home' and the 'street', and between the family – a system of hierarchical social relations and persons – and the market and free individuals. For DaMatta these divisions are less geographical or physical places than symbols of moral and ideological universes. The role of football is privileged because the personalized social world of the home and the impersonal universe of the street are combined in a public ritual (1982: 17). Impersonal rules regulating the game make possible the expression of individual qualities: 'football, in the Brazilian society, is a source of individualization . . . much more than an instrument of collectivization at the personal level' (1982: 27). The players escape from fate – the fate of class or race – and construct their own successful biographies in an open arena. Football makes it possible to experience male equality and freedom of creativity in hierarchical contexts. In order to triumph, a football player (like a *samba* dancer) must have *jogo de cintura*, the capacity to use the body to provoke confusion and fascination in the public and in their adversaries (1982: 28). A disciplined, athletic but boring player has no place in Brazilian football imagery (1982: 39). The similarities with the Argentinian imagery are, of course, striking.

The victory in the 1958 World Cup, later consolidated in 1962 and 1970, with a 'multiracial' team – a hybrid representing racial complexity and democratization – confirmed the excellence of the Brazilian style. Leite Lopes (1997) maintains that the Brazilian style of football resembles physical activities which have ethnic Afro-Brazilian origins, like the *samba* or *capoeira* (a martial sport of African origin) (see also Roberts 1972: 26–9). The European identification of a Brazilian style of playing relating football and the *samba*, manifested in the expression '*samba*-football', is therefore not an arbitrary creation; it is rooted in Brazilian self-imagery and identity. This identification establishes important cultural differences, because the existence and development of European styles of playing football are not linked to music and dance.

The first baseball match in Cuba was played in Matanzas in 1874, and four years later the first *danzón*, the seed of the *salsa*, was composed. González Echeverría (1994) maintains that music and baseball – together with literature – are the Cuban cultural products of greatest prestige and international recognition, and therefore essential as the founding myths of the 'national' in Cuba (see also González Echeverría 1998). Baseball, a North American creation imported into Cuba by the sons of the sugar plantation aristocracy, was rapidly seen as a weapon of 'resistance' against colonialism and primitive Spanish games such as bullfighting. González Echeverría writes that 'baseball was an integral part of the patriotic and anti-Spanish ideology which led towards independence' (1994: 73). By 1890 baseball had been accepted by the Hispanic and black working-class population, becoming a very popular bodily activity. From the beginning the ritual of playing was associated with dancing: 'each baseball match culminated in a magnificent dinner and dancing, for which orchestras were hired for playing *danzones*' (1994: 74). As in the case of football in Argentina and Brazil, baseball was perceived as a democratic and modern game that made it possible for young players of modest origins to experience social mobility.

It is quite interesting that both baseball and football, two team sports which originated outside the Latin American countries, were integrated into the construction of 'national masculinities'. 'Thinking national' was, thus, a typically modernist project because it was fabricated by the introduction of foreign cultural practices and not by the revival or invention of traditions – and the same can be said of the creation of the *samba*, *danzón* and *tango*. The Cuban national sport is still baseball, and outstanding players are still produced by the hundreds in the island. Baseball in Cuba, like football in Brazil and Argentina, is not related to the tradition of national romanticism that was dominant in other countries of the region.

I expect that the reader has been convinced that the Argentinian case confirms this historical and sociological trend. However, my results also demonstrate that this picture is more intricate. The creation of 'national masculinities' in Argentina combined the urban – football and the tango – with the rural – polo. This imagery reflected the fragmented, dislocated and mismatched identities, the changing character of the social classes, and gender relations where, in the tango, men and women were at the centre. I have shown that in the rapidly modernizing pampas the gauchos existed as pre-modern and romantic figures, reminding urban Argentinians and immigrants of the existence of a traditional past. With polo, a gaucho tradition was reconstituted in a context of modern competition, and it was extended to the other practices. In a newspaper chronicle published in 1932, Arlt, one of the greatest modern Argentinian writers, disagreed on the extensive use of the idea of 'gaucho' to everything that could be defined as Argentinian: polo players with names like Miles, Lacey, Harrington or Nelson; tango orchestras with musicians with names like Cattaruzzo, Nijisky, Duprot or Müller; tango singers singing tangos that had nothing to do with rural scenarios; and football players who played with '*creole* courage', 'gaucho enthusiasm' or with a 'typical *pampa* technique' (Arlt 1994: 101–4). Arlt did not realize that what he wrote confirmed that the model of transformation and hybridization was working well because immigrants in general – and independently of ethnic origin or class identification – were 'creolized' and converted into 'gauchos'. Modernism embraced romanticism. The new 'male – and female – hybrids' became models of change and tradition, of cultural continuity and creativity.

Bibliography

Abu-Lughod, L. and Lutz, C. A. (1990), 'Introduction: Emotion, Discourse, and the Politics of Everyday Life', in C. A. Lutz and L. Abu-Lughod (eds), *Language and the Politics of Emotion*, Cambridge: Cambridge University Press.

Alabarces, P. (1996), 'Fútbol y cine', in P. Alabarces and M. G. Rodríguez (eds), *Cuestión de pelotas*, Buenos Aires: Atuel.

Alberdi, J. B. (1915) [1852], *Las Bases*, ed. Ricardo Rojas, Buenos Aires.

Anderson, B. (1983), *Imagined Communities. Reflections on the Origin and Spread of Nationalism*, London: Verso.

Archetti, E. P. (1985), 'Fotball og nasjonal etos', in E. D. Olsen (ed.), *Fotball – mer enn et spill*, Oslo: Cappelen.

Archetti, E. P. (1992), 'Argentinian Football: A Ritual of Violence?', *The International Journal of the History of Sport*, vol. 9, no. 2: 209–35.

Archetti, E. P. (1994), 'Models of Masculinity in the Poetics of the Argentinian Tango', in E. P. Archetti (ed.), *Exploring the Written. Anthropology and the Multiplicity of Tango*, Oslo: Scandinavian University Press.

Archetti, E. P. (1995a), 'Estilo y virtudes masculinas en *El Gráfico*: La creación del imaginario del fútbol argentino', *Desarrollo Económico*, vol. 35, no. 139: 419–42.

Archetti, E. P. (1995b), 'Nationalisme, football et polo: tradition et créolisation dans la construction de l'Argentine moderne', *Terrain*, vol. 25: 73–90.

Archetti, E. P. (1996), 'Playing Styles and Masculine Virtues in Argentine Football', in M. Melhuus and K. A. Stølen (eds), *Machos, Mistresses, Madonnas. Contesting the Power of Latin American Gender Imagery*, London: Verso.

Archetti, E. P. (1997a), 'The Moralities of Argentinian Football', in S. Howell (ed.), *The Ethnography of Moralities*, London: Routledge.

Archetti, E. P. (1997b), '"And Give Joy to my Heart": Ideology and Emotion in the Argentinian Cult of Maradona', in G. Armstrong and R. Giulianotti (eds), *Entering the Field. New Perspectives on World Football*, Oxford: Berg Publishers.

Archetti, E. P. (1997c), 'Hibridación, diversidad y generalización en el mundo ideológico del fútbol y el polo', *Prismas. Revista de historia intelectual*, no. 1: 53–76.

Arlt, R. (1994), *Aguafuertes porteñas: cultura y política*, Buenos Aires: Losada.

Armus, D. (1996), 'La idea del verde en la ciudad moderna. Buenos Aires 1870–1940', *Entrepasados. Revista de Historia*, vol. 5, no. 10: 9–22.

Asociación Argentina de Polo (1993), *Campeonato Argentino Abierto de Polo. Cien años de historia 1893–1993*, Buenos Aires: Asociación Argentina de Polo.

Assuncao, F. O. (1959), 'El gaucho', *Revista del Instituto Histórico y Geográfico* (Montevideo): 364–918.

Augé, M. (1998), *Les formes de l'oubli*, Paris: Payot.

Azzi, M. S. (1991), *Antropología del tango. Los protagonistas*, Buenos Aires: Ediciones de Olavarría.

Bhabha, H. K. (1985), 'Signs Taken for Wonders: Questions of Ambivalence and Authority under a Tree Outside Dehli, May 1817', *Critical Inquiry*, vol. 12, no. 1: 144–65.

Bhabha, H. K. (1994), *The Location of Culture*, London: Routledge.

Bakthin, M. M. (1981), *The Dialogic Imagination: Four Essays*, Austin: University of Texas Press.

Balderston, D. and Guy, D. (eds), (1997), *Sex and Sexuality in Latin America*, New York: New York University Press.

Basave Benítez, A. (1992), *México mestizo. Análisis del nacionalismo mexicano en torno a la mestizofilia de Andrés Molina Enríquez*, México: Fondo de Cultura Económica.

Bayer, O. (1990), *Fútbol argentino*, Buenos Aires: Editorial Sudamericana.

Becco, H. J. and Dellepiane Calcena, C. (1978), *El gaucho. Documentación. Iconografía*, Buenos Aires: Editorial Plus Ultra.

Bernand, C. (1997), *Histoire de Buenos Aires*, Paris: Fayard.

Bioy Casares, A. (1970), *Memoria sobre la pampa y los gauchos*, Buenos Aires: Sur.

Borges, J. L. (1956), 'Prólogo', in S. Bullrich and J. L. Borges (eds), *El compadrito*, Buenos Aires: Emecé Editores.

Borges J. L. (1980) [1930], *Evaristo Carriego*, in *Prosa Completa*, vol. 1, Barcelona: Bruguera.

Borges, J. L. (1993) [1926], *El tamaño de mi esperanza*, Buenos aires: Seix Barral.

Borneman, J. (1996), 'Narrative, Genealogy, and the Historical Consciousness: Selfhood in a Disintegrating State', in E. Valentine Daniel and J. M. Peck (eds), *Culture/Contexture. Explorations in Anthropology and Literary Studies*, Berkeley: University of California Press.

Bourdieu, P. (1991), *Language and Symbolic Power*, Cambridge: Polity Press.

Bouysse-Cassagne, T. and Saignes, T. (1996), 'Le *cholo*, absent de l'histoire andine', in S. Gruzinski and N. Wachtel (eds), *Le Nouveau Monde. Mondes nouveaux. L'expérience américaine*, Paris: Editions Recherche sur les Civilisations–Editions de l'Ecole des Hautes Etudes en Sciences Sociales.

Brera, G. (1975), *Storia critica del calcio italiano*, Milano: Tascabili Bompiani.

Brody, E. (1987), *Paris. The Musical Kaledoiscope: 1870–1925*, New York: George Braziller.

Bruant, A. (1924), *Dans la rue*, Paris: Eugène Rey.

Bunge, C. O. (1911), 'La enseñanza de la tradición y la leyenda', *Monitor*: 263–80.

Cadícamo, E. (1969), *Café de camareras*, Buenos Aires: Editorial Acleon.

Cadícamo, E. (1975), *La historia del tango en Paris*, Buenos Aires: Corregidor.

Caldas, W. (1989), *O pontapé inicial. Memoria do futebol brasileiro (1894–1933)*, São Paulo: IBRASA.

Cantón, D. (1972), *Gardel, a quién le cantás?*, Buenos Aires: Ediciones de la Flor.

Casas, F. and Chacón, P. (1996), 'San Dieguito. La novela de Maradona. La película de Maradona', *Página 30*, vol. 5, no. 69: 6–11.

Castro, D. S. (1991), *The Argentine Tango as Social History: 1880–1955*, Lewiston: The Edwin Mellen Press.

Ceballos, F. (ed.) (1969), *El polo en la Argentina*, Buenos Aires: Comando en Jefe del Ejército.

Cechetto, C. (1993), 'Borocotó', Buenos Aires: Taller Escuela Agencia, ms.

Chiaramonte, J. C. (1989), 'Formas de identidad en el Rio de la Plata luego de 1810', *Boletin del Instituto de Historia Argentina y Americana 'Dr. E. Ravignani'*, third series, no. 1: 71–92.

Clifford, J. (1988), *The Predicament of Culture*, Cambridge, Mass.: Harvard University Press.

Cohen, A. (1994), *Self Consciousness. An Alternative Anthropology of Identity*, London: Routledge.

Cohen A. and Rapport, N. (1995), 'Introduction: Consciousness in Anthropology', in A. Cohen and N. Rapport (eds), *Question of Consciousness*, London: Routledge.

Cohen, B. J. (1974), 'Nativism and Western Myth: The Influence of Nativist Ideas on the American Self-Image', *Journal of American Studies*, vol. 8, no. 1: 23–39.

Coleman, D. C. (1973), 'Gentlemen and Players', *The Economic History Review*, second series, vol. 26, no. 1: 92–116.

Collier, S. (1986), *The Life, Music and Times of Carlos Gardel*, Pittsburgh: University of Pittsburgh Press.

Collier, S. (1995), 'The Tango Is Born: 1880s–1920s', in S. Collier, A. Cooper, M. S. Azzi and R. Martin (eds), *Tango*, London: Thames and Hudson.

Coni, E. A. (1969), *El gaucho. Argentina–Brasil–Uruguay*, Buenos Aires: Solar/Hachette.

Connerton, P. (1989), *How Societies Remember*, Cambridge: Cambridge University Press.

Cooper, A. (1995), 'Tangomania in Europe and North America: 1913–1914', in S. Collier, A. Cooper, M. S. Azzi and R. Martin, *Tango*, London: Thames and Hudson.

Cornwall, A. (1994), 'Gendered Identities and Gender Ambiguity among *Travestis* in Salvador, Bahia', in A. Cornwall and N. Lindisfarne (eds), *Dislocating Masculinity. Comparative Ethnographies*, London: Routledge.

Cornwall, A. and Lindisfarne N. (eds) (1994), *Dislocating Masculinity. Comparative Ethnographies*, London: Routledge.

Cortázar, J. (1985), *Salvo el crepúsculo*, Madrid: Ediciones Alfaguara.

Crites, S. (1971), 'The Narrative Quality of Experience', *Journal of the American Academy of Religion*, vol. 39: 291–311.

DaMatta, R. (1978), *Carnavais, Malandros e Heróis*, Rio de Janeiro: Zahar Editores.

DaMatta, R. (1982), 'Esporte na Sociedade: Um Ensaio sobre o Futebol Brasileiro', in R. DaMatta, L. F. Baêta Neves, S. L. Guedes and A. Vogel, *Universo do Futebol: Esporte e Sociedade Brasileira*, Rio de Janeiro: Edicoes Pinakotheke.

De Ipola, E. (1985), 'El tango en sus márgenes', *Punto de Vista*, vol. 25: 15–25.

Delaney, J. (1996), 'Making Sense of Modernity: Changing Attitudes toward the Immigrant and the *Gaucho* in Turn-of-the-Century Argentina', *Comparative Studies in Society and History*, vol. 38, no. 3: 434–59.

De Lara, T. and Roncetti de Panti, I. L. (1981), *El tema del tango en la literatura argentina*, Buenos Aires: Ediciones Culturales Argentinas.

Deusta Carvallo, J., Stein, S. and Stokes, S. C. (1984), 'Soccer and Social Change in Early Twentieth Century Peru', *Studies in Latin American Popular Culture*, vol. 3: 17–21.

Devoto, F. J. (1992), 'Del crisol al pluralismo. Treinta años de estudios sobre las migraciones europeas a la Argentina', *Serie Documentos de Trabajo. DTS 118*, Buenos Aires: Instituto Torcuato Di Tella.

Durkheim, E. (1915), *The Elementary Forms of Religious Life*, London: George Allen & Unwin.

Durkheim, E. (1966), *Sociologie et philosophie*, Paris: Presses Universitaires de France.

Durkheim, E. (1992), *Professional Ethics and Civic Morals*, London: Routledge.

Edel, M. and Edel, A. (1959), *Anthropology and Ethics*, Springfield, Ill.: Charles C. Thomas Publisher.

Erenberg, L. A. (1981), *Steppin' out. New York Nightlife and the Transformation of American Culture*, Chicago: Chicago University Press.

Eriksen, T. H. (1993), *Ethnicity and Nationalism. Anthropological Perspectives*, London: Pluto Press.

Escobar Bavio, E. (1923), *Historia del fútbol en el Río de la Plata*, Buenos Aires: Sports.

Escudé, C. (1990), *El fracaso del proyecto argentino. Educación e idceología*, Buenos Aires: Editorial Tesis-Instituto Torcuato Di Tella.

Evens, T. M. S. (1982), 'Two Concepts of "Society as a Moral System":
   Evans Pritchard's Heterodoxy', *Man* (n.s.), vol. 17, 2: 205–18.
Evens, T. M. S. (1993), 'Rationality, Hierarchy and Practice: Contradiction
   as Choice', *Social Anthropology*, vol. 1, no. 1B: 101–18.
Fabian, J. (1983), *Time and the Other: How Anthropology Makes its Objects*,
   New York: Colombia University Press.
Fachel Leal, O. (1989), 'The Gauchos: Male Culture and Identity in the
   Pampas', unpublished PhD thesis, University of California, Berkeley.
Fernández, J. W. (1995), 'Amazing Grace: Meaning Deficit, Displacement
   and New Consciousness in Expressive Interaction', in A. Cohen and N.
   Rapport (eds), *Question of Consciousness*, London: Routledge.
Ferrer, A. (1972), *La economía argentina*, Buenos Aires: Fondo de Cultura
   Económica.
Ferrer, H. (1960), *El tango. Su historia y evolución*, Buenos Aires: A. Peña
   Lillo editor.
Ferrer H. (1980), *El libro del tango*, 3 vol., Barcelona: Antonio Tersol Editor.
Fontanarrosa and Sanz (1994), *El pequeño diccionario ilustrado: el fútbol
   argentino*, Buenos Aires: Clarin-Aguilar.
Freire, G. (1946), *The Masters and the Slaves*, New York: Knopf.
Freundlich de Seefeld, R. (1986), 'La integración social de extranjeros en
   Buenos Aires: Según sus pautas matrimoniales, Pluralismo cultural
   o crisol de razas?', *Estudios Migratorios Latinoamericanos*, vol. 1, no. 2:
   203–31.
Friedman, J. (1997), 'Global Crises, the Struggle for Cultural Identity and
   Intellectual Porkbarrelling: Cosmopolitan Versus Locals, Ethnics and
   Nationals in an Era of De-hegemonisation', in P. Werbner and T. Modood
   (eds), *Debating Cultural Hybridity. Multi-Cultural Identities and the Politics
   of Anti-Racism*, London: Zed Books.
Frydenberg, J. (1997), 'Prácticas y valores en el proceso de popularización
   del fútbol. Buenos Aires 1900–1910', *Entrepasados. Revista de Historia*,
   vol. 6, no. 12: 7–31.
Frydenberg, J. (1998), 'Redefinición del fútbol aficionado y del fútbol
   oficial. Buenos Aires, 1912', in P. Alabarces, R. Di Giano and J. Frydenberg (eds), *Deporte y sociedad*, Buenos Aires: Eudeba.
Fuentes, C. (1992), *The Buried Mirror*, London: Andre Deutsch.
Gálvez, M. (1910), *El diario de Gabriel Quiroga: Opiniones sobre la vida
   argentina*, Buenos Aires: Arnoldo Moen & Hno.
Gálvez, M. (1930), *El solar de la raza*, Buenos Aires: Editorial 'La Facultad'.
García Canclini, N. (1995) [1990], *Hybrid Cultures. Strategies for Entering
   and Leaving Modernity*, Minneapolis: University of Minnesota Press.
García Costa, V. O. (1986), *Alfredo L. Palacios. Un socialismo argentino*,
   Buenos Aires: Centro Editor de América Latina.
Gellner, E. (1983), *Nations and Nationalism*, Oxford: Blackwell.
Gilbert, A. (1996), 'Cebolla de Fiorito. Maradona jurásico', *Página 30*, vol.
   5, no. 69: 16–21.

Gilmore, D. D. (1990), *Manhood in the Making. Cultural Concepts of Masculinity*, New Haven: Yale University Press.

Giordano, H. (1955), 'El éxodo de los jugadores argentinos a Colombia', in *Historia del fútbol argentino*, vol. III, Buenos Aires: Editorial Eiffel.

Gobello, J. (1980), *Crónica general del tango*, Buenos Aires: Editorial Fraterna.

Gobello, J. and Bossio, J. A. (1979), *Tangos y letristas*, Buenos Aires: Editorial Plus Ultra.

Gobello, J. and Stilman, E. (1966), *Las letras de tango de Villoldo a Borges*, Buenos Aires: Editorial Brújula.

Gobineau, J. A. (1983) [1853–55], *Essai sur l'inégalité des races humaines*, Paris: Gallimard.

González Echeverría, R. (1994), 'Literature, baile y béisbol en el (último) fin de siglo cubano', in J. Ludmer (ed), *Las culturas de fin de siglo en América Latina*, Rosario: Beatriz Viterbo Editora.

Gonzáles Echeverría, R. (1998), 'Tres peloteros cubanos', *Nueva Sociedad*, vol. 154: 87–100.

Goodrich, D. S. (1996), *Facundo and the Construction of Argentine Culture*, Austin: The University of Texas Press.

Gorelik, A. (1996), 'La grilla y el parque. La emergencia de un espacio público metropolitano en Buenos Aires, 1887–1936', unpublished PhD thesis, University of Buenos Aires.

Graham-Yooll, A. (1981), *The Forgotten Colony. A History of the English-Speaking Communities in Argentina*, London: Hutchinson.

Gramuglio, M. T. (1997), 'Ponencia: "La primera épica de Lugones"', *Prismas. Revista de historia intelectual*, vol, 1: 157–63.

Gutmann, M. C. (1996), *The Meanings of Macho. Being a Man in Mexico City*, Berkeley: University of California Press.

Guy, D. (1991), *Sex and Danger in Buenos Aires. Prostitution, Family, and Nation in Argentina*, Lincoln, Nebr.: University of Nebraska Press.

Hall, S. (1990), 'Cultural Identity and Diaspora', in J. Rutherford (ed.), *Identity: Community, Culture, Difference*, London: Sage in association with the Open University.

Halperín Donghi, T. (1987), *El espejo de la historia*, Buenos Aires: Editorial Sudamericana.

Hannerz, U. (1996), *Transnational Connections. Culture, People, Places*, London: Routledge.

Harris, O. (1995), 'Knowing the Past. Plural Identities and the Antinomies of Loss in Highland Bolivia', in R. Fardon (ed.), *Counterworks. Managing the Diversity of Knowledge*, London: Routledge.

Hart, A. (1994), 'Missing Masculinity ? Prostitutes' Clients in Alicante, Spain', in A. Cornwall and N. Lindisfarne (eds), *Dislocating Masculinity. Comparative Ethnographies*, London: Routledge.

Hastrup, K. (1987), 'Fieldwork among Friends: Ethnographic Exchange within the Northern Civilization', in A. Jackson (ed.), *Anthropology at Home*, London: Tavistock Publications.

Hennessy, A. (1992), 'Argentines, Anglo-Argentines and Others', in A. Hennessy and J. King (eds), *The Land that England Lost. Argentina and Britain: A Special Relationship*, London: British Academic Press.

Herzfeld, M. (1985), *The Poetics of Manhood. Contest and Identity in a Cretan Mountain Village*, Princeton: Princeton University Press.

Holt, R. (1989), *Sport and the British. A Modern History*, Oxford: Clarendon Press.

Holy, L. (ed) (1987), *Comparative Anthropology*, Oxford: Blackwell.

Holy, L. (1996), *The Little Czech and the Great Czech Nation*, Cambridge: Cambridge University Press.

Howell, S. (1997), 'Introduction', in S. Howell (ed.), *The Ethnography of Moralities*, London: Routledge.

Humphrey, C. (1997), 'Exemplars and Rules: Aspects of the Discourse of Moralities in Mongolia', in S. Howell (ed.), *The Ethnography of Moralities*, London: Routledge.

Hutchinson, J. (1992), 'Moral Innovators and the Politics of Regeneration: The Distinctive Role of Cultural Nationalists in Nation-Building', in A. D. Smith (ed.), *Ethnicity and Nationalism*, New York: E. J. Brill.

Ibarguren, C. (1934), *La inquietud de esta hora*, Buenos Aires: Roldán Editor.

Ibarguren, C. (1971), *Respuestas a un cuestionario acerca del nacionalismo 1930–1945*, Buenos Aires: n/e.

Ingenieros, J. (1956), *Tratado del amor*, Buenos Aires: Elmer Editor.

Jackson, A. (1987), 'Reflections on Ethnography at Home and the ASA', in A. Jackson (ed.), *Anthropology at Home*, London: Tavistock Publications.

Jarvie, G. and Walker, G. (1994), *Scottish Sport in the Making of the Nation. Ninety Minute Patriots?*, Leicester: Leicester University Press.

Jelavich, P. (1990), 'Modernity, Civic Identity, and Metropoloitan Entertainment: Vaudeville, Cabaret, and Revue in Berlin, 1900–1933', in C. W. Haxthausen and H. Suhr (eds), *Berlin. Culture and Metropolis*, Minneapolis: University of Minnesota Press.

Johnson, M. (1993), *Moral Imagination*, Chicago: University of Chicago Press.

Kanitkar, H. (1994), '"Real True Boys"; Moulding the Cadets of Imperialism', in A. Cornwall and H. Lindisfarne (eds), *Dislocating Masculinity: Comparative Ethnographies*, London: Routledge.

Kerby, A. (1991), *Narrative and the Self*, Bloomington: Indiana University Press.

King, J. (1992), 'The Influence of British Culture in Argentina', in A. Hennessy and J. King (eds), *The Land that England Lost. Argentina and Britain: A Special Relationship*, London: British Academic Press.

Korol, J. C. and Sábato, H. (1981), *Cómo fue la inmigración Irlandesa en Argentina*, Buenos Aires: Editorial Plus Ultra.

Krohn-Hansen, C. (1996), 'Masculinity and the Political among Dominicans: "The Dominican Tiger"', in M. Melhuus and K. A. Stølen (eds), *Machos,*

Mistresses, Madonnas. Contesting the Power of Latin American Gender Imagery, London: Verso.

Krohn-Hansen, C. (1997), 'Collective Amnesia: Race and Nation in the Dominican Republic', Department of Anthropology, University of Oslo, ms.

Kulick, D. (1997), 'The Gender of Brazilian Transgendered Prostitutes', *American Anthropologist*, vol. 99, no. 3: 574–85.

La Nación (1994), *Historia del fútbol argentino*, 3 vols, Buenos Aires: La Nación.

Laffaye, H. A. (1989), *El polo internacional argentino*, Buenos Aires: Edición del autor.

Latour, B. (1993), *We Have Never Been Modern*, London: Harvester Wheatsheaf.

Lázaro (1993), 'Doctrina de fútbol', *La Caja*, vol. 3: 30–1.

Leite Lopes, J. S. (1997), 'Succeses and Contradictions in "Multiracial" Brazilian Football', in G. Armstrong and R. Giulianotti (eds), *Entering the Field. New Perspectives on World Football*, Oxford: Berg.

Leite Lopes, J. S. and Faguer, J.-P. (1994), 'L'invention du style brésilien. Sport, journalisme et politique au Brésil', *Actes de la Recherche en Sciences Sociales*, no. 103: 27–35.

Le Wita, B. (1994), *French Bourgeois Culture*, Cambridge: Cambridge University Press–Editions de la Maison des Sciences de l'Homme Paris.

Liernur, J. F. and Silvestri, G. (1993), 'El torbellino de la electrificación. Buenos Aires, 1880-1930', in J. F. Liernur and G. Silvestri (eds), *El umbral de la metrópolis*, Buenos Aires: Editorial Sudamericana.

Liernur, J. F. (1993), 'La ciudad efímera', in J. F. Liernur and G. Silvestri (eds), *El umbral de la metrópolis*, Buenos Aires: Editorial Sudamericana.

Lindisfarne, N. (1994), 'Variant Masculinities, Variant Virginities: Rethinking "Honour and Shame"', in A. Cornwall and N. Lindisfarne (eds), *Dislocating Masculinities*, London: Routledge.

Llobera, J. (1986), 'Fieldwork in Southwestern Europe: An Anthropological Panacea or Epistemological Straitjacket', *Critique of Anthropology*, vol. 6, no. 2: 25–33.

Lorenzo, R. (1946), *25 años en el deporte*, Buenos Aires: Editorial Atlántida.

Ludmer, J. (1988), *El género gauchesco. Un tratado sobre la patria*, Buenos Aires: Editorial Sudamericana.

Lugones, L. (1961) [1916], *El payador*, Buenos Aires: Ediciones Centurión.

Luhmann, N. (1985), *El amor como pasión*, Barcelona: Ediciones Península.

Lukes, S. (1981), *Emile Durkheim*, Middlesex: Penguin.

McKendrick, N. (1986), '"Gentleman and Players" revisited: the gentlemanly ideal, the business ideal and the professional ideal in English literary culture', in N. McKendrick and R. B. Outhwaite (eds), *Business Life and Public Policy. Essays in Honour of D. C. Coleman*, Cambridge: Cambridge University Press.

Mangan J. A. (ed.) (1988), *Pleasure, Profit, Proselytism. British Culture and Sport at Home and Abroad 1700-1914*, London: Frank Cass.

Mangan, J. A. (ed.) (1996), *Tribal Identities. Nationalism, Europe, Sport*, London: Frank Cass.

Maranghello, C. (1984), 'La pantalla y el estado', in Centro Editor de América Latina, *Historia del Cine Argentino*, Buenos Aires: Centro Editor de América Latina.

Martini Real, J. C. (ed.) (1976), *La historia del tango*, vol. 1, Buenos Aires: Corregidor.

Masiello, F. (1992), *Between Civilization and Barbarism. Women, Nation and Literary Culture in Modern Argentina*, Lincoln: University of Nebraska Press.

Mason, T. (1989), 'Football', in T. Mason (ed.), *Sport in Britain. A Social History*, Cambridge: Cambridge University Press.

Mason, T. (1995), *Passion of the People? Football in South America*, London: Verso.

Matamoro, B. (1982), *La ciudad del tango*, Buenos Aires: Editorial Galerna.

Melhuus, M. (1996), 'The Troubles of Virtue: Values of Violence and Suffering in a Mexican Context', in S. Howell (ed.), *The Ethnography of Moralities*, London: Routledge.

Melhuus, M (1998), 'The Power of Penetration – The Value of Virginity: Male and Female in Mexican Heterosexual and Homosexual Relations', *Ethnos* , vol. 63, 3: 353–82.

Melhuus, M. and Stølen, K. A. (1996), 'Introduction', in M. Melhuus and K. A. Stølen (eds), *Machos, Mistresses, Madonnas. Contesting the Power of Latin American Gender Imagery*, London: Verso.

Menotti, C. L. (1980), *Fútbol: juego, deporte y profesión*, Buenos Aires: El Gráfico.

Menotti, C. L. (1993), 'Entrevista', *La Maga*, vol. 2: 2–5.

Menotti, C. L. (1994a), 'La defensa de una escuela', *La Maga Colección*, vol. 2: 51.

Menotti, C. L. (1994b), 'Entrevista abierta', *El toque*, vol. 2: 2–3.

Miller, B. (1977), 'An American Polo Club: A Study of Leisure Activity as a Process of Production and Consumption, and as a Mechanism for the Maintenance and Enhancement of Elite Status', unpublished MS thesis, Temple University.

Miller, Nicola (1997), 'The Voice of the People?: Intellectuals and the Creation of Popular National Identities in Argentina and Peru', paper presented at the 1997 meeting of the Latin American Studies Association, Guadalajara, Mexico.

Moorhouse, H. F. (1996), 'One State, Several Countries: Soccer and Nationality in a "United" Kingdom', in J. A. Mangan (ed.), *Tribal Identities. Nationalism, Europe, Sport*, London: Frank Cass.

Mörner, M. (1971), *Le Métissage dans l'histoire de l'Amérique Latine*, Paris: Fayard.

Navarro Gerassi, M. (1969), *Los nacionalistas*, Buenos Aires: Editorial Jorge Alvárez.

Mosse, G. L. (1985), *Nationalism and Sexuality. Middle-Class Morality and Sexual Norms in Modern Europe*, Wisconsin: The University of Wisconsin Press.

Mosse, G. L. (1996), *The Image of Man. The Creation of Modern Masculinity*, New York: Oxford University Press.

Nelson, J. D. (1969), 'Giras al exterior', in F. Ceballos (ed.), *El polo en la Argentina*, Buenos Aires: Comando en Jefe del Ejército.

Nencel, L. (1996), '*Pacharacas, Putas* and *Chicas de su casa*. Labelling, Femininity and Men's Sexual Selves in Lima, Peru', in M. Melhuus and K. A. Stølen (eds), *Machos, Mistresses, Madonnas, Contesting the Power of Latin American Gender Imagery*, London: Verso.

Nichols, M. W. (1942), *The Gaucho: Cattle Hunter, Cavalryman, Ideal of Romance*, Durham: Duke University Press.

Nilsson, P. (1993), *Fotbollen och Moralen*, Stockholm: HLS Förlag.

Ochoa, L. (1995), *Conquista, transculturación y mestizaje. Raíz y origen de México*, México, DF: Universidad Nacional Autonóma de México, Instituto de Investigaciones Antropológicas.

Oliven, R. G. (1996), 'A Modern Popular Culture Movement Based on Tradition: The Gaúcho Traditionalist Movement in Brazil', in T. Salman (ed.), *The Legacy of the Disinherited. Popular Culture in Latin America: Modernity, Globalization, Hybridity and Authenticity*, Amsterdam: CEDLA.

Olivera, E. (1932), *Orígenes de los deportes británicos en el Río de la Plata*, Buenos Aires: Edición del autor.

Oriard, M. (1993), *Reading Football: How the Popular Press Created an American Spectacle*, Chapel Hill: North Carolina University Press.

Padilla, E. (1969), 'El polo en el Ejército', in F. Ceballos (ed.), *El polo en la Argentina*, Buenos Aires: Comando en Jefe del Ejército.

Palmer, G. B. and Jankowiak, W. R. (1996), 'Performance and Imagination: Toward an Anthropology of the Spectacular and the Mundane', *Cultural Anthropology*, vol. 11, no. 2: 225–58.

Papastergiadis, N. (1995), 'Restless Hybrids', *Third Text*, 32: 9–18.

Papastergiadis, N. (1997), 'Tracing Hybridity in Theory', in P. Werbner and T. Modood (eds), *Debating Cultural Hybridity. Multi-Cultural Identities and the Politics of Anti-Racism*, London: Zed Books.

Parker, A., Russo, M, Summer, D. and Yaeger, P. (eds), (1992), *Nationalisms and Sexualities*, New York: Routledge.

Parkes, P. (1996), 'Indigenous Polo and the Politics of Regional Identity in Northern Pakistan', in J. MacClancy (ed.), *Sport, Identity and Ethnicity*, Oxford. Berg.

Parkin, D. (1983), 'Introduction', in D. Parkin (ed.), *The Anthropology of Evil*, Oxford: Blackwell.

Pedernera, A. (1993), *El fútbol que viví . . . y que yo siento*, Buenos Aires: Editorial Sineret SA.

Peña, M. (1991), 'Class, Gender, and Machismo: The "Treacherous Woman" Folklore of Mexican Male Workers', *Gender and Society*, vol. 5, no. 1: 30–46.

Pina-Cabral, J. (1989), 'The Mediterranean as a Category of Regional Comparison: A Critical View', *Current Anthropology*, vol. 3, no. 3: 399–406.

Pope, S. W. (1997), *Patriotic Games. Sporting Traditions in the American Imagination, 1876–1926*, New York: Oxford University Press.

Prieto A. (1988), *El discurso criollista en la formación de la Argentina moderna*, Buenos Aires: Sudamericana.

Prieur, A. (1996), 'Domination and Desire: Male Homosexuality and the Construction of Masculinity in Mexico', in M. Melhuus and K. A. Stølen (eds), *Machos, Mistresses, Madonnas. Contesting the Power of Latin American Gender Imagery*, London: Verso.

Rama, C. M. (1981), *Nacionalismo e historiografía en América Latina*, Madrid: Editorial Tecnos.

Rama, C. M. (1996), *The Lettered City*, Durham: Duke University Press.

Ramos Mejía. J. M. (1974) [1899], *Las multitudes argentinas*, Buenos Aires: Editorial Biblioteca.

Rapport, N. (1997), 'The Morality of Locality: On the Absolutism of Landownership in an English Village', in S. Howell (ed.), *The Ethnography of Moralities*, London: Routledge.

Radcliffe, S. A. (1997), 'The Geographies of Indigenous Self-representation in Ecuador: Hybridity, Gender and Resistance', *European Review of Latin American and Caribbean Studies*, 63: 9–28.

Reed-Danahay, D. E. (1997), 'Introduction', in D. E. Reed-Danahay (ed.), *Auto/Ethnography*, Oxford: Berg.

Reid, G. (1980), *The Afro-Argentines of Buenos Aires, 1800–1900*, Madison: University of Wisconsin Press.

Riekenberg, M. (1993), 'El concepto de la nación en la región del Plata (1810–1831)', *Entrepasados. Revista de Historia*, vol. 3, nos 3–4: 89–101.

Roberts, J. S. (1972), *Black Music of Two Worlds*, London: Allen Lane.

Rock, D. (1987), 'Intellectual Precursors of Conservative Nationalism in Argentina, 1900–1927', *Hispanic American Historical Review*, vol. 2: 271–300.

Rock, D. (1993), *La Argentina autoritaria. Los nacionalistas, su historia y su influencia en la vida pública*, Buenos Aires: Ariel.

Rodó, J. E. (1994) [1900], *Ariel*, Buenos Aires: Losada.

Rodríguez, M. G. (1996), '"El fútbol no es la patria" (pero se le parece)', in P. Alabarces and M. G. Rodríguez (eds), *Cuestión de pelotas*, Buenos Aires: Atuel.

Rodríguez, M. G. (1998), 'Diego, un héroe global en apuros (la agonía del último dinosaurio)', in P. Alabarces, R. Di Giano and J. Frydenberg (eds), *Deporte y sociedad*, Buenos Aires: Eudeba.

Rojas, R. (1909), *La restauración nacionalista*, Buenos Aires: Ediciones Centurión.

Rojas, R. (1912), *Blasón de plata*, Buenos Aires: Martín García Editores.

Romano, E. (1991), *Las letras del tango. Antología cronológica: 1900–1980*, Rosario: Editorial Fundación Ros.

Romano E. (1998), 'Cuando los "berretines" emigran del escenario a la pantalla', in P. Alabarces, R. Di Giano and J. Frydenberg (eds), *Deporte y sociedad*, Buenos Aires: Eudeba.

Sábato, E. (1961), *Sobre héroes y tumbas*, Buenos Aires: Fabril.

Sábato, E. (1963), *Tango. Discusión y clave*, Buenos Aires: Editorial Losada.

Salas, H. (1986), *El tango*, Buenos Aires: Planeta.

Sánchez León, A. (1993), *La balada del gol perdido*, Lima: Ediciones Noviembre Trece.

Sánchez León, A. (1998), 'El gol de América Latina', *Nueva Sociedad*, no. 154: 147–56.

Sarlo, B. (1985), *El imperio de los sentimientos*, Buenos Aires: Catálogos Editora.

Sarlo, B. (1988), *Una modernidad periférica: Buenos Aires 1920 y 1930*, Buenos Aires: Ediciones Nueva Visión.

Sarlo, B. (1993), *Jorge Luis Borges. A Writer on the Edge*, London: Verso.

Sarlo, B. (1996), 'Modernidad y mezcla cultural', in H. Vázquez Rial (ed.), *Buenos Aires 1880–1930. La capital de un imperio imaginario*, Madrid: Alianza Editorial.

Sarlo, B. 1997, 'Ponencia: "Cabezas rapadas y cintas argentinas"', *Primas. Revista de historia intelectual*, vol.1: 187–91.

Sarmiento, D. F. (1981) [1845], *Facundo*, Buenos Aires: Editorial Losada S. A.

Savigliano, M. (1995), *Tango and the Political Economy of Passion*, Boulder: Westview Press.

Scher, A. and Palomino, H. (1988), *Fútbol: pasión de multitudes y de elites*, Buenos Aires: Centro de Investigaciones Sociales sobre el Estado y la Administración.

Schneider, A. (1996), 'The Two Faces of Modernity. Concepts of the Melting Pot in Argentina', *Critique of Anthropology*, vol. 16, no. 2: 173–98.

Schneider, A. (1997), 'Discourses of Differences in Modern Argentina', paper presented at the conference 'Différence culturelle, racisme et démocratie', Forum International des Sciences Humaines, Paris.

Schwartz, S. B. (1996), 'Brazilian Ethnogenesis: *Mesticos, Mamelucos* and *Pardos*', in S. Gruzinski and N. Wachtel (eds), *Le Nouveau Monde. Mondes nouveaux. L'expérience américaine*, Paris: Editions Recherche sur les Civilisations–Editions de l'Ecole des Hautes Etudes en Sciences Sociales.

Segel, H. B. (1987), *Turn-of-the-Century Cabaret. Paris, Barcelona, Belin, Munich, Vienna, Cracow, Moscow, St Petersburg, Zurich*, New York: Columbia University Press.

Shunway, N. (1991), *The Invention of Argentina*, Berkeley: The University of California Press.

Siegel, J. (1986), *Bohemian Paris: Culture, Politics and the Boundaries of Bourgeois Life. 1830–1930*, New York: Viking.

Silvestri, G. (1993), 'La ciudad y el río', in J. F. Liernur and G. Silvestri (eds), *El umbral de la metrópolis*, Buenos Aires: Editorial Sudamericana.

Slatta, R. (1985), 'The Gaucho in Argentina's Quest for Identity', *Canadian Review of Studies in Nationalism*, vol. 12, no. 1: 23–38.

Slatta, R. (1986), 'The Demise of the Gaucho and the Rise of Equestrian Sport in Argentina', *Journal of Sport History*, vol. 13, no. 2: 97–110.

Socolow, S. M. (1996), 'Introduction', in S. Gruzinski and N. Wachtel (eds), *Le Nouveau Monde. Mondes Nouveaux. L'expérience américaine*, Paris: Editions Recherche sur les Civilisations–Editions de l'Ecole des Hautes Etudes en Science Sociales.

Solberg, C. (1970), *Immigration and Nationalism. Argentina and Chile, 1890–1914*, Austin: The University of Texas Press.

Somoza, S. M. (1953), 'Breve historia del pato', in *Resumen Deportivo del año 1952*, Buenos Aires: Editorial del Sur.

Soriano, O. (1987), *Rebeldes, soñadores y fugitivos*, Buenos Aires: Editora 12.

Stølen, K. A. (1996), *The Decency of Inequality. Gender, Power and Social Change in the Argentine Prairie*, Oslo: Scandinavian University Press.

Strathern, M. (1987), 'The Limits of Auto-anthropology', in A. Jackson (ed.), *Anthropology at Home*, London: Tavistock Publications.

Strathern, M. (1992), *After Nature. English Kinship in the Late Twentieth Century*, Cambridge: Cambridge University Press.

Strathern, M. (1996), 'Cutting the network', *The Journal of the Royal Anthropological Institute*, vol. 2, no. 3: 517–35.

Strathern, M. (1997), 'Double Standards', in S. Howell (ed.), *The Ethnography of Moralities*, London: Routledge.

Strauss, A. L. (1977), *Mirrors and Masks. The Search for Identity*, London: Martin Robertson.

Strickon, A. (1960), 'The Grandsons of the Gauchos: A Study in Subcultural Persistence', unpublished PhD thesis, Columbia University.

Tania (1973), *Discepolín y yo*, Buenos Aires: Ediciones La Bastilla.

Taylor, J. (1987), 'Tango. Ethos of Melancholy', *Cultural Anthropology*, vol. 1, no. 4: 481–93.

Thiesse, A. M. (1997), *Ils apprenainent la France. L'exaltation des régions dans le discours patriotique*, Paris: Editions de la Maison des Sciences de l'Homme.

Tocagni, H. (1987), *El caballo de polo*, Buenos Aires: Editorial Albatros.

Todorov, T. (1989), *Nous et les autres. La réflexion francaise sur la diversité humaine*, Paris: Seuil.

Traill, J. (n.d.), 'The Long Chukker', ms.

Turner, V. (1967), *The Forest of Symbols: Aspects of Ndembu Ritual*, Ithaca, NY: Cornell University Press.

Turner, V. (1969), *The Ritual Process*, Ithaca, NY: Cornell University Press.

Ulla, N. (1982), *Tango, rebelión y nostalgia*, Buenos Aires: Centro Editor de América Latina.

Valdano, J. (ed.) (1995), *Cuentos de fútbol*, Madrid: Extra Alfaguara.

Valdano, J. (1997), *Cuadernos de fútbol*, Madrid: El País-Aguilar.

Vale de Almeida, M. (1996), *The Hegemonic Male. Masculinity in a Portuguese Town*, Providence: Berghahn Books.

Vázques Rial, H. (1996), 'Superpoblación y concentrración urbana en un país desierto', in H. Vázques Rial (ed.), *Buenos Aires 1880–1930. La Capital de un imperio imaginario*, Madrid: Alianza Editorial.

Viale, C. (1937), *Jurisprudencia caballeresca argentina*, Buenos Aires: Edición del autor.

Vila, P. (1991), 'Tango to Folk: Hegemony Construction and Popular Identities in Argentina', *Studies in Latin American Popular Culture*, vol. 10: 107–39.

Vilariño, I. (1981), *Tangos. Antología*, vols 1 and 2, Buenos Aires: Centro Editor de América Latina.

Walter, R. J. (1977), *The Socialist Party of Argentina: 1890–1930*, Austin, Tex.: The University of Texas Press.

Watson, J. N. P. (1986), *The World of Polo. Past and Present*, London: The Sportman's Press.

Werbner, P. (1997), 'Introduction: The Dialectics of Cultural Hybridity', in P. Werbner and T. Modood (eds), *Debating Cultural Hybridity. Multi-Cultural Identities and the Politics of Anti-Racism*, London: Zed Books.

Willans, D. (1993), 'The Traills of Argentina', ms.

Williams, G. (1991), *The Welsh in Patagonia. The State and the Ethnic Community*, Cardiff: University of Wales Press.

Wolfram, S. (1982), 'Anthropology and Morality', *Journal of the Anthropological Society of Oxford*, vol. 13: 262–74.

Young, R. J. C. (1995), *Colonial Desire. Hybridity in Theory, Culture and Race*, London: Routledge.

Yuval-Davis, N. and Anthias, F. (eds) (1989), *Woman – Nation – State*, London: Macmillan.

Index